The Urban Voice Series, an affiliate of the Center for Urban Ministerial Education (CUME), Boston Campus of Gordon-Conwell Theological Seminary (GCTS—Boston), publishes a variety of writings for urban pastors, students of urban ministry, and other urban ministry practitioners. Promoting the best practices in urban ministry, its contents may include theological analyses, descriptive and exploratory research, quasi-experiments, assessments, and case studies around any of a variety of issues. Our contributors attempt to tackle many themes associated with the social, political, economic, and multicultural complexities of urban reality that impact individuals across their life-span in diverse groups, various churches, and communities in the urban world. In part, this publication represents the nature and values of CUME, which has as its tradition the contextualization of the mission of Gordon-Conwell Theological Seminary through urban-based theological education. It seeks to achieve the GCTS—Boston's mission of excellence in scholarship, innovation, leadership development, and the training of passionate people called to serve the gospel of Jesus Christ in the redemptive work of the urban church within the city's diverse communities. The series is produced by passionate practitioner-scholars who are committed to historical orthodoxy and the central role of the Holy Scriptures on all matters of Christian faith.

Reaching for
the New Jerusalem

Reaching for
the New Jerusalem

A Biblical and Theological Framework for the City

Edited by

Seong Hyun Park
Aída Besançon Spencer
and William David Spencer

WIPF & STOCK · Eugene, Oregon

REACHING FOR THE NEW JERUSALEM
A Biblical and Theological Framework for the City

Copyright © 2013 Wipf and Stock Publishers. All rights reserved. Except for brief quotations in critical publications or reviews, no part of this book may be repro-duced in any manner without prior written permission from the publisher. Write: Permissions. Wipf and Stock Publishers, 199 W. 8th Ave., Suite 3, Eugene, OR 97401.

Wipf & Stock
An Imprint of Wipf and Stock Publishers
199 W. 8th Ave., Suite 3
Eugene, OR 97401

www.wipfandstock.com

ISBN 13: 978-1-62564-060-4

Manufactured in the U.S.A.

Contents

Contributors

Lorraine Cleaves Anderson, in 1991, became the first ordained woman in the Conservative Baptist Association of America, and in 1998 received ministerial standing with the American Baptist Churches of Massachusetts. From 1990 to 1998, she copastored New Life Church with Revs. Ralph and Judy Kee, a church intentionally planted to host start-up churches. When it consolidated with Brighton Avenue Baptist Church in 1998 to create International Community Church (ICC), she became Senior Pastor. ICC continued hosting churches and organizations, as it became apparent that God was developing it into a Homeless Shelter for Churches—a ministry the church continues to hone and deeply enjoy. Lorraine's practical suggestions for radical hospitality may be found in *Under One Steeple: Multiple Congregations Sharing More Than Just Space.* She is a 1983 graduate of Gordon-Conwell Theological Seminary and a former teacher of the Deaf and Deaf-Blind. She resides with her husband Bob in Boston, where they raised their son Luke.

Jeffrey Bass is Executive Director of the Emmanuel Gospel Center (EGC), which seeks to equip the urban church in Greater Boston for effective community ministry. Trained as a civil engineer (Princeton University, 1981), he joined the EGC board in 1987, became Assistant Director in 1991, and Executive Director in 1999. He specializes in helping Christian leaders move from vision to reality in their ministries. Jeff and his wife Ellen have two grown sons and have lived in the Mission Hill neighborhood of Boston since 1986.

Dean Borgman became the Charles E. Culpeper Professor of Youth Ministries at Gordon-Conwell Theological Seminary, after working with youth on Manhattan's Lower East Side, and directing and teaching in Young Life's Urban Training Institute. He is the author of *Hear My Story: Understanding the Cries of Troubled Youth* and other works. He is also the founder and principal editor of The Center for Youth Studies (www.centerforyouth.org), and teaches courses in Social Ethics.

Carlot Ducasse Celestin has a DMin in Marriage and Family Counseling from Gordon-Conwell Theological Seminary, Boston Campus, where he worked as Adjunct Professor, Student Advisor, and Academic Support Coordinator of the MA in Counseling (MACO), the Master of Theology (ThM), and the Africanus Guild Programs. In addition to his role as the Assistant Pastor of Tabernacle Baptist Congregation in Roslindale, MA, and counselor at New Life Counseling Center, Randolph, MA, he is currently pursuing an academic doctoral degree in Psychoanalysis at Boston Graduate School of Psychoanalysis.

David A. Currie is the Director of the Doctor of Ministry Program and Associate Professor of Pastoral Theology at Gordon-Conwell Theological Seminary. He has also taught church history at Gordon-Conwell Theological Seminary, Boston Campus, since 1998. He received a PhD in Ecclesiastical History from the University of St. Andrews (Scotland) for a dissertation exploring the growth of Evangelicalism in the Church of Scotland in the first half of the nineteenth century. An ordained minister in the Presbyterian Church (USA), he has mainly served as a pastor, both in Pennsylvania and Scotland, primarily in church planting. As part of the New Church Development Committee of the Presbytery of Philadelphia, he helped to start new congregations with and for Chinese, Ghanaian, Pakistani, and Messianic Jewish believers.

Steve Daman is Senior Writer of the Emmanuel Gospel Center in Boston and has served in communications and development there since 1988. In 2010, he coauthored *The Cat and the Toaster: Living System Ministry in a Technological Age* with Doug and Judy Hall. Steve holds a BA from Gordon College (1973) and an MA in journalism and communications from Regent University (1986). Steve and his wife, Debby, live within commuting distance of Boston and have three adult children, a growing number of adorable grandchildren, and one incorrigible cat.

Bianca Duemling is the Assistant Director of Intercultural Ministries at Emmanuel Gospel Center, an interdenominational urban ministry organization in Boston, Massachusetts. The mission of Intercultural Ministries of EGC is *"to connect the Body of Christ across cultural lines . . . for the purpose of expressing and advancing the Kingdom of God . . . in Boston, New England,*

and around the world." Her ministry largely involves applied research, training, consulting, networking, and collaboration. Prior to joining the staff of EGC in 2010, Bianca was involved in intercultural ministry in different settings. She is a founding member of the *Forum for Intercultural Relations* of *Together for Berlin* and the *Foundation Himmelsfels*, where she served two years as the project coordinator for an intercultural reconciliation project. Bianca received her PhD at the University of Heidelberg, studying emerging immigrant churches in Germany and their relationship with mainline churches. Raised in the southern part of Germany close to the Black Forest, she earned her degree in European Community Education Studies (as a licensed social worker) from the University of Applied Science, Koblenz, Germany, and her Master of Arts in Intercultural Work and Conflict Management from the Alice-Salomon University of Applied Science in Berlin, Germany.

Douglas A. Hall is President of Emmanuel Gospel Center (EGC) in Boston, Massachusetts, where he and his wife, *Judy,* have served since 1964. The mission of EGC is *"to understand and nurture the vitality of urban churches and communities,"* and it has particularly worked with Boston's low-income and immigrant communities. Through a systemic approach to research and training, consulting and programs, EGC builds the capacity of urban churches to serve urban residents effectively, particularly in the areas of education, youth, ministry training, economic development, and addressing homelessness. By working with and through all different types of churches, EGC seeks to build a community that supports and cares for the spiritual and physical needs of *all* individuals throughout the city (www.egc.org). Doug and Judy are graduates of Moody Bible Institute (1960) and Michigan State University (1963)—Judy with a BA in Elementary Education and Douglas with a BA in Sociology and Anthropology and a Master's degree in Counseling and Guidance. Douglas is a graduate of Gordon Divinity School (1968) and was granted an honorary doctorate by Gordon-Conwell Theological Seminary in 1981. He has been teaching in the MA in Urban Ministry program of Gordon-Conwell's Boston Campus since 1973 and in the Doctor of Ministry in Complex Urban Settings Program since its inception in 1998.

Mark G. Harden is the Dean of Boston Campus and Associate Professor of Community Development and Outreach, at Gordon-Conwell Theological Seminary. He teaches in the area of practical theology and oversees every aspect of the Boston Campus. As a community development practitioner, he has organized several outreach organizations, including a school, and has directed several community outreach programs for Christian organizations such as Streetwise, Inc., World Vision (USFO), Detroit, Love INC, and Fellowship Inc. Housing Corporation. Mark is a family and child ecologist (PhD from Michigan State University), with a specialization in program development and evaluation for community development and provides intercultural competence assessment, training, and development assistance.

Teri Elliott-Hart is the Director of Leadership and Mentored Ministry Initiatives at Gordon-Conwell Theological Seminary, Boston Campus. She has a PhD from Boston College and EdM from Harvard University. Current research and teaching areas are Christian Education, Spiritual Formation, Church and Culture. She is the Christian Formation chairperson for the East Coast Conference Board of the Evangelical Covenant Church and serves as a lay leader in a small, multicultural, intergenerational church in the Jamaica Plain neighborhood of Boston. Before moving to Boston, where she now lives with her family, Teri lived in California and Jamaica, training teachers in both locations.

J. Anthony Lloyd is the senior pastor of the Greater Framingham Community Church, Framingham, MA, and an Adjunct Professor at Gordon-Conwell Theological Seminary, Boston Campus. Having served for twenty years at Gordon College as Associate Dean of students and adjunct faculty member, he has taught leadership courses at the Boston Campus for over twenty-five years. A native of Philadelphia, PA, he received his BS degree from Houghton College, Houghton, NY, his MDiv from Gordon-Conwell Theological Seminary, Hamilton Campus, and his DMin from United Theological Seminary, Dayton, OH. A pastor and educator at heart, he serves on numerous local and national boards, committees, and commissions, including Houghton College board of trustees, The Salvation Army School for Officer's Training, Advisory Council, Suffern NY, and the Advisory Board of the Boston Campus of Gordon-Conwell Theological Seminary, where he is chair, to name only a few.

David Martinez is the senior pastor of the Tabernáculo Evangélico (Tabernacle Gospel Church), Assemblies of God, in Revere, Massachusetts. Since his ordination in 1984, he has combined his pastoral role with a career in education. He is a certified elementary school teacher in Massachusetts, where he has taught in the Boston public schools. He received a master's degree in education from Cambridge College in Massachusetts in 1995, and MDiv and DMin from Gordon-Conwell Theological Seminary, Boston Campus, in 2003 and 2007, respectively. He has served the Spanish Eastern District, Assemblies of God, as Director of Home Missions, Director of Christian Education for the New England Section, and presbyter of the Northern New England Section. He currently serves on the advisory board of Gordon-Conwell Theological Seminary, Boston Campus. David lives in Everett, Massachusetts, with his wife and three daughters.

Seong Hyun Park is the Assistant Dean of Boston Campus and Assistant Professor of Old Testament, at Gordon-Conwell Theological Seminary. He oversees the academic programs of the Boston Campus, and coedits the *Africanus Journal*, the Africanus Monograph Series, and the Urban Voice Series, the affiliate publications of the Center for Urban Ministerial Education (CUME), Boston Campus of Gordon-Conwell Theological Seminary. Born in South Korea and reared in Paraguay, Seong studied and taught in Israel and Palestine, and currently lives with his family in Boston, Massachusetts, from where he reaches out to teach and preach across the cultures, both locally and internationally. He received his BA from The Hebrew University of Jerusalem, Israel, and his MA from Tel Aviv University, also in Israel. His PhD is in the Archaeology of Levant and the Hebrew Bible, from Harvard University.

John and Eliana Runyon live and minster in Lynn, Massachusetts, with their two children, Christopher and Daniela. Ordained ministers in the Foursquare Church, they currently pastor One Voice Church, a church that meets in their home. They both work in administration at Massachusetts Institute of Technology in Cambridge, MA, and serve as Adjunct Professors in Urban Ministry at the Boston Campus of Gordon-Conwell Theological Seminary.

Aída Besançon Spencer is Professor of New Testament at the Hamilton Campus of Gordon-Conwell Theological Seminary. Born and reared in Santo Domingo, Dominican Republic, she has served as a community organizer, protestant campus minister, and academic dean in a wide variety of urban settings in New Jersey. She has a PhD in New Testament from Southern Baptist Theological Seminary and an MDiv and ThM from Princeton Theological Seminary. An ordained Presbyterian minister, she is founding pastor of organization of the Pilgrim Church of Beverly, Massachusetts. She has written *Beyond the Curse: Women Called to Ministry, Paul's Literary Style, 2 Corinthians,* and *Pastoral Epistles.* She has coedited with her husband, the Rev. Dr. William David Spencer, and others, *Global Voices on Biblical Equality, God through the Looking Glass, The Goddess Revival, The Prayer Life of Jesus, The Global God, Joy through the Night, Latino Heritage Bible,* and *Marriage at the Crossroads.* She is also coeditor of the *Africanus Journal* and founder of the Africanus Guild and House of Prisca and Aquila Series.

William David Spencer has done urban ministry since 1966. He is Ranked Adjunct Professor of Theology and the Arts at the Boston Campus of Gordon-Conwell Theological Seminary, and founder of its Athanasian Teaching Scholars Program. He holds a ThD in theology and literature from Boston University School of Theology, MDiv and ThM from Princeton Theological Seminary, and his BA from Rutgers University. He has served as Protestant Chaplain at Rider College, Director of Personnel for the Alpha-Omega Community Theological School (A.C.T.S.), Adjunct Professor for New York Theological Seminary, and the Caribbean Graduate School of Theology (Kingston, JA), and teaching coordinator of the adult literacy program in Louisville, Kentucky. He helped found and still serves as Pastor of Encouragement for Pilgrim Church in Beverly, Massachusetts. Beside the books cowritten and coedited with his wife, he has written *Mysterium and Mystery: The Clerical Crime Novel, Dread Jesus,* and coedited *Chanting Down Babylon: The Rastafari Reader.* He has also authored a novel, *Name in the Papers.* He is the editor of *Priscilla Papers,* the coeditor of *Africanus Journal,* codirector of the Africanus Guild, and coproducer of the House of Prisca and Aquila Series.

Foundations of New Jerusalem—By Way of a Preface

Seong Hyun Park

> And the wall of the city had twelve foundations, and on them were
> the twelve names of the twelve apostles of the Lamb.[1]

THIS IS AN UNEXPECTED description for a city "coming down out of heaven
from God,"[2] the New Jerusalem. Its twelve foundations for the wall do not
bear the name of God, but the "names of the twelve apostles of the Lamb."
Is this unusual?

Whether Classical or pre-Classical, foundation inscriptions of the
Ancient Near East primarily served to mark the identity of the builder or
rebuilder—typically a monarch who commissioned the project.[3] The name
we would expect to see inscribed on the foundations of New Jerusalem's
wall, then, is the name of God—not the "names of the twelve apostles of the
Lamb." What is the implication? Did they, the apostles, build it—the wall of
heavenly Jerusalem?

Nehemiah did become the builder of the new walls of Jerusalem, after
the Exile, as John Runyon reminds us in his chapter, "Blueprints for the
Heart of the Rebuilder." It was within the bounds of this Old Jerusalem that
the church was birthed, and ever since then, the city (as represented by the
Old Jerusalem) has never ceased to foment missional zeal in the life of the
church (David A. Currie's chapter, "*Ecclesiapolis:* Two Millennia of Mutual
Transformation between Church and City").

---

1. Rev 21:14 ESV.

2. Rev 21:10 ESV.

3. For a classic treatise on the topic, see, Ellis, *Foundation Deposits*. A recent discussion of the topic can be found in Winter, "Babylonian Archaeologists."

Nehemiah's Jerusalem and the ensuing vision for the New Jerusalem are only half the story, however. Murder, banishment, and fear are associated with Cain the first builder of the city in Genesis—and the city he built, city of Enoch, has come to epitomize Cain's forced hope of reconnection, as well as his pain of estrangement, throughout the history of human cities. This is where the readjusting of our attitudes is required, says William David Spencer, in his chapter and introduction, "Rebuilding the City of Enoch with the Blueprints of Christ": not to yearn to return to Eden, but to move forward and join in the building of the city of God! This is a vision we have to seek purposefully according to Spencer, since the fall has conditioned us to see danger and fear, rather than a refuge of safety, in the city, and prompts us to turn to the lost garden. But the journey is only going forward, toward the city that God builds forever, not back to Eden. This is a bold proposition.

Such conditions of the fall that force our sight away from God's vision for the city are multifarious. We see the youth fall on the streets (Dean Borgman's chapter, "Roadblocks to the New Jerusalem Facing Urban Youth and Communities"); we are trapped in consumerism (Teri Elliott-Hart's chapter, "Challenges to Discipleship in the Context of Contemporary Consumer Culture"); we are torn apart ethnically and racially (Bianca Duemling's chapter, "Intercultural Unity, a Sign of the New Jerusalem: Overcoming Barriers and Getting Ready for Church Collaborations across Cultural Lines"); we are discouraged by virtue of being a minority (David Martinez's chapter, "Building *Shalom* in the City: Education Provides a Bridge between the Church and the Secular Community"); or we may be a "homeless" congregation, partnering for space to hold our worship (Lorraine Cleaves Anderson's chapter, "Under One Steeple: Biblical and Theological Foundations for Sharing Church Space"). Each of these authors grapples with the ramifications of such conditions and shares where their journey has taken them so far as God graces us to join him in the rebuilding of "the city of Enoch on the blueprint plans of the New Jerusalem."

Can the "blueprint plans" of New Jerusalem incorporate the theoretical frameworks that we formulate? Efforts are presented in the chapters mentioned above, but especially in the following three chapters: Carlot D. Celestin's in counseling ("A Conceptual Framework for Counseling City People"), Douglas A. Hall's in social systems ("Living-System Ministry Ushers in the New Jerusalem," with collaborations by Judy Hall, Steve Daman, and Jeffrey Bass), and Mark G. Harden's in human ecology ("Redeeming the City in the Margins").

"(T)welve foundations, and on them . . . the twelve names of the twelve apostles." It is my conviction that what the readers will find in the chapters that follow is how variously, and intimately, each of the authors have been engaging in living out the unfathomable depth of the grace that declares the heavenly city as ours, and us as his:

> Then I looked, and behold, on Mount Zion stood the Lamb, and with him 144,000 who had his name and his Father's name written on their foreheads.[4]

Yes, New Jerusalem is the city that bears our name, but we in turn bear God's name. As he builds us, he has us build this new city; as he loves us, he has us love this city; as he owns us, he has us own this city—the city where he will dwell with us.[5] Living out this grace, living out our New Jerusalem, is what we, the contributors to this volume, see as one important implication of having disciples' names engraved on the heavenly foundations.

What will that city be like, once the "blueprint plans" have been carried through? That is where Aída B. Spencer's chapter, "What City Are We Creating?" will take you, and I'll leave that for you to discover.

---

4. Rev 14:1 ESV.

5. Rev 21:3.

Acknowledgments

THE EDITORS ARE INDEBTED to the wonderful assistance provided by the following students of Gordon-Conwell Theological Seminary: Jet Li (Aída Besançon Spencer's Byington Scholar for 2012–13) for the formatting of the initial manuscript; Jennifer Creamer (Aída Besançon Spencer's Africanus Guild Student) for the proofreading of the manuscript; François Augustin (Seong Hyun Park's Byington Scholar for Fall, 2012) for the initial bibliographic collection; Clevette N. Greene for assistance with indexes; and Alta Bazile (Seong Hyun Park's Byington Scholar for Spring, 2013) for feedback on the contents. The editors also thank Esmé Bieberly for her superb copyediting service, Mark G. Harden for the cover-design concept, and Christian Amondson, the Assistant Managing Editor at Wipf & Stock, for overseeing the production of this volume.

The authors would like to express love and gratitude to our students at Gordon-Conwell Theological Seminary—Boston for their passionate, yet fond, presence both in the classes and in the city. David Currie expresses his appreciation to Al Padilla, the former Dean of Gordon-Conwell Theological Seminary—Boston, both for his vision and for seeing in David, "the WASPiest guy I know," the ability to teach church history in the city effectively. Carlot Celestin wishes to express his gratitude to the staff at New Life Counseling and Wellness Center, the church family, Tabernacle Baptist Congregation, his wife Carla, and his children Mischael and Jephthe. David Martinez thanks his wife Rosa and family for all their support, as well as Pastor Rafael Reyes, the Superintendent of the Spanish Eastern District of Assemblies of God, who has been his mentor and spiritual guide over 15 years of ministry. Seong Hyun Park is greatly indebted to Bill and Aída, the co-editors, for their encouragement and advice throughout the editing process of the present volume—and cannot express enough how much he loves his wife Hyun and the two jewels of their lives, Daniel and Matthew.

Finally, thanks be to God, the author of this all.

Rebuilding the City of Enoch with the Blueprints of Christ

An Introduction

WILLIAM DAVID SPENCER

SOMETIMES, WHEN YOU ARE traveling on a cloud-covered, moonless night, riding through the darkness on some empty interstate highway, perhaps in a bus, or a truck, or a car, you find the darkness so encompassing you wonder if it is playing tricks with your eyes. Perhaps you have hit a long and lonely stretch of flat, barren land. Your eyes have been straining past the headlights so long that you imagine the absence of light is complete, the night bereft of any light besides what you can generate yourself. Then, slowly, in the distance ahead, you perceive a faint glow. Of course, you wonder if it is real or a mirage. You have been so long in the darkness it seems there is no light left in the world, but the closer you get to it, the brighter it grows.

The first thing you see is light itself, glimmering in the distance. Then outlying farms and homes and businesses and factories etch out of the darkness, each with its own separate illumination. Fairly soon, reflecting signs and street lamps appear. The lights proliferate, blending together, and shortly the whole area is ablaze. For example, those who have walked the central streets of Manhattan at midnight may wonder if there is any night at all, or if the sun has stopped at high noon. Every shop appears open; all the lights are on. It is hard to miss a city that is active. And, if that city happens to be on the highest elevated spot in an area—you can see it for miles. These are the images Jesus used when addressing his disciples in the midst of a huge gathering of people.

He may himself have been out in the empty hill country, across the Sea of Galilee (the Lake of Tiberius), where he went to seek solace and respite, but a large crowd had gathered and, had they stayed, they might have been the beginning of a new city, for that is basically what a city is: a vast group of people and all their accouterments, houses, businesses, roads, conveyances, etc.

What Jesus explained to them in Matthew 5:14, addressing his disciples as the crowd listened in, was literally, "You [that is, you plural—all of you] are the light of the world. A city is not able to be kept secret [that is to say, concealed, or covered up, or hidden, or private] upon a mountain [or hill] standing." In other words, one cannot hide a city that is built on a mountaintop, towering over everything else. It is going to be obvious. We are not talking subtle here. We are not talking blend in. We are talking out front—up close and personal, in your face, in the middle of everything!

For Jesus, two positive images are linked together: light and the city. His disciples are supposed to be a source of light for everyone else—as obvious and unashamed as a great metropolis, resplendent on the highest promontory, presiding over everything, influencing culture, setting the standard, establishing the trends, making itself the center, the reference point to which everyone else in the population turns for knowledge, for enlightenment, for healing. This depiction of the city contains Jesus' intention for the Christian community: to be a city of light.

Changing Images of the City

For many today, this imagery has been lost. We no longer view the city as the positive symbol it was for Jesus. Instead, many of us fear the city. For us, it is a dangerous place. We go outside of it and seek to create "suburbs of refuge." Throughout history, however, as for Jesus, the city was the sanctuary of safety. The countryside was a wasteland of lawlessness, where brigands and bandits lurked.

Think of the story of the Good Samaritan: it was in the pass between Samaria and Jerusalem that the traveler was attacked. Had he only made it to the city—to the place where the people are, where there is safety in numbers so one is protected—he would have been fine. But he was waylaid outside in the desolation, alone, with no one to rescue him, a solitary victim.

The great African teacher, St. Augustine, who lived back in the 400s, in his seminal book *The City of God*, pointed out that evil strikes at the core of this concept of sanctuary, as the devil's definition of the city is constantly battling with God's definition in order to define humanity. Augustine wrote of these two competing populations: "The one consists of those who wish to live after the flesh, the other of those who wish to live after the spirit."[1] Obviously, many of us contemporary humans have lost both our historical consciousness that there is a battle of definitions raging around us, as well as our common sense of where we ought to be seeking community. We have been deluded into trading the center of humanity for the periphery, thereby handing the locus of action over to evil and all its nefarious work to undermine our reliance on each other, destroy community, isolate individuals, and mug them as surely as was the victim in Jesus' parable. Clearly, many of us need to rethink the city.

How Did Urban Life Begin?

A watchword in Christian studies is that all good theology goes back to Genesis. And certainly we find the beginning of our study in Genesis 4:9–17:

> Then the Lord said to Cain, "Where is your brother Abel?"
>
> "I don't know," he replied. "Am I my brother's keeper?"
>
> The Lord said, "What have you done? Listen! Your brother's blood cries out to me from the ground. Now you are under a curse and driven from the ground, which opened its mouth to receive your brother's blood from your hand. When you work the ground, it will no longer yield its crops for you. You will be a restless wanderer on the earth."
>
> Cain said to the Lord, "My punishment is more than I can bear. Today you are driving me from the land, and I will be hidden from your presence; I will be a restless wanderer on the earth, and whoever finds me will kill me."
>
> But the Lord said to him, "Not so; anyone who kills Cain will suffer vengeance seven times over." Then the Lord put a mark on Cain so that no one who found him would kill him. So Cain went out from the Lord's presence and lived in the land of Nod, east of Eden.

---

1. Augustine, *The City of God*, 14.1.

3

Cain made love to his wife, and she became pregnant and gave birth to Enoch. Cain was then building a city, and he named it after his son Enoch. (TNIV)

This is a story full of pathos. Cain, the first juvenile delinquent, gets tried and sentenced to banishment—estrangement from the Lord, the land, the love of his fellow human beings. In other words, what he robbed Abel of becomes his own punishment, his own loss.

He has made it so that Abel cannot earn a living, so now Cain's livelihood too is gone; the land is cursed because of what he has done, and he will have to struggle to wrest out a living from it. Cain has made Abel incapable of having any earthly relationships, so now Cain is driven away from communion with God and community with humanity; he is in despair. He cannot live with such estrangement.

He begs God for a lighter sentence, but God reprieves him only of the capital sentence on his life. Cain's alienation from the land and from other people remains. He has to seek out his own way to counterbalance this disenfranchisement and replace the support he once had. And, therefore, in desperation, he seeks to create a series of networks that will provide him a support base.

First, his begging God for mercy has placed a mark on him that, while not ensuring amiable relations, at least will protect him from the reprisal of capital punishment when he meets another human. Second, he and his wife have a son, creating a nuclear family. And, third, having been banished to the land of *Nod*, that is, in Hebrew, the state of wandering about,[2] he attempts to recreate for himself an extended human community to make up for the one his crime has cost him. He starts a settlement, a city, to deal with the communal level of the curse, and he names it for his son. In that decision, he displays his pain. He does not glorify himself, elevating his own name and building his empire in defiance of his just desert of isolation and shame. Rather, he names his city for his innocent child. Perhaps, he is expressing a desire that this gift, this child, will right through righteous rule his own wrong. In such a gesture, Cain would be reminiscent of his mother, as she exults at Cain's birth, "With the help of the Lord I have brought forth a man!" (Gen 4:1) Perhaps, she too had been hoping that the cataclysmic wrong her deception had instigated, which had resulted in the devastating loss of Eden's garden, would end in Cain himself, her offspring, who would be the promised one to crush the head of the serpentine evil that had

2. Feyerabend, *Langenscheidt*, 210. See also BDB, 627, col. 1.

destroyed her home in paradise. But with his vain hope, Cain, as an active agent, disappears from recorded history.

Now, we might ask, in founding his city, does Cain continue to sin? Does he, in effect, defy God by not accepting his punishment of estrangement in trying to ease his loneliness by building a family, a network, a city? No. The curses in Genesis are descriptive, not prescriptive. God, in driving Cain out of the divine and human familial circle, is describing what Cain can now expect—that terrible loneliness that plagues fallen humanity.

In 1990, in a French prison, a reporter interviewed an inmate who had committed murder as part of an armed robbery. The young prisoner reflected,

> I didn't set out to kill him, but I did so—and in cold blood—when it seemed necessary. I didn't give it another thought at the time. I thought that I would shrug it off the way I had successfully ignored all my other crimes. But I soon discovered that a man who commits murder sets himself apart from all other human beings for the rest of his life. One day I woke and felt that I had been permanently stained by my act. The feeling grew so strong that I was almost relieved to be caught.

Like Cain before him, this young inmate realized his act had driven him from God's presence as "the feeling of horror, of disgust, of shame grew." So, he reports,

> I consulted a priest in prison. He gave me a Bible and, as I began to read, I was somewhat comforted, not initially by a sense of God's forgiveness but by the conviction that He was present. The sense of separation I felt suggested the existence of a Being who was offended, who cared enough for me to be ashamed for me. I came to belief through guilt.[3]

Like this inmate, Cain, who had once known and had now lost communion with God, was not so seared in his conscience that he was tempted to lift himself up for glorification. His act was one of desperation, attempting to ameliorate his loss, to ease its ramifications by creating a support base through an expanding series of networks. The ultimate step was to create the city.

3. *Life* Magazine, "Face of God," 52.

5

In this light, a city can be defined as a network of relationships. The reason for a city's existence, after all, is to connect. Everything in it is networked. In essence, the city is itself a container of connections.

The City as a Container of Connecting Communities

A city is a kind of communal womb in whose hospitals much of the population begins. As well, it is an incubator for human creativity, where its arts and its conduits of written and transmitted media serve its multiple populations as the means for varied human expression and interchange.

In addition to an innovator, the city then becomes a repository, preserving classic expressions of art and of architecture. Its museums are archives, preserving the historical record of its communal experiences and expressions.

At the same time that it looks to the past, the city looks to the future as the capital of applied techno-culture. While technology may be created anywhere, the city is where the majority of humanity operates it, and, therefore, where it is applied most graphically.

In parallel to technology, the arts find their finest performance expressions in the city, as, within the dizzying onslaught of the future, they become a kind of safety valve, a humanizer to reflect and leaven the impersonal mechanism of technology. A Christian art, in particular, has the capacity to reaffirm human worth in the tension between human worker as commercial producer/product and the human cry, "I am worth more than a handful of bolts." The arts become a powerful tool of ministry within such a venue, telling the good news that God values people and has a destiny for humans that is not just planned obsolescence.

Since the city is the place where the greatest concentration of people live, work, and interact, it serves as a forum for debating all topics of national and international concern. Its opinions often set the trends of thinking for all in its surrounding area and beyond.

In its wider identity, the city is a global crossroads and a seat of multicultural diversity. In Boston, where the writers of this present book currently teach at Gordon-Conwell Theological Seminary's Boston Campus, we have rich church communities of African Americans; Africans of many nations, including Christian gatherings of Eritreans, Ethiopians, Cape Verdeans; Messianic Jews, Lebanese, Arabs, Syrians, and other Middle Easterners; Burmese, Cambodians, Vietnamese, Chinese, Filipinos, Indonesians,

Japanese, Koreans, and others from the Far East; Indians; Armenians, Albanians, Lithuanians, Poles, and other Eastern Europeans, including Romanians and Serbians, Russians, Latvians, Ukrainians, and the Slavonic; Greeks; Italians, Swiss, Swedes, other Scandinavians, and other Europeans; Irish, Brits, and Canadians; Barbadians, Jamaicans, Trinidadians, and other English-speaking West Indians, as well as Panamanians and Belizeans; South and Central Americans, Puerto Ricans, Cubans, Dominicans, and other West Indians, as well as Mexican Hispanics and Spaniards; Haitians and other French-speaking peoples; Brazilians and the Portuguese.[4] In this diversity, the gospel of Jesus Christ serves as a kind of common identifier, a chief promoter of cross-cultural understanding.

Most poignantly, then, the city serves as holy ground where people meet God. This is why Jesus, himself, who came among us, participating in the life of humanity, went to the cities, teaching and healing, loving and mourning his city of Enoch: "Jerusalem, Jerusalem, you who kill the prophets and stone those sent to you, how often I have longed to gather your children together, as a hen gathers her chicks under her wings, and you were not willing" (Luke 13:34 TNIV), as he worked to prepare its population for the coming of the New Jerusalem.

And all of this that was potential in the city's primordial context, what Cain set out to accomplish in founding the first city, we can see, still explains the nature of the city today. In contemporary cities, all the best of what Cain could hope to achieve in reconnecting with humanity is present. And all that remains of the estrangement is present as well.

The City in Its Biblical Significance

In the Bible, we find two urban bookends that frame human history. The primal garden is gone forever. We can forget that—dismiss it from our minds. Despite the late 1960s' pathetically hope-filled plea in Joni Mitchell's era-defining, flower-power, anthemic tribute, "Woodstock," humanity did not then, and will never be able to, get itself back to God's garden. That seminal part of human history is forever lost to us. It is never coming back. Instead, the countless generations of humans that have come about over the eons should now look forward together for an urban paradise: the city that God rules. But, in this search, as the war that began at Eden continues to rage in our world, two definitions for our ultimate urban home struggle

4. Mitchell et al., *Boston Church Directory*, 347.

against each other to become the definer of the city and, therefore, the final contextualizing means of self-understanding for humanity.

On one side is this city of Cain that began with Enoch and degenerated into Babel, with its blasphemous tower, and ultimately became Babylon, the presumptuous and lethal, both so clearly symbols of what St. Augustine meant by the city of humanity.

On the other side is the city of God, symbolized by the New Jerusalem that comes to earth in Revelation 21, after "Babylon" falls in chapter 18. This is the beautiful city—the city of Cain's and of all of our best desires—radiant in light and resplendent in purity like a chaste bride awaiting her husband (Rev 21:2). In this urban paradise, every eye will be dried, every tear will be wiped away, sorrow will be no more; no more death, no more mourning, no more crying, no more pain (Rev 21:4). Consider John's description, as the apostle reports the vision that he was given on the island of Patmos.

I never understood what this passage was about until I had the privilege to stand in that cave in which John is reported to have received the revelation. In his day, the cave's entrance was open, and John could sit and look out from the mountain height across the fishing village, down the shoreline, and out across the sea. As a child, I had imagined the exiled John, struggling for existence on a bleak and rocky volcano top that jutted out of the waters, starving no doubt, as he attempted to scrape his subsistence from its meager, weed-spotted slopes. The reality is vastly different.

Patmos is a fertile and, even in that day, inhabited island. The bitter Domitian, who had begun his rule firmly but equitably enough, had swiftly degenerated into ruthlessness after an attempted coup, altering his policy into what became known as "the terror," as he systematically terminated anyone with leadership potential.[5]

John, one of Jesus' actual disciples, would naturally attract Domitian's attention, especially being the leader of a movement that refused emperor worship in a time when complete loyalty was the besieged emperor's chief requirement. But John, the beloved disciple, was obviously harmless, and Domitian chose to banish rather than exterminate him.

Once on Patmos, rather than in a cave, John probably lived on the shoreline in a village among the fisherfolk and, periodically, perhaps daily, climbed up to the cave, from whose heights he could lift up his prayers for its inhabitants. I believe it was in such a pastoral moment that he suddenly received the gift of sight. What he saw before him was no longer the humble

5. James and Chilver, "Domitian," 360.

little fishing village, but something altogether more resplendent, the New Jerusalem, the fulfillment of all God's promises, and the end of all banishment and all human suffering. And, as he watched, from his own vantage point of exile, he realized this city, though not yet here, was truly imminent. It was the fulfillment of a long-suffering God, who waits to give opportunities to humans to avoid missing out on the promise of restoration. And, yet, this paradise was still steadily, inexorably, coming in as John wrote down what he saw. In fact, it is still coming in as I write these words, and yet still coming in as you read them.

John is startled as an angel calls out to him: "Come, I will show you the bride, the wife of the Lamb" (Rev 21:9). As John watches, awestruck, he reports,

> I saw the Holy City, the new Jerusalem, coming down out of heaven from God, prepared as a bride beautifully dressed for her husband. And I heard a loud voice from the throne saying, "Look! God's dwelling place is now among the people, and he will dwell with them. They will be his people, and God himself will be with them and be their God. 'He will wipe every tear from their eyes. There will be no more death' or mourning or crying or pain, for the old order of things has passed away."
>
> He who was seated on the throne said, "I am making everything new!"

And in this new city, John reports,

> I did not see a temple in the city, because the Lord God Almighty and the Lamb are its temple. The city does not need the sun or the moon to shine on it, for the glory of God gives it light, and the Lamb is its lamp. The nations will walk by its light, and the kings of the earth will bring their splendor into it. On no day will its gates ever be shut, for there will be no night there. The glory and honor of the nations will be brought into it. Nothing impure will ever enter it, nor will anyone who does what is shameful or deceitful, but only those whose names are written in the Lamb's book of life. (Rev 21:2–5; 22–27 TNIV)

Do we see what is happening here? Revelation 21:4 tells us that the old order has passed away. The city that Cain tried to build with all its wishes, with all its flaws, will be replaced with the city God builds forever. That is what we are all looking forward to: not the restoration of a garden, but the establishment of an eternal holy city. So, that reality determines what we followers of Jesus are all about now—helping rebuild the city of Enoch on the blueprint plans of the New Jerusalem.

Readjusting Our Attitudes to Be Architects for Christ

If anything stands in our way of accomplishing the goal of helping rebuild the city of Enoch into the New Jerusalem, it is the attitude conditioned into us by living in this fallen world. Today, the fall has conditioned us not to look to the city for a refuge of safety—even we who would like to remake the city for God. Instead, emotionally, even unconsciously, we yearn for the lost garden, as our popular cultures around the world express fear of the city in news features; action movies; and popular televised, eBook, and printed tales of suspense. For many of us around the world, it seems a given fact that the city is a dangerous place. For us, the city is Sodom and Gomorrah and Gibeah (see Judg 19), equipped with neon lights so criminals can better spot us out. But the Bible gives us a different paradigm.

In the Bible, God ordained cities of refuge, which were sanctuaries from harm, as we see in God's instructions in Numbers 35:6–15:

> "Six of the towns you give the Levites will be cities of refuge, to which a person who has killed someone may flee. In addition, give them forty-two other towns. In all you must give the Levites forty-eight towns, together with their pasturelands. The towns you give the Levites from the land the Israelites possess are to be given in proportion to the inheritance of each tribe: Take many towns from a tribe that has many, but few from one that has few."

> Then the Lord said to Moses: "Speak to the Israelites and say to them: 'When you cross the Jordan into Canaan, select some towns to be your cities of refuge, to which a person who has killed someone accidentally may flee. They will be places of refuge from the avenger, so that anyone accused of murder may not die before they stand trial before the assembly. These six towns you give will be your cities of refuge. Give three on this side of the Jordan and three in Canaan as cities of refuge. These six towns will be a place of refuge for Israelites and for foreigners residing among them, so that anyone who has killed another accidentally can flee there.'" (TNIV)

Important to note is that the tribe which presides over these urban refuges is that of Levi, the tribe of priests. Those who preside over worship give sanctuary. Anyone seeking refuge in such urban centers of safety can find respite, mercy, and then justice.

We often talk these days about bringing *shalom* to the city. What would we mean by that term if we were to expand this picture of Numbers 35 to encompass giving peace to the entire multitude following Christ from every nation, tribe, people, and language across the globe, as we see depicted in Revelation 7:9? We would see the return of a whole different attitude toward the city and the role of the Christian within it. Expanding on the vision given (perhaps one starry night) to Abraham, we would see ourselves as part of the nation of priests through whom God intended those who have come to dwell in cities around the world would be blessed (Gen 12:3).

What we are envisioning is not just a utopian dream that is reserved for a millennium when Christ must rule in person directly over the earth to order to ensure amiable relationships among people. Forty years ago, when I began to visit my wife's birth city, Santo Domingo, in the Dominican Republic, I discovered an entirely different attitude than I had known, working as I had been doing in the then riot-scarred centers of Plainfield, my birth city, Newark in New Jersey, and Philadelphia. In the late 1960s, early 1970s, two of these cities had had riots, and the third was like a war grid of armed camps, filled with racial tension, all of them plagued by sporadic violence.

In those days, in contrast, the Dominicans viewed the countryside, not the city, as wild and dangerous—out there is where anything could happen. I remember one incident that scandalized the nation. It was a carjacking, in which thieves accosted a vehicle that included a priest, stole everything from the passengers, including their clothes, and turned them out with nothing on the highway. The people shook their heads in sorrow and said, "But, that's the way it is in the countryside. No one is safe."

In Santo Domingo, in those days, one could walk out in our area at all hours of the day and night. There was an armed guard on nearly every corner, so street crime was virtually nonexistent. Of course, there was always stealing by employees and purse snatching and pickpockets abroad—and in this fallen world there will always be crimes of passion—but everyone expected to be at risk in the countryside and to find succor from being mugged if only one could manage to get across the city limits into safety.

But, today, this is no longer true. Santo Domingo, like the cities in which we now labor in the United States, and those reported by our colleagues around the world, has itself become the victim of violence, due to the invasion of street drugs. Cities all along the drug flow have been reduced to so many sites for trafficking, simply stages marking the progress, as cartels advance their wares city after city. Borders mean nothing. Politicians, customs officers, police are killed or corrupted. And that corruption seeps down into everything, becoming endemic even in the simplest aspects of life.

Several years ago, my wife had her purse snatched. Steve, our son, and I chased the thieves, as they were escaping on a moped, through crowds who would not help us stop them, despite my shouts of "Ladrones! (thieves!)" When we returned empty-handed and frustrated to Aída's home and reported the incident to a retired New York City policeman who happened to be visiting the widow whom Aída has allowed to live there with her children, he explained to us, "The people on the street could not help you. They are afraid. Most crimes these days are done by off-duty policemen. They fear reprisal." He then told us a heartrending story. His own mother had been shopping at a pharmacy when armed robbers came in to hold it up. One of them pointed with his rifle at a pendant she was wearing and the gun went off accidently and killed her. When the police made no progress, the former officer hired a detective who hunted for the killers until he suddenly stopped. The trail had led to the police station. Under a corrupt president, the situation seethed, as all night long we could hear the whirr of mopeds, as off-duty policemen went out to break into people's homes.

And then things began to change. The nation, fed up with this plight, elected an honest president. When the next atrocity occurred to us, the widow's own brother murdered by a gang for not giving them free beer from his little market, this time the government acted. The new president had fired much of the police leadership, putting in charge an honest commissioner who himself had survived an extermination attempt. Then the new president had the vice president of a leading bank arrested for financing a drug plane, and began to clean up as much of the graft in the government as he could. To the gang's dismay, the police invaded the barrio, arresting gang members and shooting those who resisted. Corrupt lawyers helped the leader escape, but the message was out. In the most graphic way, ensuring justice was restoring peace to the city.[6] It has now been four years of honest rule and a newly elected president promises to maintain the same.

6. The fight being waged in the Dominican Republic is part of the same war we are

The war to take back our cities transcends simple ideology. In 2002, my wife and I were privileged to visit Havana, Cuba, as part of a team from the Boston Theological Institute, the consortium of Boston's theological schools. We were on a religious visa to meet with the churches to see how they fared under the new relaxed policies the government had traded for help with the overwhelming social problems. On the streets, we heard the people moaning the same complaint about Havana that we ourselves were making about our own cities, which was clear evidence that communism, like capitalism, is no match for corruption in a fallen world; all human systems struggle with pervasive evil. Fidel Castro had come in half a century earlier as a reform candidate, people told us, to rid the country of North American crime syndicates who were using Cuba as their playland and stash center. Castro delivered. He just never left. But, by 2002, he had grown elderly and infirm and far less effective, and prostitution, gambling, theft, and crime were back in the streets. The Cubans also told us that they love the United States; so many of their relatives are now living in Florida, in New York, and throughout the USA, and the money they generously send back to them has become a great part of their gross national income. When the Castros pass on, many told us, they are looking forward to mending relations with the United States.

Over the years, many new and innovative ideas for reclaiming cities have been developed, from urban planning, to gentrification of former slums, to "streets for people," to solarization to replace carbon-based urban economies, to many more constructive movements. When Massachusetts Institute of Technology's press released journalist Catherine Tumber's *Small, Gritty, and Green,* a defense of the smaller industrial city to replace the mega-metropolis as the way of the future, in an interview with *The Boston Phoenix,* Tumber recalled Lewis Mumford's observation, "The modern metropolis is the urban form of financial monopoly." Although the point of this metaphor has to do with power, for example, with prestige (e.g., before the 1950s, smaller cities "were taken seriously as cities, where interesting people wanted to live. It's a self-perpetuating cycle. The more interesting people leave, the more no one wants to stay. . . . New York has a

---

fighting today in the United States. It continues. When we visited Santo Domingo in January of 2012, I read daily of drug gang struggles that have put whole districts in thrall, sophisticated rings that specialize in robbing certain kinds of vehicles or items to finance drug movements, an entire neighboring city, popular with mission groups, in which no one can venture out after 9:00 p.m. for safety's sake. But the people have elected another honest leader and correction goes on.

monopolization on high culture and the dissemination of mass culture"[7]), I could hear something more basic to the plight of Santo Domingo and Havana, as I listened to the Dominicans and the Cubans. In their complaints, I could hear echoed my own concern for the present captivity of North American cities in which I have worked for the last 47 years and in which I still work. To me, the power of Mumford's depiction lies in the metaphor of finance to represent all that draws the population to big cities. In my observation, the financially driven mass movement to larger cities has to do with opportunities to find remunerative work, to cut living expenses in the greater opportunity for consumer choice in more competitive markets, to find housing that is more affordable in more mobile and fluid markets, as well as for streams of immigrants to survive culturally in the ponds of ethnic ghettos where one can maintain an identity support base. But, there is an underside to the idea of the city as the locus of financial stability as it is expressed in the most lethal form of acquired financially-driven commodities whose rapid turnover and attractive profits thwart all attempts to remake the city, and these are what crime provides.

For an example from my own area, as a pastor of a storefront church in a small satellite city of Boston, on its North Shore, I, along with our deacons, constantly work with heroin addicts, the victims of an incredibly cheap and potent strain that has made the truly lovely North Shore simply one more stage in the flow across continents. The street word is that the drugs are floated off our shores in plastic bags, picked up, and brought in under the meager catch of fish by fisherfolk whose livelihood has been threatened by red tides and overfishing by Russian trawlers and by others who practice no conservation restraint. The drugs are processed in safe houses in suburbs and smaller towns, then distributed throughout New England as they move to their final goal, which is New York City. All along the way, churches, like our church, pick up the human flotsam and jetsam strewn in the wake of this river of death and, despite the valiant struggle of programs both secular (in our area, the Center for Addictive Behavior) and religious (for us, most notably Teen Challenge and the Salvation Army), we see very little permanent deliverance from heroin of this grade and this devastation. Jesus changes lives, but this drug is so addictive that eight years down the line of sobriety can still be lost in one afternoon of depression with a nickel bag available on so many corners. Clearly, Christians need to wake up from the stupor of thinking "getting saved," if it is divorced from the struggle of daily

7. Garelick, "Thinking Small," 14.

taking on the Lordship of Christ, is the simple answer to everything. Jesus said, "Whoever wants to be my disciple must deny themselves and take up their cross daily and follow me" (Luke 9:23). His apostle Paul wrote,

> Do you not know that in a race all the runners run, but only one gets the prize? Run in such a way as to get the prize. Everyone who competes in the games goes into strict training. They do it to get a crown that will not last, but we do it to get a crown that will last forever. Therefore I do not run like someone running aimlessly; I do not fight like a boxer beating the air. No, I strike a blow to my body and make it my slave so that after I have preached to others, I myself will not be disqualified for the prize. (1 Cor 9:24–27 TNIV)

As one very wise friend observed, when a drug addict gets saved, we now have a Christian drug addict. Corruption breeds corruption; discipline breeds discipline, which is why we support life-rebuilding programs. Following Christ begins with grace, Jesus' gift to us of salvation, and then continues with our tribute back to Christ, disciplining ourselves to become more and more the people he has commanded us to be, then collectively expanding that discipline by an entire concentrated effort to root out and change the systemic evil that seeks to define us against Christ in city and suburb.[8]

Conclusion

In summary, the garden is lost. As with Cain's city, initial founding intentions may be good ones, but the end result can produce depressed, even lethal, sections of any city that now need adjustment. In addition, the fall has conditioned us to fear the city, evoking a self-fulfilling worldview where we expect the urban environment to be unsafe for all, though, historically, God intended it to provide safety, even refuge. Instead, we have allowed

8. Here in Massachusetts, for example, there is a tremendous cultural push to decriminalize marijuana use, as if that was going to solve our drug problem. We hear how marijuana is a harmless little diversion and not the entry drug that we all imagine. I doubt if many of those who push this specious idea have worked with addicts on the same level day in and day out, year in and year out that a storefront church does. Addicts start with marijuana. Not every marijuana user ends with heroin, but every heroin user with whom I have worked over the three decades I have been a volunteer founding pastor with this church has started with marijuana. We need to wake up the people in government who make our rules, the media that pushes these ideas, and the population that receives them and espouses them like so many imitating myna birds.

crime and corruption and drugs and other evils to pollute the city and its suburbs—and even steal them from us. We have to band together and act to take back our communities. The divinely appointed task of assisting God in reconciling the world demands we adjust the values of our communities to those of God's New Jerusalem, rebuilding our own cities of Enoch on the blueprints of Christ.

Against all this confusion and fear is Jesus Christ's mandate to go into all the world and share his good news, building the Christian community along the lines of the New Jerusalem, a city of light in which God is revealed. In that way, we can help others to draw on God's power that raises consciousness and inspires all to struggle against the pervasive evil that dwells within each one of us and infects our cities like a plague.

Toward accomplishing this task, this book is an examination of the biblical and theological meaning of the city and our mission within it. We hope it is useful to you. It distills what we have learned together in the three-plus decades in which we have been training pastors at Gordon-Conwell Theological Seminary, Boston Campus, while all of us have been ministering in churches ourselves. May God bless you to be a priestly healer, bringing Christ's *shalom* to the people whom you serve, as you do your part, as we all together work to rebuild the city of Enoch into a city of God's light on the blueprints of Christ.

References for Further Study

Augustine. *The City of God*. Translated by Marcus Dods. New York: Modern Library, 1994.

Spencer, Aída Besançon, and William David Spencer, eds. *The Global God: Multicultural Evangelical Views of God*. Grand Rapids: Baker, 1998.

Tumber, Catherine. *Small, Gritty, and Green: The Promise of America's Smaller Industrial Cities in a Low-Carbon World*. Cambridge: MIT Press, 2011.

Winter, Gibson. *The Suburban Captivity of the Churches*. New York: Macmillan, 1962.

What City Are We Creating?

Aída Besançon Spencer

THE WONDERFUL IMAGE OF the New Jerusalem closes the biblical canon. In the new heaven and earth, the holy city, the New Jerusalem, portrayed as a joyful bride, comes down out of heaven to earth. In this new city, God dwells with humans, having eliminated sinners, suffering, and death. The fallen earth created by disobedient Adam and Eve is no more. This new city has a ruler, God. This city is on a great, high mountain with a great, high wall. People of all nations will dwell there with open gates. All are invited to come. But, to enter the city one must have washed robes. In the midst of the city, coming from God, is a river which brings life.[1] In this city, the architect and builder is God. This city has no temple because the Lord God Almighty and the Lamb are its temple. God's glory lights it. The city is yet to arrive.[2]

But, how does this heavenly vision of a city relate to the concept of an earthly city? How does the New Jerusalem relate to the old Jerusalem? How does this heavenly vision relate to believers now? Since the New Jerusalem is a royal city where God dwells, it is both future and present and large and small.

What Is a "City"?

To begin, what is a city? What do we call a city now? Today a city is defined as "a large or important town," "an incorporated municipality, usually governed by a mayor and a board of alderman or councilmen" (United States), or "a municipality of high rank, usually based on population" (Canada), or

---

1. Rev 21:1–22:17; Ezek 47:1, 9. All quotations are from the NRSV unless otherwise noted.

2. Heb 11:10; 13:14; Rev 3:12; Isa 60:11, 19–20.

"a borough, usually the seat of a bishop, upon which the dignity of the title has been conferred by the crown" (Great Britain), or "the major metropolitan center of a region," or "a city-state."[3] Population is a key aspect of the definition.

In the Old Testament, a city was an enclosed place: *'ir* had walls and gates. It was a fortified height and an abode for humans.[4] It was a fortified place of any size. In Greek, *polis* comes from the verb *pelomai*, which means "to dwell," originally, "fulness, throng."[5] The countryside around it was dependent on the city. The city had its community or body of citizens with the rights of citizenship. It even was a state.[6] It was a population center.[7] Originally, individuals were citizens of a city-state. Thus, the word *citizen* (*politēs* and *politeia*) is related to *polis*. To survive, it had to be united (Matt 12:25). Thus, a city is a community that dwells together in a protected stronghold.

Why Jerusalem?

What made the Jerusalem of the Old Testament special? Like any city, it was built on a mountain. Like a fortress, it had its walls and gates.[8] Like a community, people dwelled there. It had its citizens. But what made it special were two things: it was a royal city, and it was the city where the temple of God was located.

A royal city had a ruler dwelling there. Jerusalem was the city of David.[9] But, this royal city also had the ruler of all, God, "dwelling" there; therefore, it was called the "holy city." King David brought the ark with the covenant of the Lord into the tabernacle that was set up in Jerusalem.[10] Thus, the temple and the city and places of prayer became intertwined (1 Kgs 8:21–29, 44–45, 48–49). People would pray toward the temple as a symbol of God's presence. They would also confirm oaths before the altar in the temple (1 Kgs 8:29, 34–43). Solomon then built a localized temple

3. *Random House Webster's Unabridged Dictionary,* 377.

4. BDB, 746.

5. Thayer, *Lexicon,* 528.

6. LSJ, 1434; BDAG, 844.

7. BDAG, 844–45.

8. 2 Sam 5:7, 9: the stronghold or fortress of Zion became the city of David.

9. 1 Sam 27:5: royal city; Kings David and Solomon were buried there (1 Kgs 2:10; 11:43; 15:8); Thayer, *Lexicon,* 528.

10. 2 Sam 6:12–18.

to replace the tabernacle (1 Kgs 3:1). Jerusalem was the city chosen by God where the city represented the people (1 Kgs 11:32; 14:21; 2 Kgs 23:27; 2 Chr 6:6, 34–35). Therefore, God was considered to be in the midst of the city. It had a river in its midst (Ps 46:4–5). Jerusalem, the stronghold of Zion, the city of David, became the city of God, his holy mountain (Ps 48:1–9, 12; Neh 11:1; Heb 12:22), the city God loved (Ps 87:1–3). It became the city with God's name (Dan 9:18), a holy city (Matt 27:53), "the holy habitation of the Most High" (Ps 46:4; 76:2). God became the king of Jerusalem (Matt 5:35; Ps 48:1–3):

> Great is the Lord and greatly to be praised in the city of our God.
>
> His holy mountain, beautiful in elevation, is the joy of all the earth, Mount Zion, in the far north, the city of the great King.
>
> Within its citadels God has shown himself a sure defense . . . .
>
> In the city of the Lord of hosts, in the city of our God, which God establishes forever.
>
> We ponder your steadfast love, O God, in the midst of your temple.
>
> Your name, O God, like your praise, reaches to the ends of the earth. . . .
>
> Walk about Zion, go all around it, count its towers, consider well its ramparts; go through its citadels, that you may tell the next generation that this is God, our God forever and ever. He will be our guide forever. (Ps 48:1–3, 8b–10a, 12–14)

No unclean person would enter the temple, and no unclean person then could enter the city because the city had God's presence (Isa 52:1–2; 26:1–2; 60:11–22). As representative of the chosen people, the city was to be just and righteous, defending the orphan and widow, a faithful city (Isa 1:21, 23, 26–27).

The New Jerusalem includes the concept of a city, the old Jerusalem, but even more. It also includes the concept of a royal city where God dwells.[11] Like an ancient city, it is fortified, it is inhabited, but, even more so, it has a ruler, who is perfectly righteous and loving, God. Psalm 48 brings out that the Jerusalem, which is God's city, would bring joy to all the world and would keep people safe from attack. Its inhabitants would report and praise God's deeds, constant love, and justice. Therefore, God would lead them forever.[12] However, what Judah failed to remember was the city was

---

11. Bauckham (*Theology*, 136, 140) explains that the whole of the New Jerusalem is a holy of holies shaped in a perfect cube (1 Kgs 6:20).

12. Bryan writes: the focus in the heavenly sanctuary "rests on the experience of the

not a magic talisman but, rather, a symbol of what each person, household, and nation should be like and could become if God indeed led them.

Why Is Jerusalem Presented as a Bride?

Personification of cities is often feminine because both the Hebrew (*'ir*) and the Greek *(polis)* words for "city" are feminine. In Hebrew, names of countries and towns are feminine, according to Gesenius, since they are regarded as the mothers and nurses of the inhabitants.[13] For example, Isaiah described Zion as a woman in labor (Isa 66:8) and a mother who nurses (66:11) and then God as a mother who comforts (66:13). The city of Abel is called a "mother city in Israel" (2 Sam 20:19) with a wise woman leading. Jerusalem is lamented as a widow with former lovers (Lam 1:1–6), a divorced wife (Isa 50:1), and a barren wife who has been restored (Isa 54:1–8). As Jerusalem was once punished for its inhabitants' sins, so now the New Jerusalem is restored. As a bridegroom rejoices over a bride, so will the Lord rejoice over the New Jerusalem, now restored (Isa 62:5). Thus, the restored bride, the New Jerusalem, is a counterpart to the exiled bride, the old Jerusalem.[14]

In a few instances, Jesus is referred to as a bridegroom preparing for a festive occasion.[15] Paul describes the church as a chaste virgin to be presented to Christ, the bridegroom (2 Cor 11:2).[16] A marriage ceremony is a time of rejoicing (Ps 19:5). Portraying the New Jerusalem as a bride reflects this joyful moment when humanity and God are united.

---

presence of God enjoyed by the followers of Jesus, an experience that will no longer be limited by the constraints imposed on visitors to the Jerusalem Temple" ("Eschatological Temple," 197). Richard M. Davidson adds: the New Jerusalem is "the place where the saints live and serve in the Father's presence, and where the whole universe comes to worship the King of kings and Lord of lords. . . .The earth made new will be an eternal festival celebration in the Sanctuary, with the Lord God Almighty and the Lamb" ("Cosmic Metanarrative for the Coming Millenium," 119). McKelvey explains: "The new Jerusalem is the new heaven and the new earth." The church as God's temple indicates how the faithful should live: holy, united, and sacrificing (*New Temple*, 176, 183–87).

13. Kautzsch and Cowley, *Gesenius' Hebrew Grammar*, 391.

14. The woman in Rev 12 appears to represent Israel (with twelve stars representing the twelve tribes) birthing the new Israel, the Old Jerusalem birthing the New Jerusalem. The seed of the woman are the believers in Jesus (Rev 12:10, 17; 14:12). The New Jerusalem appears in its glory in Rev 21:2.

15. Matt 9:15; 25:1, 5–6, 10; Mark 2:19–20; Luke 5:34–35.

16. Not all references to the church are feminine (e.g., Eph 4:13).

We Can Live in the New Jerusalem Now

Thus, the new heavenly Jerusalem may serve as a vision toward which we look, but also as a vision that can begin now. It is not yet, but yet. If a city is a network of interrelated people, all of us live in a microcosmic "city." The Bible even describes individuals as cities:

> The wealth of the rich is their strong city; in their imagination it is like a high wall. (Prov 18:11; 10:15)

> Like a city breached, without walls, is one who lacks self-control. (Prov 25:28)

> The Lord showed his steadfast love to David when he "was beset as a city under siege." (Ps 31:21)

> The Lord told Jeremiah that he made him "a fortified city, . . . They will fight against" him but shall "not prevail" . . . for the Lord was with him. (Jer 1:18–19)

> The wise woman builds her house, but the foolish tears it down with her own hands. (Prov 14:1)

A city is also like a household, a house that extends out to many. It is enclosed, but its gates are open. For example, because David wanted to build a house for the ark of the covenant, the Lord promised David that he would make him a "house." His heritage and kingdom would be established forever (2 Sam 7:11b–19, 25–29). The house of the Rechabites, the descendants of Jonadab son of Rechab, were charged not to drink wine nor build a house nor sow seed nor plant a vineyard or even own one, but to live in tents all their days. They became an illustration of what the nation of Israel should have done. Therefore, the Rechabites would never lack a descendant (Jer 35). As the Rechabites obeyed their ancestor even when tempted by outsiders, so too all of Israel should always have obeyed their God.

The New Testament records several households who ministered. The household of Onesiphorus served at Ephesus and also made an extended effort to find and visit Paul when he was imprisoned in Rome for the final time during Nero's persecution of Christians (2 Tim 1:16–18). The household of Stephana(s) decided to minister and serve others (1 Cor 16:15–18).[17] Lydia's household, by welcoming Paul and his coworkers, ministered at Philippi (Acts 16:14–15, 40). The New Testament also records notewor-

---

17. Spencer, "'El Hogar' as Ministry Team," 69–77.

thy churches that ministered, such as Philippi, which sent money for Paul's support several times (Phil 1:5; 4:10, 14–19).

Like the wise woman, we need to build our houses by walking uprightly, fearing the Lord (Prov 14:1). Like the wise man, we want to build our houses on rock by hearing and acting on Jesus's teachings (Matt 7:24). Like a team of builders, we need to work with coworkers to build our house on the already cemented foundation which is Jesus Christ, looking forward to the Owner's reward (1 Cor 3:10–15). Hebrews explains that Christians make up "God's house" "if we hold onto our courage and the hope of which we boast" (3:6 NIV). Hebrews itself, after calling its readers to come to "the city of the living God, the heavenly Jerusalem" (12:22), exhorts its listeners to live as followers of Christ: loving one another, entertaining strangers, being empathetic to those who are suffering and willing to suffer for Christ's sake, honoring marriage, being content with what one has, imitating and obeying good leaders, following right doctrine, praising and confessing Jesus, doing good, sharing with others, and praying for each other (13:1–18).[18]

What Is the Antithesis of the New Jerusalem?

Babylon is the archetypal antithesis of the New Jerusalem. The name *Babylon* comes from the gate of Bel (*Babulōn*) and *ribel* (confusion) or the Akkadian *babilu*, the gate of god. The ancestors of Babylon are described in Genesis 10:6–10, the descendants of Ham, Cush, and Nimrod. The Jews themselves originally came from Chaldea (Gen 11:28, 31; 15:7). Babylon was the capital of the Babylonian Empire located on the Euphrates River, 300 miles north of the Persian Gulf. Babel was the city with a tower made to reach into the heavens so its inhabitants could make a name for themselves. Instead of one language, their language became confused and the city: "Babel" (Gen 11:1–9). Later, they became the vehicle of God's punishment of Judah.[19] They were deeply associated with pagan deities. Eventually they themselves were punished by being conquered by Cyrus, the Medes and Persians in 538 B.C., about 50 years after they had deported the Jews (Isa 13:17–20). They were punished because they had no mercy, and instead of

18. See also Mouw, *Kings*, 73–77; Bauckham elaborates that through their free obedience, God's servants reign with God. God's will becomes also the spontaneous desire of their hearts (*Theology*, 142–43). In that sense, the New Jerusalem is free (Gal 4:26).

19. 2 Kgs 24:1, 12; 1 Chr 9:1; 2 Chr 36:6–7, 10, 17–21; Isa 13:1; Jer 21:4–10; 25:9–12; 38:3, 18.

recognizing the living God, they made the same mistake as the inhabitants of the tower of Babel, thinking, "I am, and there is no one besides me" (Isa 47:8, 10; Zeph 2:15; Dan 4:28–33). By the time of the Christian era, during Alexander the Great's time, the city was almost uninhabited.[20] The king of Babylon became an image of the devil (Isa 14:12–15), and later Babylon became an image of fallen Rome (1 Pet 5:13; Rev 14:8; 17:1–18; 18:24).[21]

In Babylon, in contrast to the New Jerusalem, God did not dwell, nor was God recognized. Instead, Babylon was devoted to its pagan deities. It promoted injustice and sin and death instead of justice, righteousness, and life. It had been protected but was no longer.

Conclusion

What are the elements of individuals, households, churches and cities that incorporate aspects of the New Jerusalem?

(1) God's *presence* is invoked. God dwells there.

(2) Seeking to please God as a *holy* God is sought.

(3) God is the *ruler*.

(4) The entity is both *protected* from harmful outsiders yet *open* to people from all nations.

(5) The entity brings *life* to itself, to others.

Isaiah, which presages Revelation, says,

> The descendants of those who oppressed you shall come bending low to you, and all who despised you shall bow down at your feet; they shall call you the City of the Lord, the Zion of the Holy One of Israel.
>
> Whereas you have been forsaken and hated, with no one passing through, I will make you majestic forever, a joy from age to age.
>
> You shall suck the milk of nations, you shall suck the breasts of kings; and you shall know that I, the Lord, am your Savior and your Redeemer, the Mighty One of Jacob.

20. Isa 13:19–20; 14:22–23; Jer 25:12–14; 27:6–7; 50:1–3, 8–18; 51:29, 37, 60–64; Zeph 2:15.

21. In Revelation, Babylon and the New Jerusalem are presented as contrasting alternatives, contrasting feminine prototypes (Alexander, *From Eden to the New Jerusalem*, 175–187; Bauckman, *Theology*, 131–32).

Instead of bronze I will bring gold, instead of iron I will bring silver; instead of wood, bronze, instead of stones, iron.

I will appoint Peace as your overseer and Righteousness as your taskmaster.

Violence shall no more be heard in your land, devastation or destruction within your borders; you shall call your walls Salvation, and your gates Praise.

The sun shall no longer be your light by day, nor for brightness shall the moon give light to you by night; but the Lord will be your everlasting light, and your God will be your glory.

Your sun shall no more go down, or your moon withdraw itself; for the Lord will be your everlasting light, and your days of mourning shall be ended.

Your people shall all be righteous; they shall possess the land forever.

They are the shoot that I planted, the work of my hands, so that I might be glorified.

The least of them shall become a clan, and the smallest one a mighty nation;

I am the Lord; in its time I will accomplish it quickly. (Isa 60:14–22)

The vision of the New Jerusalem is one which we need to incorporate into our own "cities" now, our cities of self, household, church, and extended community. We need to be saved, redeemed, holy, peaceful, righteous, joyful, living with the Lord as our Light. God will accomplish the New Jerusalem, but also God can accomplish this vision in and through God's people today.

References for Further Study

Alexander, T. Desmond. *From Eden to the New Jerusalem: An Introduction to Biblical Theology*. Grand Rapids: Kregel, 2008.

———, and Simon Gathercole, eds. *Heaven on Earth: The Temple in Biblical Theology*. Carlisle, UK: Paternoster, 2004.

Bauckham, Richard. *The Theology of the Book of Revelation*. New Testament Theology. Cambridge: Cambridge University Press, 1993. Ch. 6.

Bryan, Steven M. "The Eschatological Temple in John 14." *Bulletin of Biblical Research* 15:2 (2005) 187–98.

Davidson, Richard M. "Cosmic Metanarrative for the Coming Millenium." *Journal of the Adventist Theological Society* 11:1–2 (Spring–Autumn 2000) 102–119.

DiTommaso, Lorenzo. *The Dead Sea New Jerusalem Text: Contents and Contexts.* Texts and Studies in Ancient Judaism 110. Tübingen: Mohr Siebeck, 2005.

Lee, Pilchan. *The New Jerusalem in the Book of Revelation: A Study of Revelation 21–22 in the Light of its Background in Jewish Tradition.* Wissenschaftliche Untersuchungen zum Neuen Testament 2. Reihe 129. Tübingen: J.C.B. Mohr, 2001.

McKelvey, R. J. *The New Temple: The Church in the New Testament.* Oxford: Oxford University Press, 1969.

Mouw, Richard J. *When the Kings Come Marching In: Isaiah and the New Jerusalem.* Grand Rapids: Eerdmans, 1983.

Blueprints for the Heart of the Rebuilder

John Runyon

FOR CENTURIES BELIEVERS HAVE waited for the New Jerusalem. In fact, from the beginning of time, the characteristic of a true believer was one "looking forward to the city with foundations, whose architect and builder is God"[1] (Heb 11:10). What this future hope of a heavenly city calls forth from us as believers here on earth gets translated in many ways. Some lose sight of the heavenly city in the walls and streets of the earthly city; others lose connection with the earthly city by dwelling on the thought of the heavenly city. Indeed, God has called his people to be salt and light in the world, co-regents with Christ, citizens and ambassadors of a heavenly country, his kingdom, synonymous with the New Jerusalem: " . . . they were longing for a better country—a heavenly one. Therefore, God is not ashamed to be called their God, for he has prepared a city for them" (Heb 11:16).

One thing is certain from the urban parables recorded in Matthew 25: Jesus will have no sympathy or room in the New Jerusalem for those who are not actively engaged in proper investment on this earth. In the parable of the ten virgins, those who just showed up and waited without planning for enough oil were left out in the dark. The servant who did not invest his talent *while his master was gone* was thrown outside. Those who did nothing to feed the hungry, visit prisoners, practice hospitality, or provide for those who were in need, were sent away to eternal punishment. It is clear from his ministry and from these parables that Jesus cared as much about the physical deliverance and well-being (*shalom*) of people on this earth during his ministry as he did about saving their souls. And "whoever claims to live in him must walk as Jesus did" (1 John 2:6).

1. All Scripture quoted from the New International Version, 2011.

If Christ was anointed to "proclaim good news to the poor," "proclaim freedom for the prisoners and recovery of sight for the blind, to set the oppressed free, to proclaim the year of the Lord's favor" (Luke 4:18–19), then how can it not be our anointing to do the same, as his body here on earth? Many interpret this message in simplistic spiritual terms, believing that, as each individual prays the sinner's prayer, somehow this manifesto is made complete. But I propose that this interpretive lamp lacks oil, because, although forgiveness of sin sets us on the right path, it is only the beginning of God's saving work. As Howard Snyder puts it, "The Bible speaks of a divine master plan for the whole creation."[2]

As Adam and Eve were entrusted with the mandate of bringing order out of chaos and ruling over the world, we as the body of the second Adam now have divine power to carry out this mandate in the face of the destruction sin has brought into the equation. Bringing order out of chaos means bringing life out of death, restoring what was taken, rebuilding that which was destroyed, and overcoming the work of the evil one—thus "bring[ing] unity to all things in heaven and on earth under Christ" (Eph 1:10b). "All things" means all things, including all of the current created order. What God has in store for a new heaven and a new earth is directly correlated to how we manage the current creation. It is clearly stated that the present creation is related to the future one in Romans 8:19–21:

> For the creation waits in eager expectation for the children of God to be revealed. For the creation was subjected to frustration, not by its own choice, but by the will of the one who subjected it, in hope that the creation itself will be liberated from its bondage to decay and brought into the freedom and glory of the children of God.

I call to our attention these correlations about the current creation, future creation, and stewardship because I want to demonstrate how clear it is that God is concerned about the current conditions of the earth we live in, which translates directly into his concern for the cities where the majority of the people now on earth live.[3] The exhortation becomes one

2. Snyder, *The Community of the King*, 62.

3. According to the Global Health Observatory, "For the first time ever, the majority of the world's population lives in a city, and this proportion continues to grow. One hundred years ago, 2 out of every 10 people lived in an urban area. By 1990, less than 40% of the global population lived in a city, but as of 2010, more than half of all people live in an urban area. By 2030, 6 out of every 10 people will live in a city, and by 2050, this proportion will increase to 7 out of 10 people. Currently, around half of all urban dwellers live in cities with between 100,000–500,000 people, and fewer than 10% of urban dwellers

to disciple all nations by demonstrating what it means to live in true harmony with God, which includes harmony with our surrounding earth.[4] This means the body of Christ must be an agent of transformation at all levels of society and in all areas of creation. The earth and everything in it, the people around us, and the organizational structures they form are all talents entrusted to our care, and we must not bury them. We must find a way to cultivate each talent into multiplicative life according to the pattern of our creative and restorative God. Anything apart from this does not fit his pattern and will be rejected and thrown out.

If we are to follow Christ, then, we must focus our eyes to look for devastation into which we can bring the restorative kingdom of God. We really must look for the gates of hell and march right into them, as Jesus did. There is the destructiveness of hell all around us, at all levels of our society and throughout creation itself, brought by humans following the patterns of Satan instead of the patterns of God. People are broken, families are torn apart, friendships are destroyed, communities are fractured, business structures are oppressive, and even cities lie in ruins, when and where true, life-giving, holistic discipleship is not carried out.

Where can we start, and what paradigm might we use to bring restoration? Nehemiah was one of the great restorers of the Bible, a type of Christ in that regard, and I have found it useful to apply many of the principles I find in his restoration of the city of Jerusalem to restoration and rebuilding in people's lives, our families, organizations, communities, and our contemporary cities.[5]

Attitudes of a Rebuilder

Nehemiah demonstrates several attitudes that stand out as clear indications of Christ-likeness and which lay a firm foundation for rebuilding. At the

---

live in megacities (defined by UN HABITAT as a city with a population of more than 10 million)," "Situation and trends in key indicators, Urban Population Growth."

4. Grigg comments, ". . . in Luke 14:26–33, Jesus himself defines discipleship in economic and social terms. For discipleship, the response to the Kingdom is not simply a spiritual relationship with God," *The Spirit of Christ and the Postmodern City*, 107.

5. Others have taken similar approach, finding Ezra and Nehemiah as essential books of wisdom for rebuilding (see Lupton, *Renewing the City*). In Africa, the books of Ezra and Nehemiah have become "the source for what African theologians have for some years been calling the theology of reconstruction," Weanzana, *Africa Bible Commentary*, 532.

outset is his heart-felt despondence when he hears of the continued state of destruction of Jerusalem (Neh 1:4). We must never get so immune to the destruction around us that our hearts do not respond to the pain and oppression that continue rampant.

Nehemiah's heart leads him into prayers of repentance, not only for his own sin, but collectively for his generation, and even for the sins of those who went before him (1:6). His prayers show that he identifies with those who are hurting, as does any good intercessor, and that he begins in humility before the God who can restore all things.

Nehemiah then positions himself in expectation that God will move on his behalf in answer to his prayers. He asks God for favor before the king and then expects that God will use his role as cupbearer to the king to bring about the reconstruction of Jerusalem (1:11). This hope was quite bold, as rebuilding a conquered capital city could easily be seen as a sign of rebellion, and Nehemiah and others could lose their lives as a result. Often, when stepping into situations of destruction and asking for permission to rebuild, the forces that destroyed in the first place pose a great threat to any rebuilding. It is amazing how often people fight to maintain a destroyed state because they exercise some kind of control over it, or gain something from that destruction. I think of people who have abused others and have utterly destroyed their "objects'" understanding of themselves; when someone comes to restore a proper understanding of self with proper boundaries, the abusers lash out with fury.

Nehemiah exercises another attitude of a good rebuilder: he prepared himself for opposition even beyond that which he might have received from the king (2:7–9). Once he saw the king was being moved by the hand of God, he asked for letters to the governors of the Trans-Euphrates on his behalf because he knew there would be opposition from somewhere. Rebuilders must always expect opposition.

Actions of a Rebuilder

Nehemiah asks for all that he needs for the journey, as well as building materials, expecting that it would be provided by the God who wants restoration. When he arrives at Jerusalem, he looks around, makes an assessment of the situation, formulates a plan, communicates the plan, and begins the work (2:11–16). Often we do not even start to formulate a plan because we feel that the devastation is too great, or perhaps there are not enough resources in the midst of the devastation. We might languish, waiting for a big grant or some other source, rather than actively engaging the situation and resources we find present, no matter how scarce and burned they are.

I find it particularly interesting that Nehemiah surveys the damage by himself, and gauges the right time to involve others (2:11–18). Many times in my own ministry, I have spoken of visions too far down the road and have lost everyone's attention because they made no sense for the current context. I find, too, that, if we are too loud about what we are setting out to do, we attract negative attention to our work and lessen our chances of success. Even in capital fundraising campaigns, there is the "silent phase," and then the "public phase," when it seems certain that all is in line for success. Good rebuilding has its "silent phase" and its "public phase," once the proper groundwork has been laid.

Surveying the damage also helped Nehemiah come to grips with the exact state the city was in (2:17). Recognizing reality is always a foundational key to good rebuilding. If we remain in denial about the level of destruction in our lives, families, and communities, then we will find ourselves wasting our efforts rebuilding roofs before walls, and gates before gateposts. As rebuilders, we must never be afraid of truth, as hard as it is to confront. We must also prepare for those who will complain that the roof is not being rebuilt while we work on the walls! Denial and avoidance of the truth result in strange ideas at times. A correctly executed "current state analysis" will help the good rebuilder set the right priorities and focus for the rebuilding project, and have answers for those who have their own opinions about what the next steps should be.

Understanding the city and its present state gave Nehemiah credibility when he began to speak to the people about rebuilding (2:17–18). They were not able to counter with the words many of us have heard many times in our lives: "You just don't understand! There's no way . . ." The work was overwhelming, the human capital low, and resources scarce, but Nehemiah was able to convince his people that rebuilding *was* possible, and they set their hands to the work.

Nehemiah involves everyone in Jerusalem in the rebuilding, with each person doing their part (3:1–32). It may be a small part, but no part is too small—all are necessary for rebuilding. It is as important for us as rebuilders to engage everyone who has a true stake in the rebuilding as it is for every organ in our bodies to work in its function. The bigger the project and the more the workers, the harder it is to engage everyone in some fashion in the rebuilding, but total involvement is necessary.

Opposition to the Rebuilding

Nehemiah needed to put his readiness for conflict into action immediately upon beginning the rebuilding. Hardly the first stone was in place when Sanballat and Tobiah showed up to ridicule them, asking, "What is this you are doing? Are you rebelling against the king?" Nehemiah had his answer: "The God of heaven will give us success. We his servants will start rebuilding, but as for you, you have no share in Jerusalem or any claim or historic right to it" (2:20). I find Nehemiah's answer applicable in so many rebuilding scenarios. When people are torn down, often they hear these whispers when they start to rebuild their lives: "What is this you are doing? Are you rebelling against this state you are in? How can you possibly think you will succeed?" Family members often hear this from each other, when they take steps to make changes: "Are you rebelling against the way our family has always done this?" And the application goes on, throughout every level of rebuilding.

Nehemiah's answer that Sanballat and Tobiah "have no share in Jerusalem or any claim or historic right to it" (2:20) is extremely important for laying the foundation for his future answers to opposition and for maintaining the focus on the real problem. Sanballat and Tobiah's claim that Nehemiah might be rebelling goes unanswered because it is not the point. The truth that lies behind the questions is that Sanballat and Tobiah feel they have a claim on the city of Jerusalem, and fear that, if it is rebuilt, they will lose their control and influence over the region, which will subsequently result in a loss of people to oppress and fleece. The oppressor is always looking for a way to maintain claim over the oppressed, and we can be sure that we will face such questions in any rebuilding that we undertake, whether internal thoughts and doubts, or outright external opposition. The key to the answer is that God has ultimate claim over our lives and spoke into existence all on earth, and no oppressor can claim otherwise. God has ultimate authority to rebuild, and, if we align ourselves with him, we can be certain that Nehemiah's answer is our answer. Satan has no claim or share or historic right to anything we are setting out to rebuild along the patterns of God.

Opposition can come from many sources. It can come from the usual suspects—Satan, haters, our own fears—but it can also come from people we care about, including friends and family members. Aside from the questions we have just discussed, there are others that come our way, with recognizable characteristics. Sanballat and Tobiah come back—with ridicule this time. Sanballat sneers, "What are those feeble Jews doing? Will they restore their wall? Will they offer sacrifices? Will they finish in a day? Can they bring the stones back to life from those heaps of rubble—burned as they are?"(4:2). And Tobiah scoffs, "What they are building—even a fox climbing up on it would break down their wall of stones!"(4:3).

All of these are answered resoundingly. The rebuilders were not feeble; they were quite resolute and strong. They did restore their wall. They did restore the sacrificial system. And, although they did not finish in one day, they finished in record time, astonishing everyone. New life was brought out of the heaps of burned rubble, a testament to the restorative power of God at work, and we'll just ignore the line about the fox!

The ridicule that may fly our way in the face of our rebuilding can be noted because it is often ridiculous. No one is building a wall in a day, and no one is building something that a fox can break. But the enemy is cunning because we often fall for such ridiculous insults. When we are asked to turn around an organization, or to help renew a community, we might often get worried that things are not progressing fast enough. I find that when we are dealing with spiritual, emotional, and organizational rebuilding, where the walls are not physical, there is even more room for feelings of inadequacy to creep in. When progress cannot be measured in bricks and stones and wall height, questions and comments like, "what do you think you are doing?" or "you'll be fired for this," or "you're the worst boss I've ever had," may have a larger impact. But we must identify such words as deterrents and stay the course.

We notice that Nehemiah did not bother to answer any of these questions. He prayed, asked God to turn the insults back on their enemies, and kept doing the work. And the very next verse states, "So we rebuilt the wall till all of it reached half its height, for the people worked with all their heart" (4:6). If our rebuilding is from God, it is God that they are challenging, not us. We turn vengeance over to him and keep our hands to the work.

The result of such progress frustrates the enemy even more. Sanballat and Tobiah realized that all their insults only led to the wall being built to half its height. Their strategy needed to change if they were going to get real results, so they resorted to fear. Not only did they spread rumors that they would mount an attack on the city, they actually held the residents of Judah who lived close to them under such a yoke of fear that they "came and told us ten times over, 'Wherever you turn, they will attack us'" (4:12). We must be ready for fear tactics that even use people who are on our side. Nehemiah posted a guard at the weak points in the wall, and, after reviewing the situation, reassured everyone that they could meet any attack mounted against them: "Don't be afraid of them. Remember the Lord, who is great and awesome, and fight for your families, your sons and your daughters, your wives and your homes" (4:14).

Then they returned to their work, but this time with weapons in one hand and tools in the other. The work goes slower this way, but they are safe. Often we get caught up in the work and forget that we must continue to carry our weapons of warfare as we complete the work. Rebuilders are warriors, too, and must keep their spiritual armor on and their spiritual weapons ready, as our battle is not against flesh and blood as much as Nehemiah's was. But it is just as real.

Good planning needs to be brought into preparations for meeting opposition because, often in situations of rebuilding, human resources are scarce, and the task at hand seems entirely impossible, not to mention meeting any opposition that might come. Nehemiah created a strategy that allowed each person to do his or her work, but that, when a concentrated effort needed to be made against a threat, would bring them together to fight. Coming together for rebuilders is extremely important, not only in terms of strength for the battle, but for encouragement and perspective as well. Good rebuilders need a clear contingency plan for meeting threats that takes into consideration the nature of the work at hand as well as the threat itself.

As the wall nears completion, Nehemiah's enemies are furious. They try another ploy—to get him out of the walls of protection he has just built onto the Plain of Ono, clearly a much more vulnerable location, for a "meeting." He stays focused, and they do too, sending the message four times! On their fifth attempt, they make use of an unsealed letter full of lies and accusations. Nehemiah surely thought about how many had seen that letter as it was being delivered. How many people were out there who now wondered if the lies in it were true? But he did not waver and responded, "Nothing like what you are saying is happening; you are just making it up out of your head" (6:8). Nehemiah has great discernment into what is happening: "They were all trying to frighten us, thinking, 'Their hands will get too weak for the work, and it will not be completed.' But I prayed, 'Now strengthen my hands'" (6:9).

Often the rebuilder will need this prayer, "Lord, strengthen my hands," particularly when there could be a myriad of people "out there" doubting his or her integrity. Depending on your personality as a rebuilder, you may find a challenge to your integrity the hardest prevarication of all to resist. Satan loves to sidetrack and preoccupy us with questions about our integrity, assurances that everyone thinks we are wrong, and slander that we are scheming to set up our own kingdom. We need resolution to strengthen our hands to complete the work given to us without turning to the left or right, or traveling out to the spiritual plains of Ono for bogus meetings that leave us exposed and vulnerable to danger.

Integrity of a Rebuilder

In chapter 5 of Nehemiah's story, we come across a social issue that Nehemiah addresses. We might not initially think that this outcry that the Jews were bringing against their fellow countrymen was directly related to the rebuilding of Jerusalem, unless we understand rebuilding in a holistic light. Nehemiah's goal was not simply to rebuild a physical wall, but beyond that to establish life-giving social and economic systems that would sustain the city and its people over the long-term. Nehemiah thinks the situation over thoroughly and then directly addresses those responsible for the oppression (5:6–7). Surprisingly (to me, at least), they were quite willing to give up their oppressive ways and return value to the oppressed. Often our fears tell us that, when we confront oppression, we will be met with deathly opposition, but we must remember that, if we present a life-giving alternative, we might encounter willingness to accept correction and even find the former oppressors praising the Lord once the yoke of oppression has been released from both parties!

Nehemiah goes on to make a few notes about his own commitment to not oppress those he governed (5:14–19). When we are rebuilding, we might have much easier opportunities to exploit because normal controls may not be in place and because often in the course of a rebuilding project people's hope is restored and they may begin to place implicit trust in their rebuilding leader. But, as Nehemiah, we must always remember that we are accountable to God and take only what is needed and not make up reasons for "needing" extra. We remember that, if we seek first his kingdom and his righteousness, all "these things" that we need will be provided to us.

Some might find it odd that Nehemiah actually asks God to remember the good things he has done in this regard, of treating the people justly and not oppressing them (5:19). I think that such prayers may actually serve as a help to us to maintain our integrity. If we can honestly pray such a prayer at the end of each day, then we can be confident that we are on the right track. It also reminds us that we may not see our reward here on earth, but, as Jesus reminds us, "Look, I am coming soon! My reward is with me, and I will give to everyone according to what they have done" (Rev 22:12 TNIV). Rewards are good, particularly if we have been good.

Completion and Continuance

In the final chapters of the book of Nehemiah, we begin to see the fullness of what it means to rebuild. Not only was it setting the economic system straight, as we just discussed, but it includes every aspect of life in the city. Nehemiah, with the help of Ezra the priest, establishes preventative measures to ensure the people do not recommit the errors that brought about the destruction in the first place. In their case (and often in ours), it was a lack of knowledge of the word of God and what he required of them that led to their destruction, aside from outright conscious refusal to obey. So, in response to this knowledge void, they restored the reading of the word. They reestablished the feasts and the rhythms of their religion that reminded them of their relationship to God. They confessed and recommitted themselves with a covenant (9:38).

It is much easier to apply these actions of re-covenanting with God, or committing to restoring the knowledge of the word of God in the life of a believer who is rebuilding his or her life, or in a Christian organization that is being reformed, than it is in attempting to reshape a secular life or a non-Christian organization, but equivalents must be found for every situation. We can build principles of justice, celebration, confession, and commitment to truth into any organization or community in which we work to rebuild. And we must. It is God's justice we are seeking in all things, after all.

Nehemiah continues to reform even after the walls are rebuilt (9:1—13:31). Continuance is just as important as the rebuilding itself. We must not stop confessing, we must not stop fostering proper attitudes in ourselves and our people, and we must not stop being vigilant to the schemes of the enemy. The people of Jerusalem continued to seek God and, as they discovered through his word more ways in which they had erred, they corrected them. There were adjustments and corrections that needed to be made to every sphere of life and relationships: work, Sabbath, temple, marriage, and foreign relations.

And, yet, even as the systems were improving and being brought into line with the word of God, we find that Tobiah himself, that fox, had moved right into the temple and was living in one of the rooms there (13:5). Often, when the walls are rebuilt, we (or someone close to us) let those who oppose us move right in and take up residence! We must take the same attitude as Nehemiah and not be afraid of offending, but we need to cast out that which needs casting out.

Letting Tobiah in was not the only area in which the Israelites regressed. They had also stopped giving their tithes, and the religious system collapsed—the Levites went back to their farms. They also began selling and buying again on the Sabbath, in direct violation of the law (13:15–18). Rebuilders will always find areas of regression, and they must face them head on. Entire structures may collapse because of regression, but each must be addressed, and the proper structure reestablished. Each part must do its work, or the entire project will succumb to the patterns of entropy, rather than those which are life-giving and multiplicative.

Conclusion

And, thus, from the narrative of Nehemiah, we can see that rebuilding is not easy. We must have the proper attitudes; make adequate assessments; face opposition of many types; put everyone to work according to their abilities; deal with spiritual, economic, social, and political structures that must be realigned; and in the end, never stop our vigilance and discipline. But rebuilding is in the heart of God. He raised up Nehemiah to rebuild Jerusalem; where is he sending you to rebuild? There are areas of vast devastation: lives, families, organizations, communities, cities, and entire countries, waiting for the ambassadors of the kingdom of life to engage them. With our hands joined with Christ's and our hearts aligned to his, it is my prayer that as we address the evils of this world, as we address oppression and need, then the words of the prophet Isaiah will be true of us:

If you do away with the yoke of oppression,
with the pointing finger and malicious talk,
and if you spend yourselves in behalf of the hungry
and satisfy the needs of the oppressed,
then your light will rise in the darkness,
and your night will become like the noonday.
The Lord will guide you always;
he will satisfy your needs in a sun-scorched land
and will strengthen your frame.
You will be like a well-watered garden,
like a spring whose waters never fail.
Your people will rebuild the ancient ruins
and will raise up the age-old foundations;
you will be called Repairer of Broken Walls,
Restorer of Streets with Dwellings.
(Isaiah 58:9b–12)

References for Further Study

Ellul, Jacques. *The Meaning of the City*. Translated by Dennis Pardee. Eugene, OR: Wipf & Stock, 2011. Originally published in 1970.

Getz, Gene A. *Nehemiah: Becoming a Disciplined Leader*. Nashville: B&H Publishing, 1995.

Linthicum, Robert. *City of God, City of Satan: A Biblical Theology of the Urban Church*. Grand Rapids: Zondervan, 1991.

McKenna, David L. *Becoming Nehemiah: Leading with Significance*. Kansas City, MO: Beacon Hill Press, 2005.

Villafañe, Eldin. *Seek the Peace of the City: Reflections on Urban Ministry*. Grand Rapids: Eerdmans, 1995.

Ecclesiapolis

Two Millennia of Mutual Transformation between Church and City

David A. Currie

Introduction

The church began in the city, Jerusalem, and the church will end in the city, the New Jerusalem (Rev 21). Therefore, viewing the broad sweep and arc of the history of how the church and the city have mutually influenced one another over the past 2000 years can help contemporary churches and ministries press into God's urban future for his people.

However, because both the church and the city have been extremely complex, dynamic entities in their own right throughout their histories, looking at their mutual interaction can seem like an impossible and potentially misleading task, destined to myopic misunderstandings such as attributing to them simplistically false cause/effect relationships: "Because the city was X at this time, the church was Y. Because the church did (or did not do) A, the city became B." To borrow the imagery of Doug Hall, this approach is to reduce two very complex cats into the simplest kinds of toasters.[1] No matter what kind of historical bread you put in—wheat, rye, pumpernickel— the end result will look the same: burnt toast.

Nonetheless, recognizing that these are complex entities with an even more complex interrelationship and refusing to press the details too strongly can still make an examination of the shared history of the church and the city potentially clarifying and beneficial. The church has transformed and been transformed by the city, and vice versa. Coining a word to capture the complexities of this dynamic, *Ecclesiapolis* (*ecclesia* = church + *polis* =

---

1. Hall, *The Cat and the Toaster*.

city), guards against simplistic, false conclusions. Exploring the history of *Ecclesiapolis* provides some helpful interpretive guides to explore mutual transformations between church and city over the past two millennia. Remember that the canvas is sweeping, and the brush strokes are broad, but an overall picture will emerge from this historical perspective that will help contemporaries see the interaction of their contexts more clearly.

The form of this overview of the relationship between the church and the city will be a quadtych, with each panel featuring major urban and parallel ecclesiastical developments. Particular kinds of cities accompanied particular kinds of church movements. In the first through fifth centuries, the cosmopolitan cities of the Roman Empire accompanied the Gentile church. Following the millennium of general decline of urban life that characterized the decline of the Roman Empire, the sixteenth and seventeenth centuries saw the rise of commercial cities parallel the Reformation. The accelerated growth of industrial cities in the eighteenth and nineteenth centuries accompanied multiple seasons of mass revivals in the church. The geometric explosion of global cities in the twentieth and twenty-first centuries has accompanied the rise of indigenous and immigrant churches.

Much more was going on in both cities and the church than these generalized characterizations can capture. Moreover, no simplistic, unidirectional causality should be inferred, as in Marxist interpretations that reduce everything to underlying economic determinism. New approaches to urban life paralleled new approaches to church life. These parallels do not mean that the church simply aped society or that the city blindly conformed to ecclesiastical expectations. Sometimes, urban dynamics seemed to shape the growth of the church, as with Paul's intentionally urban church-planting strategy. At other times, the church seemed to reshape cities into their own image, such as in Calvin's Geneva.

However, regardless of which influence seemed to have priority at particular times and situations, the overall dynamic has been more one of mutuality than manipulation. Because the church as the "people of God"[2] is inherently communal, it has been particularly compatible with the largest communities of people, cities. Because the church is also the *sent* people of God,[3] it is also inherently missional, and consequently intentional about interpenetrating the complexities of urban society as yeast, salt, and light.[4]

---

2. 1 Pet 2:10.

3. John 20:21; see also Matt 28:18–20 and Acts 1:8.

4. Matt 13:33, Matt 5:13, and especially v. 14: "You are the light of the world. A *city*

This interpenetration, when it was authentic, allowed for mutual influence from the city upon the church. Ideally, this influence shaped the context for mission—changing the kind of loaf, the dimensions of the saltshaker, or the color of the lantern that best fit that particular time and place. At times, distortion resulted as well, making the loaf inedible, the salt flavorless, and placing the lantern under a bushel.

One final caveat before looking at each panel of the quadtych of *Ecclesiapolis*: focusing upon the mutual transformation of the church and the city is neither meant to delegitimize the rural church nor to disregard historical periods such as the Middle Ages when urbanization was on the wane. God has been at work just as much in those places and times as in the city. However, because some Christians mistakenly assume the reverse—that the church is somehow more country and medieval than urban and modern, and therefore that moving to the big, bad city will inevitably cause believers to lose their faith—providing a clearer picture of some of the main developments in the church and in the city can lead to greater faithfulness in responding to the challenges and opportunities of urban ministry.

Panel 1: First through Fifth Centuries—Cosmopolitan Cities of the Roman Empire and the Gentile Church

The church was conceived and born in primarily rural Palestine, but it grew up in a predominantly urban Greco-Roman nursery. At the beginning of the book of Acts, the church is almost exclusively monocultural: Palestinian Jews who mainly spoke Aramaic from villages in Galilee. By the end of Acts, only about three decades later, the church has spread throughout the Roman Empire, primarily to the cities of the eastern half of the Empire and has become predominantly non-Jewish (drawing from multiple Gentile ethnic groups) and Greek-speaking. What accounts for this rapid and dramatic transformation?

A significant influence was the urban, multicultural character of the Roman Empire. While the church did begin in a city, Jerusalem was still mainly a monocultural context, an anomaly compared to most cities under Roman rule. As frequent riots and revolts indicated, non-Jewish presence was barely tolerated, with Gentile and Jewish cultures remaining essentially separate, like oil and water. Even after the outpouring of the Holy Spirit at Pentecost brought in non-Palestinian Jews from the diaspora, speaking

(*polis*) on a hill cannot be hidden" (NIV 84, emphasis added).

other languages, and despite the Great Commissions,[5] the church remained fairly monocultural.

Acts does not record any sustained, concerted efforts by Palestinian Jews, or even initially by diaspora Jews, to spread the gospel among Gentiles. Acts 8 describes how Philip—as a Greek-speaking leader of the Jewish church—forced out of Jerusalem by the stoning of Stephen, shared the gospel in Samaria and with an Ethiopian God-fearer, but his efforts seem piecemeal and isolated, not the new norm. In Acts 10, Peter is basically compelled to share with Cornelius even though Cornelius was already highly sympathetic to Judaism.

Not until the formation of a multiethnic, urban church outside of Palestine in Antioch does a true Gentile mission emerge, first somewhat accidentally (Acts 11:19–20), but eventually as an intentional strategy (Acts 13:1–3). The diverse leadership of the Antioch church (note the African representation) reflected the multicultural character of a crossroads city such as Antioch, which was the third largest city in the Empire after Rome and Alexandria. Not surprisingly, the missionaries sent out by such a church, initially Barnabas and Paul, who eventually each led their own team, adopted an intentionally urban church-planting strategy.[6]

The latter part of Acts does not describe missionaries seeking to spread the gospel out in the countryside or even in villages, but concentrating on primary urban centers, usually the provincial capitals, in Asia Minor, Greece, and Macedonia. The expectation was that preexisting patterns of interaction would eventually carry Christ's message throughout a region once a strong church was established in a central urban area. This expectation undergirds Paul's bold claim that "there is no more place for me to work in these regions" (Rom 15:23 NIV), in describing his desire to shift his ministry from the eastern to the western half of the Roman Empire.

The church emerged in an urban environment already well established by the first century. Cities were the embodiment of Greco-Roman culture, reflecting both its origins in city-states and its self-confidence. Roman engineers constructed imposing buildings, usually far more impressive than anything the locals had ever built; Roman lawyers governed these cities with a comprehensive system of laws; and Roman generals kept them safe—at least until the fifth century—because Roman legions could move about quickly on the efficient road system that linked urban centers

5. E.g., Acts 1:8, Matt 28:18–20.

6. Allen, *Missionary Methods*.

together. Most conquered peoples readily embraced the urban lifestyle and values that followed the legions, transforming traditional rural cultures.

These urban structural, intellectual, and cultural developments facilitated the spread of a Gentile church, despite Christianity's strong Palestinian Jewish origins. Concentrating population in cities made it easier to spread the gospel message to many more people in a relatively short period of time than if people were dispersed throughout the countryside. Secure roads and shipping lanes made it possible for missionaries to travel easily, as Paul's missionary journeys demonstrate. These are a few reasons why Christianity initially was primarily an urban religion and was less prevalent in rural areas.[7]

Another, more subtle, reason for the urban character of the early church reflected a new approach to religion that emerged in the Roman Empire, *choice*. Religious choice grew out of a broader imperial value, *cosmopolitanism*. People who now viewed themselves primarily as world citizens (*cosmo* = world + *politan* = city citizen) instead of members of particular tribal or ethnic groups were far more exposed to new religions—particularly in diverse, multiethnic urban contexts—and far more open to embracing them.[8]

Within the region around the Mediterranean basin that became the bulk of the Roman Empire, religions were originally local and tribal. People worshiped the gods according to the customs of their ancestors because they had always done it that way. Romans made sacrifices to Jupiter, Greeks to Zeus, Egyptians to Isis, and Hebrews to Yahweh. In most traditional areas, especially rural ones, this was probably the only religious option available. Religion was primarily a matter of birth, not of choice.

As the Roman Empire expanded into this region and people began to move around much farther, more freely and frequently—sometimes involuntarily as a result of forced relocation after conquest, but more often as the result of serving in the army or pursuing economic opportunities made possible in urban centers—new religious options emerged. Religiously, this cosmopolitan environment created three groups of people: the "natives" who stayed in the home country and continued worshiping their traditional gods the way they always had; the "diaspora" who traveled outside of the homeland, but took their gods with them and worshiped them in their new foreign environment (e.g., the Jewish diaspora); and the "hangers on"

7. Meeks, *The First Urban Christians*.

8. Perrin, *The New Testament: An Introduction*, 4–35.

who were attracted to the non-indigenous religions that they saw practiced by the diaspora (e.g. Gentile God-fearers with Judaism).

The latter two groups, the diaspora and the hangers on, worshiped primarily as a result of personal choice, not simply because of where they happened to live. Even traditionalists had to exercise some element of choice as awareness and acceptance of other religions became more prominent. Introducing choice to religion in the Roman Empire was somewhat like introducing choice to telephone service in America. After the breakup of AT&T, Americans who had only had the choice of "Ma Bell" or nothing, now had multiple and proliferating options.

Such a cosmopolitan approach to religion led to many religions spreading throughout the Roman Empire, far beyond where they initially arose as tribal religions, and attracting adherents other than their originating ethnic groups. Christianity was one of numerous religions that proliferated as a result of this pluralistic social and cultural context that introduced choice to religion. Compared to Mithraism from Asia and Isis worship from Egypt,[9] Christianity seemed like a fairly minor sect of Judaism, unlikely to gain broad popularity.

However, the introduction of choice to religion in the Roman cosmopolitan urban environment created social space for the Gentile church to emerge. Judaism and its culture were not seen as intrinsic to the choice of following Jesus. Nevertheless, the trans-cultural character of Christianity was not merely a consequence of choice, and its exclusivism in this fanatically pluralistic context was radically countercultural. Moreover, the vision of the church as the new people of God, a distinctive community drawn from existing communities of all ethnicities, ultimately came from its founder, Jesus, who made more explicit what was already hinted at in the Old Testament.[10]

Nonetheless, this vision was not fully realized until the church moved more extensively into urban contexts, which were self-consciously cosmopolitan and voluntary in their approach to religion. Christianity fit many aspects of this prevailing religious temperament, though Christ's exclusive claims and high moral standards were highly contrary. This social and cultural compatibility is one reason that Christianity was more prevalent in the cities and in the more urban, eastern part of the Empire. The emergence of the Gentile church out of what could have been seen as a tribal religion

9. Celebrated in the second-century Latin work by Apuleius, *The Golden Ass.*
10. E.g., in the Suffering Servant songs in Isaiah 42:6 and 49:6.

was the first manifestation of *Ecclesiapolis*, the dynamic mutual transformation of the church and the city.

The late second-century apologetic writing, *The Epistle to Diognetus*, beautifully captures the transcultural, voluntary nature of the Gentile church, distinguishing it from Judaism and other tribal religions and highlighting its strong urban connections:

> For Christians cannot be distinguished from the rest of the human race by country or language or customs. They do not live in *cities* of their own; they do not use a peculiar form of speech; they do not follow an eccentric manner of life . . . Yet, although they live in Greek and barbarian *cities* alike, as each man's lot has been cast, and follow the customs of the country in clothing and food and other matters of daily living, at the same time they give proof of the remarkable and admittedly extraordinary constitution of their own commonwealth. They live in their own countries, but only as aliens. They have a share in everything as citizens, and endure everything as foreigners. Every foreign land is their fatherland, and yet for them every fatherland is a foreign land. They marry, like everyone else, and they beget children, but they do not cast out their offspring. They share their board with each other, but not their marriage bed. It is true that they are "in the flesh," but they do not live "according to the flesh." They busy themselves on earth, but their citizenship is in heaven. They obey the established laws, but in their own lives they go far beyond what the laws require. They love all men, and by all men are persecuted . . . To put it simply: What the soul is in the body, that Christians are in the world. The soul is dispersed through all the members of the body, and Christians are scattered through all the *cities* of the world.[11]

As the Gentile church continued to multiply throughout the Roman Empire in the third century, gaining ascendancy in the fourth century after the conversion of Constantine, it grew in influence, particularly transforming cities. Signs of this transformation included the subtraction of lethal combat from urban arenas and the addition of basilicas to urban skylines. However, in the fifth century, the sack of Rome by the Visigoths in A.D. 410 exposed complexities in the relationship between church and city, which Augustine of Hippo explored at great length in his analysis of these events in *The City of God*.

---

11. "Epistle of Mathetes to Diognetus" 5:1–6:1, emphasis added.

Unlike many of his theological predecessors,[12] Augustine rejected the notion that the Roman Empire was a significant moment in salvation history, and consequently the sack of Rome did not require theodicy to explain. Rome was just another example of the Worldly City, constituted by a mutual love of temporal things, and hence temporary, rising and falling according to God's judgment. In contrast, the Heavenly City of God is bound together by a mutual love of God, and is eternal, the goal toward which all history is moving. The cross relativizes every act in history, even Rome. The church is the only human community through which God works to build the City of God. Notice that the vision for the community of faith is still fundamentally urban, just no longer exclusively Roman. *Ecclesiapolis* will take new forms alongside of new forms of cities.

Panel 2: Sixteenth and Seventeenth Centuries—Commercial Cities and the Reformation

Urban decline accompanied the decline of the Roman Empire as a result of successive barbarian invasions and continuing internal disarray in the fifth century and beyond. Cities still existed, but on a lesser scale and with less importance because political and economic power decentralized. The church partly filled the vacuum and provided what central authority there was for most of the Middle Ages, with the bishop in his cathedral in the city or town balancing the lord in his castle in the country.

Town life in western Europe experienced a partial revival in the eleventh century as trade began to resume somewhat again.[13] Population in general grew, but cities—while still small compared to Roman and modern ones—grew fastest and attracted population from the countryside. The church struggled to meet these growing spiritual needs by traditional approaches such as forming additional parishes and through the new mendicant orders of Franciscan and Dominican itinerant preachers.

Major urban development does not kick in until the sixteenth and seventeenth centuries with the accelerated growth of commercial cities, accompanied by the Reformation in the church.[14] Economic and political power centralized in areas of population density as a result of commerce, or trade, buying and selling things beyond what was needed for bare survival.

12. E.g., Eusebius of Caesarea.
13. McNeese, *The Middle Ages,* 20.
14. Ozment, *The Reformation in the Cities.*

The commercial city contrasted with the medieval ideal of the self-sufficient country estate or village which grew all its own food, made all of its own clothes, and generally had as little interaction as possible with the outside world.

This ideal of self-sufficiency made sense in the chaotic aftermath of the fall of the Roman Empire and the decentralized structure of feudalism, but it was economically limited. Commerce grew as the result of multiple, interrelated developments in technology, transportation, and banking. For example, cheaper paper manufacturing and the invention of the printing press created a much broader market for books. After Johannes Gutenberg made moveable type commercially viable around 1450 in Mainz and presses spread throughout Europe, many more books were printed between 1460 and 1500 than had been hand copied during the entire Middle Ages.[15] Trade was expanded by oceanic exploration (e.g., Columbus in 1492) and made safer as greater central political organization and control reduced piracy at sea and banditry on land. Money administered by bankers (e.g., the Fuggers in Germany) increasingly replaced the barter system, making it possible to engage in trade beyond one's immediate area.

A growing commercial economy supported significant population growth in Europe. Bubonic plague and famine had halved the population in some areas in the early fourteenth century, but by 1500 numbers had rebounded and multiplied to seventy million, reaching ninety-one million in 1600 before stabilizing to a little over one hundred million in the seventeenth century.[16] Most Europeans still lived in the countryside, but cities and towns, while still a small fraction overall, were growing fastest, with many doubling in size.

These growing commercial urban areas often were the most receptive to religious change in the sixteenth and seventeenth centuries. The Reformation was a religious embodiment of the trade approach that was proving so fruitful economically and socially. The Reformation was certainly far more than just urban merchants at prayer, and justification by faith alone was heartily embraced in rural areas as well, but commercial cities proved to be particularly compatible with this new movement and a catalyst for its success when earlier efforts with similar ideas remained localized (e.g., Waldensians, Hussites).

15. "Gutenberg's Legacy."
16. Malanima, *Pre-Modern European Economy,* 9.

Markets grew up in cities and towns, with multiple merchants offering new kinds of wares for sale. Choices increased, especially as exotic products were imported from newly discovered lands and technological innovations multiplied. This environment also encouraged a market approach to ideas as trade brought urbanites into regular contact with outsiders and their possible alternative worldviews. Tradition alone was no longer sufficient to commend a concept or even a doctrine.

The rise of universities through the fifteenth century, mainly in towns and cities, accelerated this process as they served as marketplaces for ideas. New ideas, particularly social and religious criticism, could be nurtured and shaped in this more secular, nationalistic environment until they could stand on their own. These urban academic environments helped to shape the thinking of Luther, Zwingli, Calvin, and many early Anabaptist leaders.

The new ideas of these Reformation thinkers could then be spread quickly and broadly through books and pamphlets since most printing presses were in towns and cities that also were linked together by regular book fairs. As with the early church, concentrations of population made it easier to reach more people in less time with a message before authorities could squelch it.

Commerce created a new class of urban elites—merchants, bankers, and artisans—who were often cut off from the hereditary, land-based traditional, political, and religious power structures. These urbanites increasingly resented what they perceived as the church hierarchy's greedy efforts to coerce them out of their wealth through expanding forms of ecclesiastical taxation and fees. To make matters worse, the corruption and inefficiency of church authorities in overseeing markets and property transfers through canon law deepened resentment and nurtured resistance. Wealthy burghers asked themselves why their church should be a conduit for their hard-earned money to go to Rome, which under a series of particularly unspiritual popes seemed like just another competing city-state.

This growing dissatisfaction with the status quo made the citizens of Zurich, Wittenberg, Geneva, and similar cities more open to change, both with regard to the existing ecclesiastical-political system and to its doctrinal rationale. As citizens embraced these changes in the church, the church also sought to change the city. Sometimes this involved taking up arms as Zwingli did in Zurich, but more often it involved legal and social transformation—on a small scale in Lutheran towns in Germany and much more extensively in Geneva under Calvin. Thus, the commercial city paralleled the Reformation church in this sixteenth and seventeenth-century mani-festation of *Ecclesiapolis.*

Panel 3: Eighteenth and Nineteenth Centuries—Industrial Cities and Revivals

The pace of urbanization accelerated by the development of commercial cities in the sixteenth and seventeenth centuries was increased all the more by industrialization in the eighteenth and nineteenth centuries. Once trad-ing goods and services beyond what was needed for self-sufficiency within a local area became not merely possible, but acceptable and even desirable, efforts to expand the means of production and delivery burgeoned into multiple industries. The resulting efficiencies generated wealth, particularly for the owners of these industries, but also raised standards of living in general that led to an urban population explosion, creating opportunities and challenges for city churches exemplified by revivals.

A variety of organizational as well as technological developments made the growth of industry in this period possible. The guild approach of the self-sufficient village craftsman who participated in every step of the economic process gave way to forms of urban mass production. The shoemaker who bought leather from the local tanner and then made each part of a shoe by hand and sold the finished product from a home shop was replaced by the shoe factory.

In contrast, the factory was owned by a non-worker, increasingly a corporation instead of an individual, because of the large amounts of capi-tal needed for acquiring and maintaining the machines that made mass production possible. Workers concentrated on a single part of the produc-tion process, for example, with one cutting out the pieces, another sewing together the uppers, and another attaching the soles. Multiple specialized factory workers could make far more shoes than the same number of shoemakers, so factories tended to be near centers of population to ensure an adequate labor supply. The finished product was then sold wholesale to retailers who distributed the shoes far from the factory to other urban centers.

The joint-stock company made large-scale projects like factories possible. Pooling resources and distributing risk allowed corporations to pursue projects beyond the means of even the wealthiest individuals. Un-like earlier top-down approaches to corporate organization such as royal charters, which, for example, created the British East India Company, joint-stock companies reflected a more democratic, bottom-up structure. Having capital to invest became more important than being a crony of the king. As financial markets grew more sophisticated, even small investors could participate, nurturing a sense of ownership in what seemed to be a grand enterprise. Increasingly, the ability to persuade a mass of shareholders, large and small, to buy into a company's plans became more important than having the king's ear.

The potential of industry became revolutionary when the organizational capacity of joint-stock companies was harnessed to successive waves of technological advances. Water mills and power looms launched the first advance in textile manufacturing. With the development of the steam engine, heavy industries such as coal, iron, and steel followed in the 1820s and 30s, paralleled by advances in transportation, such as railroads and steamships, made possible by these technologies. Farm machinery and improved approaches to agriculture distanced the threat of starvation, but also reduced the number of farm workers needed. This surplus labor tended to leave the countryside, attracted to factory jobs in industrial cities.

Industrialization led to urbanization by raising the overall standards of living that contributed to an urban population explosion, since the death rate was decreasing at the same time as the birth rate was increasing. Opportunities for unskilled workers to escape rural poverty attracted many to industrial centers. For example, the population of Glasgow, Scotland, tripled within one generation, from 40,000 in 1780 to more than 120,000 in 1815, reflecting the growth of manufacturing from almost none to fifty-two cotton mills.[17]

This kind of rapid population growth contributed to severe social problems such as insufficient housing, sanitation, and medical care—the slum conditions explored in the novels of Charles Dickens. The increasing concentration of people in towns and cities instead of being spread out in stable villages led to a breakdown of a strong sense of community. The church was no longer at the center geographically, socially, or spiritually. Population increased far faster than existing congregations could keep up, especially in contexts with an established church where it literally took an act of parliament to create a new parish. As old approaches seemed increasingly insufficient, people turned to adapting elements of urban, industrial society to respond more effectively.

17. Brown, *Thomas Chalmers*, 95.

Successive waves of mass revivals in the eighteenth and nineteenth centuries embodied an industrial approach to religion. George Whitefield, a catalyst of the first Great Awakening around the middle of the eighteenth century, invented the role of the international, itinerant evangelist. Improvements in transportation allowed him to travel extensively throughout Britain and America, and he shrewdly used both his own and the general urban press to publicize his visits to cities in advance, helping to gather crowds in the thousands to which he regularly preached. Adapting the strategy of the traveling salesman who took the product to the customers, Whitefield took the gospel to the masses through extraordinary means such as open-air preaching.[18]

John Wesley helped to organize the movement catalyzed by Whitefield during the first Great Awakening. He not only preached in the open air, focusing on the urban and industrial poor—such as coal miners, whom existing churches were either unwilling or unable to reach—but "franchised" the role of itinerant evangelists through the development of the Methodist system of circuit riders and lay-led classes.[19]

During the second Great Awakening of the early nineteenth century, believers adapted other elements of urban, industrial society to catalyze and organize the church to respond to rapid cultural changes. Advances in papermaking and printing helped make the first long-term religious periodicals possible, sustaining the influence that Whitefield's more ephemeral publications had.[20]

The organizational strategy of joint-stock companies generated a religious form in the creation of voluntary societies, which provided the practical support to make the spiritual means of revival available on a broad scale.[21] While the first voluntary societies focused on foreign missions, the vast majority addressed needs closer to home. While some of them may have seemed primarily "spiritual" in their orientation, such as Bible societies, even these grew out of a belief that Bible reading would improve society as a whole, and many were direct responses to growing urban problems. For example, many cities had "Magdalene" societies for the reformation of

18. Stout, *The Divine Dramatist*.

19. Collins, *A Real Christian*.

20. For an extended discussion of the development of religious periodicals in this period, see Currie, "The Growth of Evangelicalism," Section I—Periodicals: Evangelicalism's Communications Network, 10–138.

21. For an extended discussion, see Currie, "The Growth of Evangelicalism," Section II—Societies: Evangelicalism's Active Expression, 139–275.

urban prostitutes, and interdenominational "City Missions" were formed in most major metropolitan areas to provide direct aid as well as evangelism to the poor.

As important as the direct effects of these voluntary societies were, the indirect benefits to their supporters, particularly the many working-class contributors to "penny-a-week" schemes connected with urban factories, were also highly valued. Here is a particularly glowing, though by no mean atypical, description from an annual report of one association from the early nineteenth century:

> It must form an interesting and delightful consideration to the poorest of our subscribers to reflect, that his penny is divided among so many excellent Societies, and that, through the medium of this Association, he discharges his duty to them all. . . . Their connection with, and lively interest in, these Societies, . . . have an unquestionable tendency to increase the influence of vital religion in their own hearts.[22]

Like the small shareholder in a textile or steel mill, the awakened contributor to a voluntary society gained a sense of investing in something far larger, the expansion of Christ's kingdom. Because the needs of the industrial city could seem so overwhelming, voluntary societies proved highly popular, providing a sense that ordinary people could do something small, yet tangible, to address these massive problems. Even established churches came to incorporate aspects of the voluntary society/joint-stock company into their organizational structures, and this tendency was even more pronounced in the United States, where no single denomination could dominate.

How effective voluntary societies actually were in combating the multitude of industrial urban problems was debated even by proponents. Some, such as the Rev. Thomas Chalmers in Glasgow, attempted to turn back the clock and recreate a village parish model of pastoral care in the slums. Chalmers and a committed band of lay leaders labored vigorously on behalf of the poor and seemed to reduce the need for direct relief and to improve the spiritual and social conditions within their new parish in the short term, as he described in his influential work, *The Christian and Civic Economy of Large Towns*.[23] In contrast, William and Catherine Booth took

22. Calton and Bridgeton (Scotland) Association for Religious Purposes, "Annual Report for 1816," 130–31.

23. Published in three volumes between 1819 and 1826; see Brown, *Thomas Chalmers*, 94.

a more radical approach of essentially transforming a voluntary society into a church through the development of The Salvation Army in London toward the latter part of the nineteenth century.[24] Nonetheless, the efforts of both Chalmers and the Booths reflected the ongoing mutual influence of the industrial city and the church, a continuation of *Ecclesiapolis* as both the ecclesiastical and urban environments underwent rapid changes.

In the middle of the nineteenth century, a third wave of mass revivals with a particularly urban character swept over much of the Protestant world. Beginning in New York City as a businessmen's midday prayer meeting in 1857 under the leadership of an urban missioner, Jeremiah Lanphier, this movement quickly spread to most other major metropolitan areas in North America over the next three years. Characterized by prayer and lay leadership, this prayer revival also saw major gains in church membership in almost all denominations and was covered regularly by city newspapers.[25]

Throughout much of the remainder of the nineteenth century, the spirit of the prayer revival was carried on by D. L. Moody, whose work with slum Sunday Schools and urban Y.M.C.A.s in Chicago reflected the strategies of earlier awakenings. His later career as an itinerant evangelist, preaching to large crowds in many cities in North America, Britain, and Ireland echoed the work of Whitefield and Wesley. A more long-lasting contribution to urban ministry came through his establishment of a training school for men and women that now bears his name, Moody Bible Institute in Chicago.[26]

While mass revivals were not merely an industrial approach to religion, the aggregation of large populations of urban workers in cities created an environment conducive to the rapid and extensive spread of powerful religious experiences. Improvements in transportation and communications facilitated these developments, and the wealth generated by industry—whether in the form of penny-a-week contributions by workers or the largess of factory owners—supported a variety of innovative efforts to deepen and extend the faith. Both the city and the church—*Ecclesiapolis*—were transformed as urban blight and spiritual awakening ebbed and flowed throughout the eighteenth and nineteenth centuries.

24. Hattersley, *Blood and Fire.*
25. "Revival Born in a Prayer Meeting," *Knowing and Doing* (Fall 2004).
26. Dorsett, *A Passion for Souls.*

Panel 4: Twentieth and Twenty-First Centuries—Global Cities and Indigenous and Immigrant Churches

In the twentieth and twenty-first centuries, cities carried on commercial elements from the sixteenth and seventeenth centuries and industrial characteristics from the eighteenth and nineteenth centuries, with churches continuing to reflect these contexts as well. However, as urbanization accelerated throughout these past two centuries, cities became increasingly global, drawing new residents not only from the countryside of their own nation, but immigrants from around the world, aided by continued advancements in transportation and the growing interconnectedness of the economy. The world as a whole became predominantly urban, with the majority of the world's population living in or near a city for the first time in history in 2008, a trend that shows no sign of diminishing.[27]

While cities are growing in all regions, over 90 percent of urbanization is taking place in the developing world.[28] "Megacities" such as Mumbai, India, or Mexico City usually grab the headlines, but more than half of the world's urban population lives in cities of 500,000 or less—which, according to Todd Johnson, director of the Center for the Study of Global Christianity at Gordon-Conwell Theological Seminary, tend to be the location of revivals, which then connect with the rest of the world through global cities. The church provides a new community for immigrants, who are often far more open to embracing a different religion in a foreign urban setting than in their traditional rural homeland.[29]

Boston's "Quiet Revival" exemplifies this contemporary dynamic of *Ecclesiapolis*, with declining mainline congregations being replaced and eventually outpaced by congregations planted for and by successive waves of immigrants from Haiti, Latin America, the Caribbean, and various parts of Asia and Africa since 1970. Over one hundred nations are represented in Boston churches, with an increasing number of congregations having a vibrant mix of several ethnic cultures, races, and nationalities.[30]

Much of the growth of urban Christianity, particularly in the developing world, has been among and by "Renewalists" (Pentecostals/

---

27. "Urbanization: A Majority in Cities."
28. World Bank, "6th Urban Research and Knowledge Symposium."
29. Koons, "Urbanization Hasn't Pushed Religion Aside, U.N. Says."
30. Mitchell, "An Introduction to Boston's Quiet Revival."

Charismatics and similar indigenous movements).[31] Pentecostalism began as an urban movement, growing out of the reports of widespread speaking in tongues at a multiracial Apostolic Faith Gospel Mission on Azusa Street in an industrial section of Los Angeles in 1906. Railroad and steamship connections to other cities in the United States and around the world helped to spread this movement rapidly, reaching urban centers such as Portland, Chicago, Memphis, New York, Winnipeg, Toronto, Oslo, Johannesburg, and Odessa in just a few years and radiating out beyond to cities in Sweden, Argentina, Brazil, Chile, and Korea.[32] Pentecostalism continues to manifest itself primarily as an urban phenomenon even in majority world contexts such as Kenya.[33]

Paralleling the spread of Pentecostalism in the United States was the growth of Black churches in northern cities following "The Great Migration," as large numbers of African Americans relocated from the rural South to fill the need for unskilled labor caused by the reduction of the flow of European immigrants due to World War I and extending through World War II to western cities.[34] Whether a tiny storefront or a megachurch, these congregations helped recreate a sense of "home" and provided spiritual, emotional, and practical support for the many individuals and families displaced by one of the largest internal movements of people in history.

While the Great Migration in the United States indirectly led to the Black church becoming an increasingly urban institution, other Christian movements more intentionally focused upon the city as the key to effective evangelism and discipleship.[35] For example, African Enterprise, founded in 1961 by the South African evangelist, Michael Cassidy, has made it its mission "to evangelize the cities of Africa, through word and deed, in partnership with the Church."[36] African Enterprise has been intentionally multiracial and interdenominational, recognizing that representatives of the whole church reaching cities of Africa are the best means to reach the entire continent. The complexity of the city requires multiple strategies for

31. Johnson and Ross, eds., *Atlas of Global Christianity*, 100.

32. Synan, *The Holiness-Pentecostal Tradition*, 84–142.

33. Parsitau and Mwaura, "God in the City," 95–112.

34. Gregory, *The Southern Diaspora*, ch. 6: "Gospel Highways."

35. See, for example, the strong emphasis upon the city in the Lausanne Congress' "Manila Manifesto" in 1989.

36. See descriptions of African Enterprise's strategies and ministries, online: http://www.africanenterprise.org.

effective outreach, involving spiritual warfare and stratified evangelism, not simply a large stadium event. Scores of African Enterprise and local evangelists take the gospel to every conceivable section and stratum of the community, ranging from marketplaces, street corners, schools, and colleges to prisons, as well as throughout business, civic, professional, and political contexts.

Urban church planting also has arisen more spontaneously, following various ethnic diasporas that had a significant Christian community in the homeland. As a result, there are vibrant Chinese congregations in Boston and Berlin, in Singapore and San Francisco, in Toronto and Tokyo. During the height of Communist repression of Christianity on the mainland, these diaspora Chinese urban churches preserved an authentically Chinese expression of the faith and helped to reevangelize China, particularly through outreach with graduate students who returned to start "house" churches in their apartment buildings. As emigration from the mainland has increased over the past several decades, preexisting believers have also spread their fervent faith back to more secularized Christian and non-Christian members of the diaspora.

Even nations without official repression of Christianity have seen similar patterns of indigenous urban church growth and renewal following the ebb and flow of their diasporas out to various countries and then back to the homeland, reflecting the interconnectedness of the global economy among diverse cities on multiple continents. As a result, there are Korean congregations in both North and South American cities, as well as in most urban centers in Asia. The Brazilian diaspora exhibits a similar pattern, with more concentration in Europe than in Asia, particularly returning to reevangelize their fellow Portuguese speakers. African and Caribbean immigrants are also seeking to plant churches, not only among their fellow newcomers, but also among their secular, post-Christendom former colonizers. The global, multicultural character of the twenty-first-century *Ecclesiapolis* creates seemingly unusual developments, such as the largest congregation in the city of Kiev, and perhaps all of Europe, being pastored by a Nigerian.[37]

---

37. Imade-Babs and Lawal, "Nigerian Pastor of Europe's Biggest Church."

Conclusion

The characteristic growth of indigenous and immigrant churches in twentieth and twenty-first-century global cities reflects similar developments in the cosmopolitan cities of the Roman Empire and the emergence of the Gentile church, suggesting some enduring dynamics for *Ecclesiapolis* over the past two millennia. The cosmos is now global instead of just the Mediterranean basin, and the polis is far larger as well, but the multicultural, religiously pluralistic urban context still provides a far higher level of and value in choice for religion than in traditional, rural areas.

While this dynamic is threatening to church adherence as an inherited practice, leading to justifiable concerns that "our youth may stop going to church if they move to the big city," it is not inimical to authentic faith. Indeed, a sense of being chosen and choosing, not because of family custom or ethnic identity, but as part of a new community drawn from every nation, tribe, people, and language (Rev 7:9) seems more consistent with what Jesus intended for those who would become his disciples (Matt 28:19; Acts 1:8). A historical perspective of what happened in the commercial cities of the sixteenth and seventeenth centuries and the industrial cities of the eighteenth and nineteenth centuries can also be a source of hope in these times of growing urbanization, both for those who seek to reform churches that seem to have departed from biblical faith and practice and for those who pray for revival among the masses who seem dead to Christ.

Caution is always wise in trying to predict precisely what will happen in the short term for as complex and interrelated an entity as *Ecclesiapolis*. However, the dynamic interplay of church and city sets the agenda for the future, which pastors and urban planners alike will see more clearly if they view it through the lens of their shared historical context, for history will conclude with the ultimate *Ecclesiapolis*:

> I saw the Holy City, the new Jerusalem, coming down out of heaven from God, prepared as a bride beautifully dressed for her husband. And I heard a loud voice from the throne saying, "Look! God's dwelling place is now among the people, and he will dwell with them. They will be his people, and God himself will be with them and be their God. He will wipe every tear from their eyes. There will be no more death or mourning or crying or pain, for the old order of things has passed away." (Rev 21:2–4 NIV)

References for Further Study (in Historical Order)

Meeks, Wayne A. *The First Urban Christians: the Social World of the Apostle Paul.* 2nd ed. New Haven: Yale University Press, 2003.

Allen, Roland. *Missionary Methods: St. Paul's or Ours?: A Study of the Church in the Four Provinces.* Grand Rapids: ReadaClassic.com, 2012.

Ozment, Steven. *The Reformation in the Cities: The Appeal of Protestantism to Sixteenth-Century Germany and Switzerland.* New Haven: Yale University Press, 1980.

Stout, Harry S. *The Divine Dramatist: George Whitefield and the Rise of Modern Evangelicalism.* Grand Rapids: Eerdmans, 1991.

Chalmers, Thomas. *The Christian and Civic Economy of Large Towns.* 3 vols. Glasgow: William Collins, 1819–1826.

Hattersley, Roy. *Blood and Fire: William and Catherine Booth and Their Salvation Army.* New York: Doubleday, 2000.

Synan, Vinson. *The Holiness-Pentecostal Tradition: Charismatic Movements in the Twentieth Century.* 2nd ed. Grand Rapids: Eerdmans, 1997.

Gregory, James N. *The Southern Diaspora: How the Great Migrations of Black and White Southerners Transformed America.* Chapel Hill: The University of North Carolina Press, 2005.

Johnson, Todd M. and Kenneth R. Ross, eds. *Atlas of Global Christianity 1910–2010.* Edinburgh: Edinburgh University Press, 2010.

Redeeming the City in the Margins

MARK G. HARDEN

THOSE WHO LIVE AND dwell in cities occupy and share private and public spaces among a diverse array of acquaintances and strangers on a daily basis. Each day brings with it challenges related to social and economic disparities in social spaces shared by both the righteous and the "stranger." Disparities in the system perpetuate social inequities that lead to adverse conditions in the city that do not reflect God's desire for humanity. Social inequities that adversely affect individuals and families routinely go unaddressed. Nonetheless, this problem provides unlimited opportunities for the church to engage in meaningful ministry that reflects its sacred character and purpose in the world. During the public ministry of Jesus and his disciples, the gospel found its way into public spaces, creating opportunities for men and women to become free and making God's people meaningful agents of change. When the church engages effectively in the redemptive work of God, the people and spaces in the city become communal spaces that reflect a church "reaching for the New Jerusalem." Being the "marginalized" refers to the disadvantaged who have little or no access to social and economic opportunities that would make a qualitative difference in their lives. The challenge for the church is to understand the needs of the people we seek to serve, know the best ways to deliver transformational ministry, and learn how to empower the "stranger" in the city to preserve human dignity.

This treatment on the topic of "Reaching for the New Jerusalem" is a basis for developing a practical theology for the urban church that desires to serve those in the margins of the city who are part of an insular struggle for social and economic justice. This chapter is about the opportunity for the urban church, supported by the inimitable work of the Holy Spirit, to avoid paternalistic ministry, and address the consequences of social inequities that strip people of their human dignity and quality of life, and push them further into a life in the margins.

In order to set the stage for action from the perspective of my discipline, which is human ecology in practical theology, I introduce and integrate concepts such as time, space, and economy to expand on the biblical meaning of *household*. I also attempt to outline a theological perspective using a human ecosystems framework, making the point that God empowers the church to transform people's social spaces in the city into communal spaces in a way that welcomes strangers and preserves their dignity, as does the very process of creating those spaces. Moreover, I will argue that the task of addressing the causes and consequences of social inequities requires the prophetic force of an empathetic ministry that includes compassion for the stranger. Although I forgo addressing the nature and the causes of social inequities in depth, I discuss in detail the nature of the struggle against the conditions of poverty, and how addressing these issues challenges the church to achieve its mission. My thesis is that, when one understands how the church participates in the economies of God, God compels and empowers one to act and to engage in non-paternalistic ways to get others to participate in this divine economy for their own sake.

The Church Being the Church

How can an empowered church function as a transforming agent for people of the city, particularly, those suffering from restrictions and limitations in various social spaces in the city? What can the church do to make a difference in the lives of those who become marginalized due to the dynamic consequences of disparities in the city? Specifically, how can the urban church make a difference in the city? Observing how the church and the marginalized and/or poor interact in a shared social space in the city is a wonderful place to start thinking about how one does ministry in the city. This task involves posing the right questions and learning how to develop an agenda or strategy for achieving meaningful outcomes associated with improving the quality of life among individuals and families in need.

In human ecology, the word *household* refers to a household system that consists of one or more members who share resources in order to achieve a common goal. Hence, one or more household systems constitute a shared social space. Likewise, the biblical term for *household* in the

New Testament often refers to members of the "household of God" or the "church," in which members share in the divine call to serve in faithful obedience to Jesus Christ (1 Tim 3:15 and other corroborating Scriptures, including 1 Cor 14). The word *ecology* in human ecology converges with the biblical idea of household. There are two common New Testament Greek words as a case in point: *oikos* and *oikonomos*. *Oikos* in New Testament Greek means "household." Part of the second Greek word *oikonomos* is *nemo*, which means to dispense or manage. *Oikonomos* translated can mean the "manager of a household."[1] These ancient concepts are where we get our English ideas for "ecology" and "economy." Ecology is a concept that refers to a context or the environment, while economy refers to managing things within and among "households." The "house" or a "household economy" constitutes a managed ecosystem in the context of its members or components—the household. Hence, as a human ecologist and practical theologian, I draw upon these biblical concepts to make an analysis of the church in the context of the marginalized that dwell in the city. The ecosystem in this instance is a complex system of members, each with a unique function or role that seeks to achieve the goal of the whole using shared resources. "Household" members work in community (or fellowship) as they are interdependent parts of the whole.

Time and space as human ecosystem principles work together as useful concepts in the context of ministry. In human ecosystems, time and space either expand or contract, restricting and limiting opportunities for people in the city. Time spent by individuals in the struggle to achieve social and economic goals, however, does not have to be time lost. The church can assist people in redeeming time for a greater investment of time and energy. For instance, the church can change the social and economic conditions in a person's environment in such a way that empowers individuals or families to achieve social and economic goals through various ministries. Ministries that address the economic issues include workforce development, food cooperative organizing, and affordable childcare for single mothers. Engaging others in public ministry to address needs in shared social spaces in the city creates additional time and space for other things to happen that would not otherwise happen. The church can generate a plethora of pastoral responses to address social inequities in the city and meet the needs of those relegated to the margins by social and economic circumstances.

1. *LSJ*, 1204, 1167.

Churches can advocate for youth unfairly targeted by law enforcement, form a coalition to leverage resources, educate people about pervasiveness of commercial predators, and create afterschool activities for youth to reduce crime and drug use. Time and space are created when the church is actively addressing a community-based need in the city. Instead of establishing one location to address an issue, churches can work together with other community stakeholders to establish multiple locations to address issues. This strategic approach aims at changing the conditions in the environment for people in need. It empowers the church and the community to eradicate pervasive conditions in the community that limit freedom and access to social and economic opportunities for those in the margins. Not every Christian shares the same passion to address human needs for those in the margins. Different issues and needs move different people to compassion. Therefore, organization and targeted efforts are essential.

From a human ecologist point of view, the city is made up of diverse human micro systems nested in a multi-layered environment from which people naturally draw social and economic resources in order to thrive and sustain life in the city. In this purview, the poor, the rich, and the church draw on a different range of social and economic resources in order to thrive or survive in the same multi-layered environment. These people, in their most basic sense, are human systems nested together in a multi-layered environment. Human ecosystems are individuals, families, children, men, women, or any groups of individuals seen as interacting with and within their environments. They not only interact with their environments, they are interdependent as two parts of the whole, an ecosystem. They are human subcomponents of the whole—the city. Therefore, from a Christian human ecologist perspective, the city is a composite of human ecosystems that includes the marginalized and/or the poor.

Christian human ecologists (e.g., family ecologists, child ecologists, community developers, family therapists, etc.) are those who seek to understand and service people in relationship to their environment and never apart from it. Human ecosystems interface with the church in everyday situations. All human ecosystems in the city constitute a web of interconnected and nested households among households. These ecosystems include people interacting in the workplace, institutions, schools, merchant centers, parks, jails, hospitals, and churches. When one walks down the street minding one's own business, a connection exists with the unknown person who is walking in the opposite direction by virtue of being members of the same community and sharing a social space.

The Household Economy of God

This approach even contains implications for how we think about the Trinity. Is it a divine household? How are the Son and the Holy Spirit dependent on the Father? When does one divine person of the Trinity act apart from the other? The interconnectedness of the will and nature of God expressed in the Trinity constitutes an ideal household or ecosystem that unites the people of God in fellowship. For our purposes, how does the church become a part of the divine household? As an ideal household, the Trinity becomes manifested in the city when the members of the household of God, the church, perform according to his will in ministry in a shared social space. Therefore, the "economies of God" refers to how the church participates in the redemptive work of God through Christian service in public ministry. The economies of God are the earthly activities of the Father, Son, and Holy Spirit in the life of the church in the city (and in the world). The success of the public ministry, therefore, depends on members of the church participating in the economies of God. Members of the church are household stewards that manage how ministry unfolds in the public sphere or social spaces in the city. In this ideal divine household, that is to say, the heavenly ecosystem, the church participates in the economies of God through faith. The believer becomes a change agent as a member of the household of God. The house of God is at work for God's redemptive purpose to reconcile humanity to himself (Col 1:20).

Invoking God's presence, then, requires intentional public ministry by the church as an instrument of God's redemptive work. God empowers his church to transform shared social spaces into communal spaces so that those at-risk due to adverse social and economic conditions can become free to achieve social and economic success, free from the clutches of an oppressive system. Therefore, the church that takes action in the city is a church that creates a communal space where individuals and groups may find freedom and justice. It is in this light that the church can and ought to provide access to the benefits of God's divine economy by transforming a shared social space into a communal space.

Reaching for the New Jerusalem involves transforming public or shared social spaces in the city into "communal" spaces so the marginalized can also find righteousness. When the church appropriately intervenes in a social space on behalf of the poor, it is an act of compassion couched in hospitality. "Compassion" is an important biblical concept. Some scholars have helped us to understand that compassion has to do with how considerate and caring we should be toward one another. For instance, John Pilch writes,

> The Hebrew word for compassion derives from the word for womb (*rhm*), but this etymology does not designate the value as particular to women so much as it reflects the cultural belief that children of the same mother . . . are the most closely bonded of all kin and ought to be most considerate of one another.

He further states,

> . . . compassion is a peripheral value, that is, it is specific to given interactions, namely those guided and governed by kinship considerations. Compassion would thus be defined as the caring concern that ought to be felt and acted upon between real or fictive kin.[2]

The relationship between Christian and the "stranger" in the social space is one of a communal nature when there is an act of compassion. Therefore, compassionate ministry is what ministry leaders should seek when addressing social inequities in the city. Compassion requires having the utmost care and concern for an "other-centered" approach that represents God's will in the city. Those demonstrating a need and who share the social space with the church are brought into a communal space because of this relational approach to ministry. Indeed, this perspective encourages the church to adopt a love ethic. In turn, this love ethic empowers the church to facilitate the transformation of social spaces in the city into communal spaces.

The parable of the Good Samaritan is an excellent example of compassion as a love ethic. It becomes the mandate for the righteous to address the needs of the marginalized in the city. The parable instructs us to move beyond our comfort zones and prejudices toward making a genuine effort to help our neighbor. The social space in this instance was a road shared by religious leaders, an unnamed Samaritan, and an injured stranger lying on the road. The people who are under scrutiny are the ones who fail to show "pity" for an injured stranger. Of all of the individuals in society, the

2. Pilch and Malina, *Handbook of Biblical Social Values*, 30.

stranger that occupies a social space in our lives is the most likely to be taken for granted and, at the same time, the least likely to be known or understood as a neighbor.

We need not only to ask, "Who is our neighbor?" as does the lawyer in this story, but we also need to act based on what Jesus is indicating in the story, when he addresses the question, "How do you respond as a neighbor?" (Luke 10:29). Although the former question has to do with the awareness of who is one's neighbor, the latter question has to do with a love ethic one must possess for a stranger—compassion.

Scriptural themes about "strangers" suggest that otherness should not be a factor that deters action, but spurs action. The stranger is identified in the gospel of Matthew as "Lord" when the "sheep" ask the question, "Lord, when did we do all of these things?" (Matt 25:37–39) The stranger is the one whom we must recognize as though he or she is "Jesus." One can argue that there is an echo of the theme of Jesus as "the stranger" in the appearance of Jesus to Cleopas on the Emmaus road (Luke 24:18). This biblical concept and value of compassion helps us to avoid casting an image upon the stranger that not only makes our actions paternalistic but demoralizes the "stranger." In fact, compassion should elevate the stranger to equal or greater status. Is this how the church should treat those who share social spaces in the city? The treatment of the stranger is also an Old Testament theme in reference to Israel and the commandment to care for the "stranger" who is within their "gates" (Deut 10:19).

Failing to act for social and economic justice on behalf of the poor, when it is God's will, and when it is within our power to do so, contributes to maintaining and perpetuating an unjust system. God teaches us to love the poor as He loves the poor. The process of receiving a "stranger" into one's space and treating him or her like a guest is a distinctive pattern in the tradition of Christian ministry. The poorest and most marginalized in the Scriptures are similar to the groups and individuals we find in the city. That is, they are the seniors, widows, disabled, and single women with children who require a communal system of support. In the books of Deuteronomy (15:7–8, 10–11) and Exodus (22:21–24) in the Old Testament, God clearly expresses a strong desire to address the needs of the poor among his people and in relationship to the stranger. Serious consequences are levied for failing to act on behalf of the poor and marginalized in several other Old Testament books (2 Sam 12:1–6; Prov 14:31; 17:5; 21:13; Amos 2:6–8; Mal 3:1–5). In the New Testament, it is also clear that God loves the poor. The poor are highly favored and are the focus of the ministry of Jesus (Matt 6:2–4; 19:30; 22; 25:34–40; Luke 4:16–19; 10:25–37; 11:37–41; 12:32–34). The teachings in the Scriptures about the poor versus the wealthy, God's desire to bless the poor, and God's commands that the church acts on behalf of the poor and marginalized are too numerous to list. Suffice it to say, acting on behalf of the marginalized and the poor is what God requires of the church (Matt 25:34–40).

Conclusion

God does not require each church to resolve or right all the wrongs of the whole city or human ecosystem. However, God does require his people to respond to the wrongs inflicted upon individuals and groups who share social spaces with the church, particularly among the socially and economically marginalized. There is a clear biblical, ethical perspective related to what the church ought to do when it shares a social space in the city with the marginalized.

Resources in the city are not equally distributed and accessible to everyone. As in other systems, time and space restrict and limit what resources and opportunities people have. Time and space in this instance are defined as the freedom one possesses to participate in and access social and economic resources. This is why the church of Jesus Christ must be active in helping correct an imperfect system that promotes social inequities and thereby maintains a system of haves versus have-nots even among people who share the same social (public) space. The church addressing and correcting such issues of social and economic justice will assist God in reconciling the world and creating a New Jerusalem in the city.

References for Further Study

Myers, Bryant L. *Walking with the Poor: Principles and Practices of Transformational Development*. Maryknoll, NY: Orbis, 1999.

Pilch, J. J., and B. Malina, eds. *Handbook of Biblical Social Values*. Peabody, MA: Hendrickson, 1998.

Stassen, Glen H., and David P. Gushee. *Kingdom Ethics: Following Jesus in Contemporary Context*. Downers Grove: InterVarsity, 2003.

Volf, Miroslav, and Dorothy Bass, eds. *Practicing Theology: Beliefs and Practices in Christian Life*. Grand Rapids: Eerdmans, 2002.

Roadblocks to the New Jerusalem Facing Urban Youth and Communities

DEAN BORGMAN

> *Almighty God of our Creation and our Redemption, thy kingdom come, thy will be done, here in our place and time before the coming of the King of justice and peace. And this we ask at the urgings of the prophets and mandates of our Lord and Savior Jesus Christ. Amen.*

Theological Introduction: What Is the New Jerusalem?

Most Christians and churches pray the Lord's Prayer, the "Our Father." We will assume that the New Jerusalem is roughly synonymous with the kingdom of God and hope that all or most Christians are united in accepting the Lord's Prayer as central petitions of the church. The New Jerusalem, then, is what we pray for when we ask, ". . . thy kingdom come, thy will be done on earth." Still, the "New Jerusalem" seems open to a broad range of interpretations. Some see the kingdom not as a future hope but only as a present reality.[1] Others insist the kingdom will come at some future time totally apart from human endeavors.[2] Still others see the kingdom as an individual spiritual experience, an existential interpretation of eschatology[3]

1. Adolph von Harnack, a leader in liberal theological thinking, takes a non-eschatological perspective on the kingdom of God. It is rather the present realization of biblical prophecy, emphasizing the universal fatherhood of God, brotherhood of man, and a strong ethic of love. See von Harnack, *What Is Christianity?*

2. Dr. J. Vernon McGee taught that Christians today cannot do one thing to bring about God's kingdom on earth, *Thru the Bible with Dr. J. Vernon McGee*, online: http://www.oneplace.com/ministries/thru-the-bible-with-j-vernon-mcgee/listen/. See also any edition of the *Scofield Reference Bible*, notes for John 1:14 and Acts 2:1.

3. Eschatology: having to do with the end of the world, the culmination of salvation

rather than as a future reality.[4] This chapter first assumes that God's king-dom, the perfect New Jerusalem, is realized both in the future coming of Jesus Christ and in the breaking out of God's kingdom in mysterious ways and forms today. Both take place at God's initiative. The second assumption sees God enlisting us as his partners. As Christians we are called upon to bring a taste and reflection of God's will into contemporary society. Christ challenged us to be salt and light in a world that needs healing and light. Some will apply the salt and light metaphors only spiritually rather than regard them as a challenge to enlighten, irritate, heal, and change our worldly environment. This chapter sees the church working toward a New Jerusalem—and, to that end, speaking prophetically and working for social change. Others put more emphasis upon the church being a better church. For them, the church's primary mission is to model a radical and holy com-munity as the kingdom of God.[5] Within these differences we will suggest a general strategy for church and society to transform disadvantaged families and youth in the urban context.

A few significant attempts to interpret the New Jerusalem in the year 2012 are worth noting. From one side, the Christian Right picked up Ayn Rand's Objectivist views of a city founded on strong individualism and tending toward an anti-government stance.[6] From the other, Witness Lee's Living Stream Ministry, a radical, anti-church (Roman Catholic and Prot-estant denominations) movement, published the latest issue—"The New Jerusalem"—of its polished journal *Affirmation & Critique*.[7] A more cen-trist, conservative evangelical position was expressed in *Awaiting the City: Poverty, Ecology and Morality in Today's Political Economy*.[8]

To understand the New Jerusalem is a challenging task. Most agree the Bible needs theological interpretation, and, further, that the New Jeru-salem is Scripture's contrast to its symbolic Babylon.[9] Obviously the New

---

history. We speak of the "not yet" as God's final perfection of history, and the "already" as the partial realization of God's kingdom in our times.

4. Bultmann, *History and Eschatology*.

5. See Hauerwas and Willimon, *Resident Aliens*.

6. Consider Stephen Richer, "Paul Ryan's Ayn Rand Offense," *Forbes*, 30 August 2012, online: http://www.forbes.com/sites/stephenricher/2012/08/30/paul-ryans-ayn-rand-offense/.

7. Ron Kangas, "I Saw the Holy City, New Jerusalem," 3–12.

8. Brand and Pratt, *Awaiting the City*, 240.

9. Babylon: Some have adopted the terms "The Empire" or "The Matrix" for the se-ductive, consumerist, and oppressive power-structure portrayed also in Rev 16:19 and

Jerusalem stands in contrast to Old Jerusalem, both as a real city and as a metaphor for the Old Covenant. Considering the New Jerusalem requires more than comparison to the old Jerusalem; it takes us back to the Garden of Eden—God's original intention for perfect harmony and human relations. About Eden in Genesis 1 and 2, Karl Barth thought no more can be known but that

> . . . real man could be there on the real earth, and to this day cannot overlook or forget but must always *remember* that among all the known and accessible places on earth there was and is also that unknown and inaccessible place, that in addition to his own place there is also that which is lost to him, and that that place is his home.[10]

Theological reflection, then, must *remember* Eden as the original intent of a divine partnership between God and human beings presiding over the earth with justice and shalom (peace and well-being). Imagining Eden past and the heavenly city coming begins to make sense of the mystery of God's partnership with human beings. We more fully appreciate the Divine Drama (above all earthly dramas of good and evil, of apocalypse and super heroes) as the fullness of God in human community. Our hearts begin to appreciate the grand drama of evil against good, of oppressive and unjust divisions between extreme wealth and extreme poverty. The words of biblical prophets take on contemporary meaning, and a sense of urgency takes hold.

Introduction to the Roadblocks Hindering the New Jerusalem

The year 2012 closed with shock and sadness over the slaughter of 6- and 7-year-old innocents. The small town of Newtown, Connecticut, struggled to survive the loss of 20 innocent children and 6 valiant educators. Beyond this close community, a country tried to comprehend, "How could it happen? Why did it happen? How can it be prevented?" A president, having attended four such slaughters in his first term, and after attempting to comfort families for hours, appeared before the American people and

---

chapter 17.

10. Barth, *CD* 3/3: 253; italics mine.

urged, "We can't tolerate this anymore. These tragedies must end . . . Surely we can do better."[11]

It took only days, however, for a similar number of people to be gunned down on urban streets unheralded—and in a short time-span, for urban bullets to strike down twice as many innocent children.[12] Somehow, it is difficult to rouse national concern over the loss of black and brown children and youth hidden away from those of us who live more comfortably.

After senseless slaughters of seemingly innocent youths on Boston streets, I have heard leaders and preachers cry out, "Why do they kill?" Actually, we should know by now why they kill and how it might be prevented. But instead we seek piecemeal solutions and are paralyzed by partisan polarization. Even those of us in touch with realities on urban streets and well-read on urban violence are still struck with shock by the latest killings and may ask, "Why?" That's one way we register response to senseless killings—even though the how's and why's have been well researched. That is what this chapter is about.

Research: Youth Stripped of Dignity and Dreams

The emptiness and hopelessness of many disadvantaged youth were studied and recorded by Jay MacLeod in his *Ain't No Making It: Aspirations & Attainment in a Low-Income Neighborhood* and by Alex Kotlowitz, *There Are No Children Here: The Story of Two Boys Growing Up in the Other America.* Amos N. Wilson has taken a close look at the angry reaction to disadvantage, lack of positive male role models, and empty dreams in *Understanding Black Adolescent Male Violence: Its Remediation and Prevention.* Nuance and detail are added to Wilson's diagnosis by Pedro A. Noguera's *The Trouble with Black Boys: . . . And Other Reflections on Race, Equity, and the Future of Public Education.*[13]

11. CNN Wire Staff, "Transcript: 'We have wept with you,' Obama says in Newtown speech," online: http://politicalticker.blogs.cnn.com/2012/12/16/breaking-we-have-wept-with-you-obama-says-in-newtown-speech/.

12. Chris Kirk and Dan Kois, "How Many People Have Been Killed by Guns Since Newtown?" Online: http://www.slate.com/articles/news_and_politics/crime/2012/12/gun_death_tally_every_american_gun_death_since_newtown_sandy_hook_shooting.html; Janell Ross, "Child Gun Deaths Nationwide Number Nearly 6 Newtown Massacres," online: http://www.huffingtonpost.com/2012/12/21/child-gun-deaths-newtown_n_2347920.html.

13. Noguera, *The Trouble with Black Boys.*

David Isay gave tape recorders to two perceptive young boys who lived around the Ida G. Wells projects of South Chicago. Isay encouraged them to help us understand their lives and environment through "qualitative research." They describe life in urban projects and its possible effects in remarkably insightful ways. Their chronicle includes a frightful description of how a few pre-gang-aged kids "punished" a boy for refusing to steal candy from a local market by luring two brothers up to their "clubhouse" and then dropping the boy's younger brother to his death from a 21st floor project window.[14] Elijah Anderson's research explains why urban youth kill in his widely read article "The Code of the Streets"[15] and his subsequent book, *Code of the Street*.[16]

Stories from those who have committed homicide and other crimes often describe receiving little or no special attention growing up in their homes. Fraser Mustard and the Founders Network in Canada studied the importance of early childhood stimulation.[17] Countries that ensured quality early childhood education under professional supervision had lower school dropout and crime rates. Without malicious intent, our society has programmed some disadvantaged youth for failure.

Research: School Dropouts

A child's brain is pruned and developed in the first months and years of life. Primary stimulation, limited to TV and video games, hinders later possibilities of high academic achievement. In contrast, children growing up in wealthy suburban communities receive nurture and stimulation from several adult caregivers. Such towns give a high percentage of their budgets to their schools, while cities, providing all manner of services to their suburban business workers and visitors, distribute only a small percentage of their budgets to public education. Schools with inadequate resources and weak teachers, often protected by teacher unions and lacking administrative support for discipline issues, create an atmosphere that too often

---

14. Jones et al., *Our America*, 89–99.

15. Elijah Anderson, "The Code of the Streets," online: http://www.theatlantic.com/magazine/archive/1994/05/the-code-of-the-streets/306601/.

16. Anderson, *Code of the Street*.

17. "Early World of Learning—Dr. Fraser Mustard," online: http://earlyworldoflearning.com/knowledge-centre/scientists/dr-fraser-mustard/.

encourages youth, coming from a culture devaluing academic success, to drop out:

> The vast majority of kids in the developed world finish high school—but not in the United States. More than a million kids drop out every year, around 7,000 a day, and the numbers are rising. An even higher number fail to graduate.[18]

Russell Rumberger's *Dropping Out* is one of the most complete and recent analyses of the dropout problem. He deals comprehensively with factors causing students to drop out and goes on to describe what could be done to reverse this trend. Rumsberger offers evidence such as the following: *TIME* magazine's April 9, 2006, issue noted America's dropout crisis with a cover article titled "Dropout Nation."

> On March 1, 2010. . . President Barack Obama stated, "This is a problem we cannot afford to accept and we cannot afford to ignore. The stakes are too high—for our children, for our economy, and for our country. It's time for all of us to come together—parents, students, principals and teachers, business leaders and elected officials from across the political spectrum—to end America's dropout crisis.[19]

Emphasizing the entire ecological context and the need for holistic responses to this crisis, Rumberger's work concludes,

> . . . without a clear and focused effort to improve the capacity at all levels of the educational system—the federal level, the state level, the local level and school level—these efforts will likely fail.
>
> School-based approaches alone, even with the addition of targeted dropout interventions, are also unlikely to solve the dropout crisis without providing adequate support to families and communities.
>
> One valuable investment is in early childhood education and preschool. Numerous studies have documented the educational benefits of preschool, including improved graduation and reduced crime.
>
> Improving U.S. dropout and graduation rates is likely to be a never-ending goal, akin to improving health care or the environment.[20]

18. Rumberger, *Dropping Out*, back cover.

19. Ibid., 3.

20. Ibid., 273–6.

Research: Social Costs of Gross Inequality

About poverty, Marshall Sahlins has written, "Poverty is not a certain small amount of goods, nor is it just a relationship between means and ends; above all it is a relationship between people. Poverty is a social status. . . . It has grown as an invidious distinction between classes and more importantly as a tributary relation."[21] As we consider poverty and class inequalities, it is important to keep the relativity of wealth, social opportunity, and social status in mind. Poverty involves what others think of you and how you think about yourself.

Research has gone beyond attributing urban street violence to poverty. Of course, poverty is a critical factor. But the inequality between the rich and poor tends to create more violence in one society than another—it has to do with status, appearances, and opportunities.

A number of further global studies bear this out. Richard Wilkinson and Kate Pickett are British epidemiologists[22] who worked for decades exploring the relationship of income inequalities to health and life span. Gradually, they began looking at other factors: general well-being, crime, and violence. They observed,

> It is a remarkable paradox that, at the pinnacle of human material and technical achievement, we find ourselves anxiety-ridden, prone to depression, worried about how others see us, unsure of our friendships, driven to consume and with little or no community life. . . . How is it that we have created so much mental and emotional suffering despite levels of wealth and comfort unprecedented in human history? . . . .
>
> Sooner or later in the long history of economic growth, countries inevitably reach a level of affluence where "diminishing returns" set in and additional income buys less and less additional health, happiness or wellbeing.[23]

Here two highly trained epidemiologists are interpreting data in a systemic and holistic manner. And they are able to declare serious inequalities to be public health concerns—matters that call for social action at all levels of society. They also explain paradoxes—how those not able to pay basic bills or put healthy food on the table may feel forced to buy cell phones and

---

21. Marshall Sahlins, "The Original Affluent Society," online: http://www.primitivism.com/original-affluent.htm.

22. Epidemiologists study causes of disease and pathologies in various populations.

23. Wilkinson and Pickett, *The Spirit Level*, 3, 10.

expensive footwear, forced in order to maintain basic human respect and dignity in their neighborhood. Let's read on:

> In Chapters 4–12 we focus on a series of health and social problems like violence, mental illness, teenage births and educational failure, which within each country are all more common among the poor than the rich.[24]

From the Postscript of this second edition comes this interesting finding:

> When we wrote *The Spirit Level*, we knew of no other studies of income inequality and child conflict, but a recent study of 37 countries finds higher levels of bullying in more unequal countries. Support from family and friends was associated with less bullying, but neither this nor differences in family wealth trumped the effect of income inequality.[25]

We know that the ratio of difference between top business executives and their workers has increased in the U.S. many times over during the past half century and that it stands far higher than in most other countries. *The Economist* sums up our financial inequality this way:

> The annual household income of America's ultra-wealthy, the 0.1 percent of the population is at least $1.5m, and the top 0.01 percent have an annual income of $8m or more. Over the past 30 years incomes have soared both among the wealthy and the ultra-wealthy. The higher up the income ladder, the bigger the rise has been. The result has been a huge, and widening, gap—financially, socially and geographically—between America's elite and the rest of the country.[26]

The conclusion of Wilkinson and Pickett's vast study is that

> the quality of social relations in a society is built on material foundations. The scale of income difference has a powerful effect on how we relate to one another. Rather than blaming parents, religion, values, education or the penal system, we. . . show that

24. Ibid., 11.

25. Ibid., 293.

26. Michael Morgenstern, "The Rich and the Rest: American Inequality Is a Tale of Two Countries," online: http://www.economist.com/node/21564418.

the scale of inequality provides a powerful policy lever on the psychological wellbeing for all of us.[27]

"At an intuitive level people have always recognized that inequality is socially corrosive,"[28] according to these authors, and they cite one study finding that 90 percent of Americans say they would be happy with a more equitable income differential. We are not talking about some kind of utopian egalitarianism; it would be enough for the United States to be comparable to other developed countries. We are talking about what seems to be fair and just.

Two respected economists refer to, and back up, the research of Wilkinson and Pickett. The work of Joseph Stiglitz can be found in *The Price of Inequality*.[29] Stewart Lansley's *The Cost of Inequality* describes the same negative effects of inequality and shows that a more equitable social system can aid economic recovery and prosperity from a British and European perspective.[30]

Biblical Interlude

Our line of thought has not lost scriptural direction in wandering off into economics and politics—by no means. The Torah (first five books of the Bible), the Psalms, and the Prophets continually speak of economic fairness and warn against political injustice toward the poor.[31] We are reminded again of the Virgin Mary's clear words in the Magnificat: The Lord "has cast down the mighty. . . and has lifted up the lowly. He has filled the hungry with good things, and the rich He has sent away empty."[32] Jesus himself spoke more about money than about the issues many Christians are arguing about today. The fact that these days Christianity has little voice and power on the economics of Wall Street or politics of Washington—in the real world where we live and work, buy and sell—should not be considered normative. The people of God's Covenant are expected to ameliorate the ills of society and encourage positive action toward the common good.

27. Wilkinson and Pickett, 4–5.

28. Ibid., x.

29. Stiglitz, *The Price of Inequality*.

30. Lansley, *The Cost of Inequality*.

31. Lev 25; Deut 15; Ps 72; and Amos 2:6; 4:1; 5:11 are just the beginning of examples.

32. Luke 1:52–53 (*Book of Common Prayer*, 119).

Research: Dropping out to Prison

Catherine Kim and colleagues in *The School-to-Prison Pipeline* provide
well-researched analyses of the almost necessary pathway from inadequate
schools to inadequate prisons. School dropouts in disadvantaged neighborhoods see few opportunities except in gangs and the drug business. Seemingly successful male role models are there to encourage and mentor them
in the ways of a street economy and its culture of violence:

> The School-to-Prison Pipeline thus refers to the confluence of
> educational policies in underresourced public schools and a pre-
> dominantly punitive juvenile justice system that fails to provide
> education and mental health services for our most at-risk students
> and drastically increases the likelihood that these children will end
> up with a criminal record rather than a high school diploma. Given
> the devastating impact, not only on the children themselves, but
> also the communities in which they live, challenging and limiting
> the pipeline presents one of the most urgent challenges in civil
> rights today.
>
> . . . each year across the nation, "police make 2.2 million ju-
> venile arrests, 1.7 million cases are referred to juvenile courts; an
> estimated 400,000 youngsters cycle through juvenile detention
> centers; and nearly 100,000 youth are confined in juvenile jails,
> prisons, boot camps, and other residential facilities on any given
> night. . . ." A growing number (of these children) are being re-
> ferred directly by their schools; in South Carolina, the single most
> common offense resulting in a juvenile court referral during the
> 2007–2008 school year was "disturbing schools."[33]

In January 2013, a suit was filed by the Justice Department against
Meridian, Mississippi. A joint report by the NAACP and ACLU claims of-
ficials there are running a "school-to-prison pipeline." The District Court in
Jackson claims students are being sent into detention for minor infractions
such as dress code violations and even flatulence. The report cites a study of
115 Mississippi school districts finding that black students are three times
more likely to receive out-of-school suspensions than whites. Scott Rob-
erts, coordinator of the Mississippi Coalition for the Prevention of School-
house to Jailhouse and the Advancement Project, says, "The bottom line is

33. Kim et al., *The School-to-Prison Pipeline*, 4, 128.

that there are no successful schools in America that have high expulsion, suspension, and arrest rates."[34]

Our tendency to solve youthful social misbehavior by incarceration cannot continue. Burgeoning criminal justice costs (from police to lawyers, judges, probationary officers, etc.) are contributing to overburdened budgets at all levels. The cost of putting a young person in prison for one year is estimated at four million dollars. But not only costs beg reconsideration of our criminal—and especially juvenile—justice system.[35]

A highly respected legal scholar, William Stuntz, has studied our current system and found it to be arbitrary, discriminatory, and either too punitive or too lenient.[36] The weakening of local democracy, the great increase of judicial discretionary power, and surging class and racial discrimination make our criminal justice system unjust or unfair. Stuntz' analysis also points to the amazing rise in court costs because of Earl Warren's emphasis on procedural protections. On the other hand, prosecutors are able to convince some 90 percent of those charged with crimes that they are better off entering a plea bargain. Among other things, Stuntz advocates for a return to local trials.

The United States has been called the world's leading jailor with a higher percentage of our population incarcerated than any other country. Today, 2 million Americans are behind bars. According to a Pew study, 1 in 100 United States adults are in prison or jail. 70 percent of those incarcerated are non-white.[37]

Michelle Alexander picks up on Stuntz's charge of discrimination in our criminal justice system, strengthening this chapter's argument, in her critical study, *The New Jim Crow*.[38] For many Americans, the integration of black images into media, the presence of African-American athletes at

34. Mohr, "Mississippi Criticized on School Discipline," A11.

35. See Kim et al., *The School-To-Prison Pipeline*, 128–144; California's Legislative Analyst's Office, "How Much Does Juvenile Crime Cost?" online: http://www.lao.ca.gov/1995/050195_juv_crime/kkpart6.aspx; and Jorge Rivas, "Study: Incarcerating Hordes of Youth Is Costly and Ineffective," Color Lines News for Action, online: http://colorlines.com/archives/2011/10/study_locking_juvenile_offenders_behind_bars_is_costly_and_ineffective.html.

36. Stuntz, *The Collapse of American Criminal Justice*, 281.

37. Adam Liptak, "More Than 1 in 100 U.S. Adults Are in Prison," *The New York Times*, online: http://www.nytimes.com/2008/02/29/world/americas/29iht-29prison.10561202.html?_r=0.

38. Alexander, *The New Jim Crow*.

all levels of sports, the popularity of Colin Powell, the political victories of Barack Obama, and the financial success of Oprah Winfrey all prove that America has attained a state of color blindness. On the contrary, legal scholar Alexander points to an emerging and alarming tendency to target men of color in our battle against urban crime and our "War on Drugs." It is difficult but important to follow her detailed analysis of the ways a mainly white power system is, largely through its "War on Drugs," creating a lower caste of black felons who can hardly support themselves, care for families, or contribute to their communities after release from prison. Too easily incarcerated, they return home with permanently imposed disabilities, and little opportunity for employment, housing, or public benefits. The old Jim Crow, Alexander argues effectively, has not been abolished; it has been re-designed. This study should be on the reading list for most Americans.

In a sense, we have completed the social cycle of discrimination, deprivation, and loss of human dignity. The returning felons will father children and, particularly, sons destined to continue the cycle of disadvantage, loss of privilege, feelings of hopelessness. There will be programs that catch a few, and some will overcome disadvantage by sheer human giftedness and effort. But many will step out of their apartments every day with zero-sum status and little control over their lives. They will feel the need to show "juice" or power and control that leads to urban mayhem. Hardwired to connect, human beings will turn to negative groups like gangs rather than be stranded in social limbo.

Conclusion

This chapter has provided only the findings and conclusions of research—important though these are. Real-life stories are missing. Personal accounts are needed from those affected by the trends crippling a society as it deals with crime and violence. Only by listening to stories of the marginalized can people of privilege, isolated from the power of the streets, begin to comprehend the dilemma of systemic disadvantage and discrimination.

Top-down government agencies, isolated social programs and organizations, and divided churches hack away at our enormous challenge, claim small victories, and struggle for funding. Urban programs like Communities in Schools[39] and the Harlem Children's Zone[40] point the way to a sys-

39. Community in Schools, online: http://www.communitiesinschools.org.

40. Harlem Children's Zone, online: http://hcz.org/about-us/history.

temic, holistic solution. Their success points to the possibility of new cities, offering valuable models, but they cannot provide an overall solution.

What is needed is a whole new vision of the way society might work for the common good of all. How might our thinking, our compassion, and our commitment for the rights and dignity of all be realized? Can we not turn from negative protective sanctions to positive actions in the life of every child from gestation to adulthood? Should not the crippling costs of failing schools and the criminal justice system be reinvested in building positive environments and supports for the lives of all our citizens?

Citizens of the New Jerusalem, we argue, ought to be in the vanguard of voices and actors in re-visioning and reenacting cities of our present societies. Understanding full well that human dysfunction and oppressive powers will not be overcome completely until the Prince of the New Jerusalem arrives in final glory, we still stand together as perpetual revolutionaries in the Christ-renewal of culture. And we will glory both in dramatic, as well as small successes, worshiping the Lord of justice and peace.

When the church proclaims, "Christ has died, Christ is risen, *Christ will come again*," it is expressing the mystery of the New Jerusalem's final realization. *When* and *how* the divine/human drama will be completed at the end of time is a mystery held strongly by faith. Similarly, the extent of the New Jerusalem's coming in the present time is a mystery grasped tenaciously by faith. Social change modeled by William Wilberforce and Dr. Martin Luther King, Jr. offers tangible encouragement. With such examples, all people on earth should take hope and give praise.

Laudate Omnes Gentes; Laudate Dominum

Laudate Omnes Gentes; Laudate Dominum.[41]

Give the (Ruler) your justice, O God,
And your righteousness to the Ruler's Son.
That He may rule your people righteously
And the poor with justice. . . .
He shall defend the needy among the people,
He shall rescue the poor and crush the oppressor.[42]

41. Taize chant: "Praise all people; praise the Lord."
42. Ps 72:1, 2, 4 (author's paraphrase).

And I John saw the holy city, new Jerusalem, coming down from God out of heaven . . .[43]

References for Further Study

Alexander, Michelle. *The New Jim Crow: Mass Incarceration in the Age of Colorblindness.* New York, NY: New Press, 2012.

Lansley, Stewart. *The Cost of Inequality: Why Economic Equality Is Essential for Recovery.* London: Gibson Square, 2012.

McLaren, Brian D. *Everything Must Change : Jesus, Global Crises, and a Revolution of Hope.* Nashville: Thomas Nelson, 2007.

Mott, S. Charles. *Biblical Ethics and Social Change.* 2nd ed. New York: Oxford University Press, 2011.

Rumberger, Russell W. *Dropping Out: Why Students Drop Out of High School and What Can Be Done About It.* Cambridge, MA: Harvard University Press, 2011.

43. Rev 21:2a NRSV.

Living-System Ministry Ushers in the New Jerusalem[1]

Douglas A. Hall with Judy Hall, Steve Daman, and Jeffrey Bass

His Ways Are Higher Than Ours

The Bible describes the church as a body, an organism. Yet, in our Western culture, we have grown accustomed to thinking of churches in terms of organizations or buildings because our culture is very organizationally and technologically centered. God is always at work, and, as his children, we want to participate with him in his work. If we use our simple organizational mental models to work with living systems such as churches, neighborhoods, and cities, unknowingly we cause much long-term harm instead of good. To avoid that, we need to learn to adopt living-system mental models. Through our friendship with Jesus Christ, we find that his ways are higher than ours, and, through a consistent process of redemptive thinking, we internalize his ways of growing and nurturing what is alive. More like farmers than technicians, we learn, through this redemptive process, to be involved in and "in tune with" what causes fruitfulness. We never "cause" fruit to happen! God does! As our work becomes aligned with what God is already doing in his complex living-system environment, and as his vitality begins to flow through the veins and arteries of the living social systems, there is an explosion of life within us and around us. Multiplication of this life is the natural outcome of living-system ministry. It is our joy to discover it and to give all honor and praise to God.

1. This chapter is adapted from Hall, *The Cat and the Toaster*.

Understanding Our Times

> These are the words of the Amen, the faithful and true witness, the
> ruler of God's creation. I know your deeds, that you are neither
> cold nor hot. I wish you were either one or the other! So, because
> you are lukewarm—neither hot nor cold—I am about to spit you
> out of my mouth. (Rev 3:14b–16)[2]

Overwhelmed by Complexity

We (Doug and Judy) came to Boston in 1964. Now it is five decades later.
We're still here. Same neighborhood. Same church. Same job. But in many
ways, *everything* has changed! From the very first day on the job, we were
hit with a sense of tearing fragmentation. We felt pulled in a million different directions at once. As the days, weeks, and months went by, we
longed to focus on just one task, but it seemed as if we were always trying
to manage eight or nine mammoth projects at the same time, the whole
while being interrupted by many people and their immediate needs. We
felt manipulated by the restless city and overwhelmed by the complexities
of the lives of its individuals.

We had been on the job five months when Judy and I decided to report
to our board every job, duty, and act we had performed to date, no matter how menial or insignificant. We put down how many hours we spent
on each activity. When Judy typed it up, we had filled six two-columned,
single-spaced pages.

The process of compiling that report caused Judy and me to step back
and begin to think objectively about what we were doing. It also reinforced
the feeling that our lives were fragmented and that the needs and complexity of the city were overwhelming us. I began to ask myself if we were really
doing any good. What were we trying to do in the chaos? What were our
goals?

Apart from the original board mandate to "get people saved and into
a good church," it seemed like our basic, working goal in this harsh environment was fairly low—just to be active in ministry without causing too
much damage. I realized I had no idea how to understand what was going
on around us, much less what good or bad we were doing.

---

2. Unless otherwise noted, all Scripture quoted from the New International Version,
2011.

At the end of any day, a huge number of unplanned activities had occurred over which we had no control. It seemed to me at the time that reality was so chaotic that the practical, Western approach of trying to divide these many needs and activities into manageable pieces and dealing with them separately would have only burned us out.

"I'm not going to just be manipulated by all these forces," I announced to Judy one night. "Somehow we're going to get above that; we're going to make a major shift in our thinking." We began to keep our eyes and ears open to discover how the system worked and how we could work within the chaos for the good of the kingdom.

It appeared that everything was constantly moving. Did anything in the city not move? I reasoned that, if I could find something stable, like some truths about society that were consistent across thousands of years, then I would be onto something, and I would have something firm to build on, a place to stand in the midst of the chaos of the inner city.

As I searched for answers to understand our times and how to do ministry in my difficult urban environment, I leaned on God all the harder and prayed all the more. The feelings of desperation in my heart kindled within me a desire for "doing the Bible." Please understand I mean more than "doing what it says," which is a starting point. By "doing the Bible," I mean that I want to see that the things that happen in my life are biblical things, the experiences I have are biblical experiences, and the patterns I see working in my life I also see working in the lives of people in the Bible. For example, if I am to live biblically here and now, if what happened in the Bible is going to happen in my life, I would expect to see churches as a result of my ministry!

In those early days, neither Judy nor I could have imagined how God would eventually use the Emmanuel Gospel Center to support the birth and growth of literally hundreds of new churches in the coming decades through various supportive ministries and partnerships. We have seen the book of Acts demonstrated in our city!

Understanding My Culture

As Judy and I armed ourselves with determination to figure out how the complexity of the city really worked, one of the first things we stumbled upon was a social construct that has become a cornerstone of how we do and teach ministry. It started when Judy noticed that our neighbors had a very basic way of classifying people into two groups, as epitomized in a statement a woman named Rose made to her:

> At first I was really afraid to meet you, but I found out you're like a real person I can talk to—not like a social worker.

Judy was pretty flabbergasted until she realized that Rose was not castigating all social workers. Rather, Rose was referring to the estrangement she felt relating to professional people. When talking with a social worker, a person who was talking to her for some practical reason, she experienced an "us/them" dichotomy of herself as the "client" versus "the professional person in charge behind the desk," a person "who does not really know me."

We began to see this dichotomy everywhere. On one end, close, personal, first-order or primary relationships shaped the way our local neighbors related to each other. At the other end, these local people's lives were shaped by impersonal, second-order or secondary relationships beyond their control. As we continued to explore these ideas, it was very easy for us to see the mainstream culture of the broader society as being dominantly secondary in nature. That is, most of the people in the culture had secondary relational characteristics. We began to call the broader culture *secondary culture.* We also began to see that many people from the various ethnic cultures exhibited more primary relational characteristics, and so we began to talk of groups of people who collectively took on characteristics of the relational dimension as *primary culture.*

In my lifetime, I have seen one of the most dramatic cultural shifts in all of human history. The world has changed! Since the middle of the twentieth century, it seems the entire Western culture has shifted from being the relationship-centered, primary culture it was for most of human history to becoming a construct-centered, technologically based, secondary culture. We now live in a dominantly secondary culture where the majority of the people are secondary in relational orientation. This societal change I call the *Great Transition.*

There has been a huge shift in the balance—or in where we find ourselves along the continuum—of primary and secondary aspects of culture in our Western world. Not only in the Western world, but also increasingly in many parts of the developing world, the masses of many cultures are now living as did the small elites of the past. All these cultures are increasingly dominantly secondary. That was not true for my grandparents, or even for my parents.

I wonder about what the Great Transition means for Christianity. To-day, the masses of the populations in our Western culture are secondary in orientation, in contrast with other, more relational cultures, where the masses are dominantly primary. And here is what particularly troubles me. I am not alone in hoping that God will soon send a new, great revival to our city of Boston. My hope is that the Quiet Revival, which we have now been experiencing for forty years, as aggressive church planting has produced a 50 percent growth in churches since the 1960s, will expand into a larger movement of God. But how can revival come to Western Christianity if we no longer have a relational orientation, which was the social seedbed of the revivals of the past? Can there be spiritual vitality contextualized to an impersonal, secondary culture?

Does Christianity fit the culture around me? Is the gospel message relevant and alive in today's world? Of course it is! I am convinced now that our new, dominantly secondary culture can actually nurture a vital Christianity!

Understanding the Urban Church

One day, I invited a small but growing African-American, urban, storefront church from our own neighborhood to hold a service at our little neighbor-hood mission. The leaders happily agreed. They were not familiar with the mission tradition and did not know how we normally operated, so, on their scheduled day, instead of sending a preacher and a song leader, The Mount Calvary Baptist Church brought their entire robed choir and much of their forty-plus member congregation. The music, praying, and preaching were breathtaking!

We were so surprised! It was a wonderful fellowship service. Some-thing I saw that evening changed me, and I have never been the same. The change in me eventually brought about changes in the strategy of our entire ministry. As I looked around the Emmanuel Gospel Center that night, I realized that our people were not being "preached at"—they were a church congregation having fellowship with another Christian church. At the close of the service, Mount Calvary invited us to do the same. They did not play the games we suddenly discovered we had been taught to play. For the folks at Mount Calvary, there was no room for an "us" and "them" dichotomy. They loved us openly and treated us like family. This was not a mission service. This was *church!*

This was one experience that introduced me to the indigenous church in the city, churches that I discovered had an invisible quality of spiritual vitality. I have thought a lot about the kind of spiritual vitality I was looking for, and I am learning to describe what was just an inner urge back then. To me, true spiritual vitality is found when an organic Christian community is outwardly fulfilling its highest purpose in ministry. By "its highest purpose," I mean being in tune with God's will for us and doing all that we do in a way that follows his designs. When something is spiritually vital, discernment, teaching, leadership, and outgrowth flow from prayer. A shared inner faith experience evidences the community's alignment with the Bible. In a vital church, mutual honesty, learning, and true caring characterize people's relationships with God and with each other. Further, there is a shared sense of mystery about the living dynamic that generates exciting Christian experience and expression.

Understanding the City

Many of the first lessons we learned were lessons of the street—things that you pick up when your hands get dirty doing grassroots ministry. But a more conceptual framework came along to help me understand our complex urban environment—a new social science birthed across the river from us at the Massachusetts Institute of Technology. What surprised us was that we were already learning some of the same things these social systems theorists were writing about.

In 1971, I read *Urban Dynamics* by Jay W. Forrester,[3] who is considered the founder of the social science of *systems thinking*. Systems thinking looks at large systems like businesses, organizations, cities, and cultures from a wide perspective, taking in overall patterns and cycles in the whole system instead of focusing on isolated fragments or single events. This broad view can help us identify the real system-level problems in our world and understand how to address them so that real change can take place. When I first looked at Forrester's book, its extensive math and statistical analysis was mostly a maze of information out of my reach, yet I sensed immediately that what he was observing about complex systems was very critical information for us as we sought to understand how to do the Bible in the city. One by one, I explored the different parts of his theory, and, in time, found each of them relevant to urban ministry.

3. Forrester, *Urban Dynamics*.

Several of Forrester's concepts explained why working in a complex environment such as a city is so difficult. These include the following:

- The system's tendency to drift to low performance
- Our intuitive solutions to problems are often countered by the system
- The system's insensitivity to parameter change
- The system's resistance to policy change

Other concepts described how to take a positive approach, including,

- Internal revitalization and the city as a life form
- Leverage points
- Simulation models

Understanding God's Living-System Design

The corporate church in the city is a living system. The word of God speaks to an organic unity called "the church," not to a collection of individuals, nor to an organization. Are we thinking the same way when we think about our church? When we make decisions, are we considering how those decisions will affect the *entire* body of Christ, which is one body according to Scripture? Are we truly aware that the church is a living body as the Bible teaches? Or do we think of our church as just the folks who show up on Sundays in one particular place?

Throughout his life, Paul centered his missionary work in cities, with people who had various complex networks. Why did he do that? I think he saw the city as an organism strategically designed by God that could, by its living, dynamic design, help extend the work of the kingdom of God. He realized that the city would spontaneously export Christianity to the region around the city.

In 1993 the common assumption was that Christianity was dying in the city. But we discovered the Quiet Revival—that Christianity had 50 percent more churches and had grown in many ways while no one noticed. Yet, we could identify no program or person responsible for this growth. So where did all these churches come from? Beyond the obvious answer of "God did it," which is correct, I wanted to know *how* God did it. In trying to answer that question, the only answer I could come up with—looking at it from dozens of angles over and over again—was that the Bible does have a method of ministry that fits the first century as well as the twenty-first. This biblical method is based on something so basic that it hasn't changed in more than two thousand years. And the only thing that made sense to me was that the Quiet Revival happened because (1) the body of Christ, as well as the city, really are living systems, (2) and since they are, in fact, living, we know they receive their life from God, and (3) that life in Christ produced the Quiet Revival.

Understanding Our Cat-and-Toaster World

We Westerners need to learn to understand our times and understand how the world that God created works. To help my students understand the nature of God's world, I always ask them, "What is the difference between a cat and a toaster?" They can easily visualize how using a pliers and screwdriver will work to fix a broken toaster, but not to heal the cat's urinary tract infection. The cat, representing the living creations that God makes, is a highly complex and thoroughly interrelated living system. The toaster, representing what people make, is a comparatively simple constructed thing.

We understand the nature of organic *(cat)* growth in the *physical* world of God's creation, but for some reason we have trouble seeing organic growth when it comes to our ministry or God's living *social systems*. We go about our work in ministry assuming that everything in our world is of the same nature, fashioned in a simplistic cause-and-effect *toaster* design, easily understood and easily fixed. We need to break out of that box.

Jesus observed the Laodiceans. He knew their actions and found they did not measure up to his standard. He challenged them about their deeds, and that same challenge comes to us today. As they were found wanting, so are we! We're like the Laodiceans: dependence on our riches and technology has made us wretched, pitiful, poor, blind, and naked. We need to own this and repent. How can we avoid continuing down this path? It starts with the way we think.

Embracing Our Poverty

> You say, "I am rich; I have acquired wealth and do not need a thing." But you do not realize that you are wretched, pitiful, poor, blind and naked. (Rev 3:17)

The Laodiceans feel rich. Jesus says they are poor. Which is true? Why would these mature Christians have the opposite viewpoint from Jesus?

Regardless of how long we have known Christ, and regardless of how much we think we are doing for him, are we also subconsciously harboring opinions that are in conflict with the mind of Christ? I think we are! And not only that, I think our problem is a lot closer to the Laodiceans' problem than we would care to admit. Like the people of Laodicea, we as Western Christians are leaning heavily on our abilities and our resources. I don't think God is impressed by this. Instead, he sees the Laodiceans wallowing in deep poverty. I think that, as a church, we need to own this for ourselves as well and repent of our self-sufficiency, agreeing with God that we are in inner poverty and that the shiny resources surrounding us are only empty shells!

Faulty Mental Models

Jesus had carefully listened to what the Laodiceans were saying to themselves deep inside, though perhaps not consciously, and he put his finger on the crux of the problem of why they were lukewarm. The problem stemmed from their faulty perception of themselves: "I am rich . . . and do not need a thing."

They assumed their wealth, resources, and influence could do whatever needed doing, that using these tools would address the way things work in the real world. They may not have realized that this was what they were thinking, but when Jesus put it so clearly, it showed them where they had gone wrong. Their unconscious mental model was telling them to do things in the world through reliance on their own resources instead of on the indwelling Spirit of God.

I think many of us Western Christians have mental models very similar to those of the Laodiceans. We see ourselves as educated, rich, influential, well resourced, and as people who do good things. But, like the Laodiceans, our mental perceptions of ourselves can get us into trouble. As Westerners, we tend to think, "We're okay. Everything is going well. We'll make it. Our programs are progressing nicely. And if, God forbid, they should falter, we know how to fix them." Our basic underlying assumption is that our programs and activities are what is needed to make it in the kingdom of God. Jesus lets us know that there is something wrong with that assumption by saying, "You are poor, blind, and naked."

Once our faulty mental models are exposed, we realize they are not even rational. It is better to bring them out into the open, where they can be addressed—better yet is to be able to expose our faulty mental models with respect and humor, in a safe environment.

Peter Senge challenges his readers to identify their mental models and—particularly when things have not worked out well in what they are doing—to correct not only what they did wrong, but also the thinking process that incorrectly made them even think that it was the right thing to do. Senge uses the word *metanoia,* which he defines as "a shift of mind." He says, "To grasp the meaning of 'metanoia' is to grasp the deeper meaning of 'learning,' for learning also involves a fundamental shift or movement of mind."[4]

Metanoia is the New Testament Greek word used for repentance. True repentance, this shifting of the mind from faulty mental models, is a prerequisite for operating appropriately in our world. An attitude of ongoing repentance is key to redemptive thinking.

We find in the Gospels that Jesus, too, spent a lot of time challenging people's mental models through his stories, teachings, and miracles. So, it's imperative that we answer the question, "What do you have in mind?" Do we have in mind the thoughts that God has or the thoughts that are inconsistent with what God thinks? If our subconscious mental models are inconsistent with the way God thinks, we may actually be out of sync in our thinking with the reality of God's entire living system, and our actions, which flow from our thinking, will be out of sync with what God is doing—and yet we may not even know it!

Shedding faulty mental models and finding new ones that line up with the greater reality of God's truth is an important part of the discipleship process. It is not just our actions, but also our thinking that Christ needs to redeem. This applies not only to individuals, but to our culture as well.

The "Works" Mental Model Doesn't Work

If I am fixing a toaster, the see-a-need, make-and-do-a-plan, and get-returns "works" method works just fine. Our culture developed it along with the Industrial Revolution because it works. It's great for building bridges, cleaning the house, and thousands of other tasks.

4. Senge, *The Fifth Discipline*, 13.

However, as soon as we introduce people or any living system into the works equation, it is inevitable that unintended negative returns will result, and instead of solving a problem, we will make things worse. I call it the Law of Unintended Negative Returns: *Whatever we do to accomplish something has an unintended negative return that undoes what we are trying to do.* Invariably, unintended negative things will happen, bringing the opposite result of what we are expecting to accomplish. The "works" mental model does not work for solving problems that involve people. It is a flawed mental model because of unintended negative returns that it has no mechanism to address.

But if we start with the recognition that "I cannot solve problems" because "I live in a fallen world," we begin to transform the very essence of the way we go about ministry activities. When we begin any plan or activity with the realization that it could very well blow up in our faces, that we may do more damage than good, that we could easily reap a harvest of unintended negative returns, that we inevitably tend to be counterproductive in all our actions, that we can reap death instead of life—then we are beginning from a place where fruitfulness begins! When we embrace our poverty, then we can begin to discover our wealth. The starting point is to place ourselves in a position of humility and dependence upon God.

Discovering Our Wealth

> I counsel you to buy from me gold refined in the fire, so you can become rich; and white clothes to wear, so you can cover your shameful nakedness; and salve to put on your eyes, so you can see. (Rev 3:18)

How do you describe redemption? Can you identify the steps you took when you came to Christ for salvation? It is likely that your journey may have followed a basic pattern something like this:

When you recognized your fallenness and came to God the Father and his Son Jesus Christ to find real life, at some point you *confessed and repented* of your sins. Confession and repentance are our natural reactions when we recognize that we are in the presence of a holy God and we sense the responsibility we have for our own sins. The next thing you probably did was to reach out in faith and *receive the forgiveness and cleansing* that was made possible through the sacrifice of Christ's physical body and his shed blood on the cross. The third phase of your redemption was when you realized that something deep inside you had changed: Your old self was pronounced dead at the scene, and your new self in Christ was born! *You passed from death to life.* Your baptism demonstrated this truth.

To summarize, redemption is at work when (1) we confess and repent, (2) we receive Christ's forgiveness, and (3) we exchange our death for his life.

I see this pattern in Jesus' counsel to the Christians in Laodicea to buy from him gold, white clothes, and eye salve. Jesus uses these three commodities that were so much a part of the life in their community to contextualize the reality of redemption in words and symbols these people understood, and which we can understand in our own lives as well.

The need for "gold refined in the fire" is our *confession and repentance* that we are doing things wrong, that we are not in tune with his creation. "White clothes" show that we are *forgiven* for the wrong things we have done and for our misleading faulty mental models. "Eye salve" is having a redeemed vision so we can see God's better substitute. Taken successively, these form a pattern we can follow in ministry. This pattern is what I call the *redemptive method.* Consistently engaging in this pattern will enable us to be genuinely productive over the long term.

As we work in God's world, we will need to *confess* the specific un-intended negative returns that our actions are causing and *repent* of the inadequate mental models that made us think our actions would work. We then can receive *forgiveness* for those wrong mental models, actions, and negative returns. Through that learning experience we can apprehend God's better substitute and *exchange* what does not work for mental models and actions that will work in harmony with God's created, living order.

Gold Refined in the Fire

Jesus counsels the Laodiceans, "Buy gold refined in the fire so you can become rich." His warning shows that the mental models of the Christians in Laodicea needed to be refined. The Christians in Laodicea thought they had true riches already, but Jesus' admonition shows that their dependence on resources for ministry was clearly tainted. Because they thought they could use their gold to do ministry, their wealth was impure to them.

When their ministry was based on a resource-dependent and simplistic "see-a-need, make-and-do-a-plan" *works* approach, a "take control" approach, it produced lukewarm results. Rather than making excuses for lukewarm results, they and we should *be glad* for unintended negative returns, because these returns force us to wake up and seek a better solution!

When we really believe that "works" does not work, and that applying the works method of problem solving to living systems and organisms yields death instead of life, then we are ready to begin to learn a new way of doing work in the world. But, we must be diligent to combat our old thinking with the new so that we will consistently flag our wrong thinking, and, when we approach a problem or a need, we will be on guard not to use the works method.

The same way humans purify gold by a refining process, God wants to purify our approach to doing his work so that we learn to participate with him in a pure form of ministry that is in tune with how he works. Engaging in his continual refining process by constant identification of negative unintended returns and the mental models that caused them will help purify our motivations. This "burning off the dross" will yield lives characterized by constant prayer and healthy spiritual disciplines. Eventually, with practice, we will increasingly see the limitations of the works method. To me, pure, refined gold is envisioning the highest goals, true riches, the living "fruit that remains," and not lowering those goals. Burning off the dross is confessing the things that did not meet our expectations and exploring why they did not work. Burning off the dross is seeing the unintended negative returns that resulted from our actions, taking responsibility for them, repenting of them, and seeking forgiveness.

Repent early and often! It is not a one-time event, but a lifestyle. As we confess what has gone wrong, we can go on to the next step—a joyful one—of receiving forgiveness!

White Clothes to Wear

Examples abound of anointed, gifted, Spirit-filled Christian pastors and leaders who have fallen into sin. Sin happens. But grace also happens. In God's grace, we can gain forgiveness from the penalty and results of personal sin. But we also need forgiveness for our ministry actions that result in unintended negative returns. We need safe environments in which to confess negative returns to each other, places to reflect together with others the wrong mental models that caused us to do them. Sometimes we need the loving input of other people to help us overcome our blind spots.

Repentance from and forgiveness for our actions and thinking can be a healthy, corporate activity that Christians should practice more.

The white robes we receive from Christ show us that we, too, are given a second chance. When we are clothed with Christ, God sees his own white clothes on us. We are accepted.

Salve to Put on Your Eyes

I remember reading in some systems-thinking materials that our brains are capable of processing only seven variables at a time. Therefore, we employ various techniques to reduce complexity to something we can get our brains around. Sadly, when we reduce the complexity of the living-system world around us to something we can process with our cognitive minds, we do not see things clearly. I have found that people of a more dominantly primary culture seem to employ a different thinking process that enables them to perceive complex reality with *subconscious* thinking. While our cognitive brain is limited by design, our subconscious brain is far better designed to work with complex, high-definition reality.

As secondary-culture, post-Great Transition people, most of us Westerners have so lost touch with our inner abilities to apprehend complexity subconsciously that we interpret highly complex forms of reality—especially *social* reality—as chaos! However, when it comes to observing the *physical* part of God's creation, we do a little better. Maybe that is because our own physical bodies are very familiar to us, or maybe because our subconscious brains are actively running our physical systems. Yet, while we tend to be able to recognize the complex reality of the *physical* world and comprehend the reality of its high-definition detail, we are, for some reason, more limited in our ability to perceive complex realities in the *social* realm, and we are extremely poor in processing complexity in *spiritual* reality.

And this seems to be how we approach life today. Westerners want to see things done quickly. We don't want to be encumbered with all the details. Give me a short list. Just tell me what you want me to do, and I'll do it.

Today we are in somewhat of a paradox. On the one hand, our digital age pushes us toward a new high-definition understanding of complexity, while on the other hand, we live with the legacy of our recent past: low-definition, simplistic, Western problem-solving that makes us think we can do almost anything. We can put a man on the moon. Anything is possible. Just break the problem down into bits, and we can make it happen. We walk a fine line between the increasingly complex sciences and our popular, low-definition, reductionist, "break-it- into-parts" mental models.

We need a breakthrough in understanding that will help us once again see the high-definition reality in the living-system world that God created. We have to overcome the many flawed mental models that keep us believing in low-definition simplistic reality and blind to its complex high-definition fulfilled counterpart.

If we insist on seeing God's complex activity as chaotic, we will probably miss recognizing what God is doing and how he is doing it. And, even more sobering, our reductionism will give us false vision, and we may be engaging in a heretical understanding of God and his activities.

When our ministry activities are not working as we expect they will, it may be because we cannot see the myriad, complex factors affecting them. Our thinking has to adapt to the fact that the situation is more complicated than we realize. We have to confess that the way we think is wrong and that we need to see reality in high definition.

Nevertheless, there is hope for secondary culture! With the redemptive treasure of eye salve that Jesus gives us, we can begin to see with new eyes and discern the living system. It is as if Jesus' eye salve helps us regain the primary culture's ability to see in high definition. He allows us the privilege of learning to see what is actually there. He is treating us more like friends than servants.

As we see the living system in high definition, we can begin to understand how the system itself gets things done, how things work. Knowing how a living system operates helps us see where ministry activities are actually happening in any particular living system and how those actions are working in tune with that system.

This understanding helps us identify additional and better ways of doing ministry that are more in tune with living systems in general. This will make our own ministry systems and organizations work properly. With the eye salve, we can learn to plan and design ministry approaches that do what really needs to be done in the context of our complex, living-system churches, communities, and cities.

Aligning Our Actions

> Those whom I love I rebuke and discipline. So be earnest and repent. (Rev 3:19)

God gives us many tools that help us see beyond our own perception threshold so we can discern any system's plans and structure. Some of these tools include the following:

Be Immersed in the Living System. The best place to start to learn both consciously and subconsciously about living systems is by living in the social system in which we work and minister. It takes time to become immersed in your social system. You have to develop trust. I often tell young seminarians wanting to plant a church in the city, especially among people with many personal struggles, not to expect to be supported by the church for six years. Whether or not the number is six, the point is, it takes years to discern the living system in the community and become part of it. It takes years to form community because it is a living social system. Even when a church grows rapidly, it can take several years for it to develop its fully functioning organic nature.

Uncover the Principles. A social system's inner principles describe its inner character. Because principles focus on this inner, organic part of a ministry or social system, and not on the more structured organizational part, by discerning its true principles, we may be able to hear the system talk. Once we have identified the principles, and we begin to make our ministry decisions based on those principles, we put ourselves in a position to keep listening to the organic part of our system. Our resulting actions, then, will be aligned with the life of our system. Principles define a positive existing dynamic we don't want to lose! Principles, rather than policies, are influence points that move us in a positive direction.

Ask System Questions. If you want high-order results, you cannot say, "How do I do the job?" We rephrase the question, "How does the job get done?" We form the question that way because, realistically, in a social system, there are simply too many factors at work. No one person or organization can orchestrate any significant change in any complex social system through Western organizational activity, even those that are well funded. When you figure out what the real system is that drives the activity (by wording the question properly), you can learn how to participate successfully in the activity, because you are then using the whole system to do the job and not just your individual effort or that of your organization. For example, we want to do evangelism and church planting and ministry training the way the kingdom and the broader social system works, not just the way our own organization works. This is how we can begin to align our actions with the system.

Opening Our Doors

> Here I am! I stand at the door and knock. If anyone hears my voice and opens the door, I will come in and eat with that person, and they with me. (Rev 3:20)

A Practitioner Science for Working with Living Systems

Contemporary, secondary-culture Christianity needs intentionally to use the discipline of systems thinking. It is a practitioner-friendly social science well suited to ministry. When Christian missionary strategists began to employ the practitioner-oriented social science of cultural anthropology in the 1950s, it transformed missions. Christianity went from being a Western religion to a world religion in a generation. To nurture secondary-culture Christianity, a similar practitioner-oriented, systemic social science is needed. What science should it be? Based on my experience here in Boston, I think it should be systems thinking.

Secondary-culture Christianity has not yet used systems thinking on the practitioner level. By not integrating this systemic, practitioner-friendly social science into local missiology, we have ended up with ineffective, low-level ministry that focuses on our limited organizations and programs, rather than effective ministry that focuses on highly complex and powerful living systems. Properly implanted into contemporary Christian ministry, systems thinking can empower contemporary, secondary-culture Christianity, even as the use of cultural anthropology helped the modern missionary movement following World War II.

Working with God

To work in God's field, rather than taking charge and doing our plan as we used to do, we need to take a humble and respectful approach before the Creator and his large living systems. We then learn to participate in meeting needs by *transplanting* living subsystems and *implanting* inorganic constructs into the living social system. Just as Paul planted and Apollos watered, we, too, have our unique tasks as technicians, systems actors, and systems thinkers—but God and only God makes all things grow.

God is at work! While what he is doing may at first be invisible to us, we can learn to discover a way to both *uncover* and *interact* with what he is doing simultaneously within us and in the social ecosystem around and beyond us. This discovery is thrilling! When our ministry is aligned with what God is doing in a complex living-system environment, and vitality begins to flow through the veins and arteries of the living social ecosystems, there is an explosion of life. We can't help but celebrate that God's returns are very much alive and healthy, and we watch in wonder and amazement as we see God's living systems multiply abundantly! Engaging in systemic multiplication is critical if secondary cultures are to produce the same multiplying developments as primary cultures have done.

Entering the Doors of the New Jerusalem

> To him who overcomes, I will give the right to sit with me on my throne, as I also overcame and sat down with my Father on his throne. (Rev 3:21)

Theologically speaking, heaven is the ultimate reality. And, philosophically speaking, I find that heaven fulfills my own loftiest, overall personal goal in that it embodies "the highest good for the longest time period." That perspective, which is part of systems thinking, makes heaven very exciting for me.

Heaven is that very practical and very real goal that can give shape to the way we live here and now. The new Jerusalem, with its perfect technology, is the perfect interrelationship of the three realms of reality—the physical, social, and spiritual creation, all operating as one living system, together eternally giving glory to the King, Jesus Christ, who was, is, and always will be the Ruler of God's creation.

References for Further Study

Africanus Journal 4:1 (April 2012).

Forrester, Jay W. *Urban Dynamics.* Cambridge, MA: MIT Press, 1969.

Hall, Douglas A., with Judy Hall, and Steve Daman. *The Cat and the Toaster: Living System Ministry in a Technological Age.* Urban Voice Series. Eugene, OR: Wipf & Stock, 2010.

Schwartz, Peter. *The Art of the Long View: Planning for the Future in an Uncertain World.* New York: Doubleday/Currency, 1996.

Intercultural Unity, a Sign of the New Jerusalem

Overcoming Barriers and Getting Ready for Church Collaborations across Cultural Lines

BIANCA DUEMLING

THE NEW JERUSALEM IS described as a beautiful city, a bride awaiting her husband. God himself will be dwelling among the people: "He will wipe every tear from their eyes. There will be no more death or mourning or crying or pain, for the old order of things has passed away" (Rev 21:4).[1] As William David Spencer laid out in the introduction to this book, the New Jerusalem is where God's kingdom is established, where God's promises are fulfilled, where all human suffering and humiliation is ended, where *shalom* (wholeness in body, soul, and spirit) exists, where neither race nor gender, neither economic nor social status elicit discrimination.

In Revelation 7:9, we also get a glimpse of the residents of the New Jerusalem: "After this I looked, and there before me was a great multitude that no one could count, from every nation, tribe, people and language, standing before the throne and before the Lamb." Diversity is the nature of the New Jerusalem, the kingdom of God. In this vision, no one is fitted into the same form or dress, but the people gather before God in their differences and cultural distinctiveness.

The fascinating aspect about the kingdom of God is that Jesus has started to establish it already among us, in our cities. We do not have to sit around and wait passively for Jesus' return. We are called to use our creativity and abilities in this building process, to be on Jesus's team, to be the ambassadors of the New Jerusalem, and invite others into his kingdom.

---

1. All quotations are from the NIV (2011), unless otherwise noted.

What implication has this fascinating truth for us, and for the Church[2] in our cities? How can the cities we live in become more like the New Jerusalem? As discussed in the different chapters of this book, the New Jerusalem has many implications. The focus of this chapter will be intercultural unity among the body of Christ in a city, as this is essential to building the New Jerusalem.

The face of the United States of America, especially in urban centers, is changing and diversifying rapidly; therefore, more possibilities than ever before exist to witness the nature of the New Jerusalem. The Immigration and Nationality Act of 1965 as well as following changes in immigration policies have been opening doors for an influx of new immigrants.[3] The United States has certainly diversified religiously; however, the majority of new immigrants are Christians. This means, according to R. Stephen Warner, "that the new immigrants represent not the de-Christianization of American society but the de-Europeanization of American Christianity."[4] The steady growth of ethnic-focused churches is a result not only of the continuous arrival of Christian immigrants, but also of immigrants from non-traditional Christian home countries who converted to Christianity in the United States.[5] This new reality impacts and changes the dynamics within the Church, especially in urban centers. In the combined communities of Boston, Cambridge, and Brookline, Massachusetts, for example, 82.5 percent of the churches are minority or ethnic-focused churches.[6]

In their relationships, urban church leaders are forced to navigate not only denominational or theological differences, but also cultural differences and related power dynamics. Also, though there have never been as many multicultural churches in history before, the reality is that still 90 percent of churches are mono-ethnic.[7] The Church in the United States has

---

2. The Church with a capital C refers to the one city-wide, nation-wide, or world-wide Church with Jesus as its head in its wholeness. When I refer to church with a lower c, it stands for a specific congregation.

3. Other important acts have been the United States Refugee Act of 1980, which opened the door for more African refugees, and the Immigration Act of 1990 that created the congressionally mandated Diversity Immigrant Visa Program. *New England's Book of Acts* is a good reference to explore the growth of churches of the different ethnic groups in New England. See Emmanuel Gospel Center, *New England's Book of Acts*.

4. Warner, "Coming to America," 20; see also Balmer, "Crossing the Borders," 55.

5. Chen, *Getting Saved in America*.

6. Emmanuel Gospel Center, "Church Directory."

7. DeYoung et al., *United by Faith*, 2.

certainly made progress, but there is still a long journey ahead. The Rev. Martin Luther King Jr.'s often quoted statement that 11:00 a.m. on Sunday morning is the most segregated hour in North America is still, for the most part, true.

Worship and fellowship within one's own language and cultural groups is important and a place of security especially for new immigrants—assuming that "if the Gospel is to speak to people with intimacy and more than a veneer of spirituality then it must be spoken in their mother tongue. This stresses the importance and beauty of the language and culture of every person who is addressed."[8] The ultimate call, however, is to be in relationship with each other, to work alongside each other, and to demonstrate the interdependence of the body of Christ to the world no matter whether we worship in ethnic-focused or multi-ethnic churches. As will be discussed later, it certainly is not acceptable to co-exist next to each other and to be isolated.

Collaboration should not be understood as an occasional intercultural worship service or the polite acknowledgement of each other's merits. Because words like *cooperation, coordination,* and *collaboration* are often used interchangeably, I want to specify how the word *collaboration* is used in the context of this chapter. To do so, I refer to Michael Winer and Karen Ray, who describe *cooperation, coordination,* and *collaboration* as a "continuum of increasing intensity for building relationships and doing work."[9] Intensity includes the level of risk, the time needed, and the opportunity given. The starting point is cooperation and the move is to collaboration: "Collaboration is a more durable and pervasive relationship. Participants bring separate organizations into a new structure with full commitment to a common mission . . . Partners pool or jointly secure the resources, and share the results and rewards."[10]

From a Christian perspective, communion or *koinonia,* as described in Acts 2:42–47, needs to be added as another, ultimate level of relationship. In any case, building strong relationships and successful collaborations to manifest intercultural unity is a process, a journey that takes time and commitment.

I also want to point out that there is a difference between doing cross-cultural ministries overseas and in one's own local neighborhood, especially

8. Jackson and Passarelli, *Mapping Migration,* 22.

9. Winer and Ray, *Collaboration Handbook,* 23.

10. Ibid.

from the perspective of the majority culture. As a missionary goes overseas, an intentional decision has been made to leave one's home country and to immerse oneself in a new country, structure, and culture. Hopefully, missionaries are trained and culturally sensitive. Living in a different culture is always challenging; however, there is a certain control over the length of the stay. Moreover, in times of struggle with cultural differences, language barriers, smell of food, noise, and overwhelming cultural diversity, there is the knowledge or hope of coming back to the familiar, comfortable birth home.

The fact that a neighborhood is diversifying, however, is not under the control of an individual. The buzz of different languages in shopping malls or the different smells of food might lose their exoticness. Diversity might come across as a threat to "the way it always has been."

In "Missions Theology and Practice," there has been a paradigm shift from Western-led and dominating international ministry to Western servant partnerships, working along with indigenous leaders to achieve more of an incarnational approach that empowers natives in leadership positions.[11] Such a paradigm shift is largely missing, however, regarding cross-cultural ministry in the United States.

This chapter hopes to provide an insight into the context of collaboration across cultural lines. The focus is, however, not primarily to provide a program or a model, but to initiate reflection and awareness and to help readers overcome barriers and get ready for reconciling and fruitful collaboration. In order to look at the journey of intercultural unity from different angles, the chapter is divided into three parts. First, I want to elaborate on the theological basis for intercultural unity and the call to reconciliation. Second, I will identify barriers to intercultural unity in our cities. Third and finally, I will point out some approaches to witness intercultural unity, hence participating in establishing the New Jerusalem on earth.

Theological Basis for Intercultural Unity

As described above, in Revelation 7:9 we get a glimpse of God's ultimate vision, a multitude of diverse people all standing before the throne and the lamb. Jesus has invited us, as his ambassadors, to establish the New Jerusalem in our present day's reality.

In every aspect of life, Jesus calls us to follow his example and to be aligned with him and his vision. In fulfilling his purpose on earth, Jesus

11. Borthwick, *Western Christians.*

crossed multiple cultural lines—for example, when he actively approached the Samaritan women in John 4. Moreover, he put urgency behind the vision of intercultural unity. In John 17:21, Jesus prayed shortly before he died that "all of them may be one, Father, just as you are in me and I am in you. May they also be in us so that the world may believe that you have sent me." The nature of relationship between the Father and the Son, their oneness, their intimacy, is the standard we have to strive for in our relationships with each other. This prayer also reflects a strong missional implication as it connects being one with revival—"that the world may believe." John 17:21 states clearly that intercultural unity is a key to renewal and revival in our cities. Moreover, intercultural unity is a witness to the "world" that Jesus is still relevant today, that he bridges the gap of segregation and brings peace and reconciliation. Collaboration across cultural lines also has practical applications as it helps to meet overwhelming social and spiritual needs in the city that not one congregation alone can address. Thus, through intercultural unity the Church fulfills other aspects it is called to address, such as seeking the peace and welfare of the city, and caring for the poor and marginalized.[12] At heart, to use Edward Gilbreath's words, "Unity in the body of Christ is an essential part of our mission as ambassadors of the Gospel. Without unity, we will never shine as God intends."[13]

The Body of Christ and the Interdependence among Christians and Churches

The image of the body of Christ in 1 Corinthians 12 is essential for the nature of intercultural unity. Paul did not refer to a mystical or abstract theory when he wrote about the body of Christ, but to a social organism with a clearly defined sociological profile. Consequently, the church is not only called to think about the body of Christ theoretically, but to put its conclusions into practice.[14]

The core message of this passage is Paul's description of the church as one interconnected body. He writes, "Just as a body, though one, has many parts, but all its many parts form one body, so it is with Christ. For we were all baptized by one Spirit so as to form one body—whether Jews or

---

12. A few examples include the following: Lev 19:10; Ps 82:3; Jer 29:7; Mic 6:8; Matt 25:31–46; Luke 3:11; 1 John 3:17.

13. Gilbreath, *Reconciliation Blues*, 80.

14. Hollenweger, *Erfahrungen*, 36.

Gentiles, slave or free—and we were all given the one Spirit to drink. Even so the body is not made up of one part but of many" (1 Cor 12:12–14). Miroslav Volf points out that "baptism into Christ creates a people as the differentiated body of Christ. Bodily inscribed differences are brought together, not removed. The body of Christ lives as a complex interplay of differentiated bodies . . . At the same time, no culture can retain its own tribal deities; religion must be de-ethicized so that ethnicity can be de-sacralized. Paul deprived each culture of ultimacy in order to given them all legitimacy in the wider family of culture."[15]

Culture is part of how God has created us in his image; God reveals himself through every culture. However, there is neither cultural supremacy nor self-sufficiency of any group. We are called to be who God made us to be, not to be isolated but to bless each other.

Later in verses 24–26, Paul elaborates on the implication of this interdependence: "But God has put the body together, giving greater honor to the parts that lacked it, so that there should be no division in the body, but that its parts should have equal concern for each other. If one part suffers, every part suffers with it; if one part is honored, every part rejoices with it."

The interdependence among the body of Christ does not only refer to the need of support in times of distress and suffering, but also to the building up and equipping of each other in order to participate in the process of establishing the New Jerusalem. The church community is designed to bring the best out of us, helping us to identify the blind spots and assisting us to become who God intended us to be. In Ephesians 4:11–13, Paul fleshes that out beautifully: "So Christ himself gave the apostles, the prophets, the evangelists, the pastors and teachers, to equip his people for works of service, so that the body of Christ may be built up until we all reach unity in the faith and in the knowledge of the Son of God and become mature, attaining to the whole measure of the fullness of Christ." We need each other to grow. We need each other to move forward and to experience "the whole measure of the fullness of Christ."

The image of the body of Christ is in line with Jesus' new commandment to love one another (John 13:34–35). Love is always more than words. Love implies consequences as described in 1 Corinthians 13. Love also means to serve one another humbly, as stated in Galatians 5:13.

The biblical standards for intercultural unity and the nature of the relationships among the body of Christ are laid out in the passage above.

15. Volf, *Exclusion and Embrace*, 48–49.

The body of Christ needs each other to fulfill God's commands. The reality, however, is very different. As the Church, we do not live up to the standards, to the intimacy that is required to be one as the Father is one with the Son. What we all experience in our cities is that the body of Christ is scattered; thus, relating, especially across cultures, is a challenge to us.

There are two primary questions we need to ask ourselves: (1) Why is the reality so different from what we are intended to be, and how are we called to act? (2) How can we navigate through the tensions between call and reality?

Answers to both questions are found in the Bible. We all know the story of the fall in Genesis 3; consequently, we live in a fallen and broken world, a world full of sin. Our reality and relationships are so different from God's original intentions of how this world should be. Sin interferes with the way God intended it to be. As it is beyond the scope of this chapter to discuss the theological nature and implication of sin, I want to point to George Yancey's elaboration on sin especially in the context of racial segregation.[16]

The sinful nature of our humanness is why we need first and foremost the redemption and salvation given by Jesus Christ on the cross. As sin penetrates our world, we need constant transformation and reconciliation in ourselves and in our interactions with each other. The constant call to reconciliation is the answer to the second question, which will be laid out in the next section.

Call to Reconciliation

The challenge of intercultural unity and the reality of division within the body of Christ are not new phenomena. They were constant challenges for the churches in the rising multicultural cities of the New Testament contexts. They are why Paul had to address the issue of intercultural unity and reconciliation repeatedly in his letters to the Galatians, Ephesians, and Corinthians.

The necessity of reconciliation is not removed from our daily experience or associated with escalating conflicts, the civil rights movement, past segregation and apartheid, or a genocide that happened on another continent. Reconciliation is a constant practice in our relationships with God and each other.

16. Yancey, *Beyond Racial Gridlock,* chapters 7 and 8.

The first and initial step is to be reconciled with God. In 2 Corinthians 5:17–19, Paul writes about the new body and new creation, hence the New Jerusalem that has come into being through Christ: "Therefore, if anyone is in Christ, the new creation has come: The old has gone, the new is here! All this is from God, who reconciled us to himself through Christ and gave us the ministry of reconciliation: that God was reconciling the world to himself in Christ, not counting people's sins against them. And he has committed to us the message of reconciliation." God not only wants us be reconciled with him, but "he has committed to us the message of reconciliation." We all are called to be reconcilers. We are the people God wants to use not only to bring people to God, but also to heal the divisions between people and be reconciled to one another. Similarly, Paul emphasizes in Ephesians 2:14–16: "For he himself is our peace, who has made the two groups one and has destroyed the barrier, the dividing wall of hostility, by setting aside in his flesh the law with its commands and regulations. His purpose was to create in himself one new humanity out of the two, thus making peace, and in one body to reconcile both of them to God through the cross, by which he put to death their hostility."

The good news is that the initial work of reconciliation has been done through Christ: the barriers are destroyed; the dividing wall of hostility has been torn down. Nevertheless, we are called to live according to this reality and put it into practice as Paul later points out in Ephesians 4:3: "Make every effort to keep the unity of the Spirit through the bond of peace." Moreover, Jesus calls us to "first go and be reconciled to your brother; then come and offer your gift" (Matt 5:24). Reconciliation is not a one-way street. Jesus not only calls for repentance, but also for forgiveness. In the Lord's Prayer, he prays, "And forgive us our debts, as we also have forgiven our debtors" (Matt 6:12). As Jesus is aware of the reality and brokenness of our human nature, that we are hurt by the same people again and again, he calls Peter and us to forgive seventy-seven times (Matt 18:21–22). Reconciliation is serious business, and it requires mutual participation and responsibility. Edward Gilbreath rightly points out that every believer's job description is to be a reconciler.[17]

Reconciliation is the practice and discipline of building and preserving intercultural unity on a daily basis. The reality is that, in our interactions and relationships, there is a tendency to build up barriers and walls, the walls that Christ has already destroyed. In order to practice reconciliation,

17. Gilbreath, *Reconciliation Blues*, 48.

we need to understand the existing barriers and related dynamics. Therefore, the next part of this chapter uncovers some of the existing barriers
that hinder collaboration across cultural lines and quell the witness of intercultural unity.

Identifying Barriers to Intercultural Unity

Few Christian leaders would openly argue against collaboration across
cultural lines; many emphasize the importance of it, in theory. In practice,
however, it turns out to be very different and difficult. There are attempts to
collaborate across cultural lines, but often these stay on the surface or fail.
Assuming there is a genuine desire for intercultural unity, why is collaborating across cultural lines so difficult? Why is the body of Christ not able
to manifest the beauty of unity in diversity for everyone visibly?

There are many obstacles and barriers that are hindering churches in
doing kingdom work collaboratively and in building the New Jerusalem in
our cities. Hence, in order to develop intercultural unity, an honest assessment of reality needs to take place, without pretending that everything is
fine. There is the need to ask tough questions to identify our current location on our journey toward intercultural unity. The fact is that barriers and
walls are put up from both sides, from the majority and minority culture
groups. The difference, however, is that the power structure of our society
favors the majority culture group in being self-sufficient. It is provided with
much more effective tools to build walls and create barriers.

In conversations about barriers to intercultural unity, issues such
as language, busyness, or logistics are often brought up. Although these
aspects are real challenges and require intentional effort to overcome, I,
however, think that they are secondary and easily used as excuses. Our
mental models[18] and attitudes are the real barriers. Therefore, I will focus
on identifying them in order to help us all get ready for healthy and reconciling collaboration across cultural lines. Even though I will address the
barriers separately, they are all interconnected. The list of identified barriers
below is certainly not complete and might need adjustments depending on
the context and the lenses employed to interpret these barriers.

18. Mental models "are deeply ingrained assumptions, generalizations, or even pic-
tures of images that influence how we understand the world and how we take action,"
Senge, *The Fifth Discipline*, 8.

My hope is, nevertheless, that this section will spark some reflection and self-analysis. As we consider barriers to intercultural unity, I want to emphasize again that we live in a fallen world. Our society is polarized and divided along cultural, social, economic, and political lines. The world is full of sin; our thinking and acting is—often more than we acknowledge—driven by our sinful humanness. This reality, however, should not prevent us from striving for what God has in mind for us.

Indifference

Being on a journey toward intercultural unity is challenging. Interacting with people from different ethnic backgrounds tests one's own thinking and may point out each participant's cultural blind spots. It can be a very uncomfortable endeavor. Instead of seeing intercultural encounter as an opportunity to grow and mature, to change and be transformed, the experience can be perceived as threatening. Hence, it is much easier, at least subconsciously, to leave things as they are for one's own comfort. Why should each one of us enter a painful and time-intensive process, if one can simply fondly acknowledge the congregation or ethnic group from across the street and keep interactions at their superficial level?

The desire to wrestle with differences and work toward reconciliation and intercultural unity is very low. Today, there is seldom openly expressed hostility. Indifference toward each other and ignorance of the need for communion and interdependence are the big issues. To use Gary A. Parrett's words, "The tragedy is complicated today by the fact that many churches do not struggle with this reconciliation reality at all. We simply ignore it. We envision that we are reconciled to God in a way that does not require reconciliation with 'the other' . . . Christ may have destroyed the wall of hostility between us, but we have grown so accustomed to the wall that we live as though it were still standing. Theoretically, we may affirm that there is but one body in Christ. Practically, however, most of us seem to live as though it were otherwise."[19]

Many churches have, for the most part, given up wrestling with the reconciliation reality and the acknowledging of mutual interdependence, which are so closely tied to intercultural unity. In different conversations, but especially during interviews in the context of the Diverse Leadership

---

19. Parrett, "Wondrous Cross," 75.

Project,[20] the lack of prioritizing or seeing value in cross-cultural collaboration emerges independent of ethnic backgrounds. A Chinese pastor, for example, said that many of his colleagues and staff think that the Chinese culture and the needs of their congregations are so different that there are no overlapping areas to learn from other churches. Moreover, there is a prevalent feeling that they cannot contribute something of value for others. Similar remarks have been made by Hispanic pastors.

In the majority culture churches, the lack of value for cross-cultural partnerships exists as well, not necessarily because of the feeling that they cannot contribute, but because of self-sufficiency and the lack of openness to learn from people who might be financially, socially, and culturally marginalized in the United States, but who, nevertheless, have enormous spiritual wisdom to contribute.

Colorblindness

Another barrier on the journey toward intercultural unity is the concept of "colorblindness." It is based on the idea that ignoring or overlooking racial and ethnic differences promotes racial harmony. The concept has been developed with the best intentions and assumes, in theory, that race and culture are not decisive elements in social interactions and relations. Moreover, it is based on the mental model that racism is largely conquered and does not need to be addressed anymore.[21] In the Christian context, colorblindness can be disguised in spiritual expressions such as, "We are all the same in Christ" or "Through Christ we are new creatures; race and culture do not matter anymore."

Challenges to this perspective are that, first, cultural distinctiveness does matter and, second, for people of minority cultures, ignoring this fact does not promote racial harmony. On the contrary, "colorblindness creates a society that denies their negative racial experiences, rejects their cultural heritage, and invalidates their unique perspectives . . . When race-related problems arise, colorblindness tends to individualize conflicts and shortcomings, rather than examining the larger picture with cultural differences, stereotypes, and values placed into context."[22]

20. Learn more about the Diverse Leadership Project, Duemling, "Diverse Leadership."

21. Yancey, *Beyond Racial Gridlock,* 37.

22. Williams, "Colorblind Ideology," lines 24–51. See also Bonilla-Silva, *Racism*

The ethnic, racial, and cultural differences within the church context should not be a barrier for intercultural unity. However, ignoring and denying these differences only lead to a wider gap between majority and minority Christians.

Lack of Understanding of the Impact of Culture and the Related Power Dynamics

There are European-American Christians who genuinely want to serve in an urban neighborhood and collaborate across cultural lines. As they come into the city to offer support and advice, a common experience is rejection. A European-American pastor once told me that he invited a group of immigrant pastors to an event, but none of them showed up. He interpreted this incident as lack of willingness to collaborate.

In another context, after a gathering with a diverse group of pastors, the European-American host reflected that mostly people with European-American descent were talking, and he wondered why the Asian or Latino pastors did not speak up, even though they were invited. He also was discussing whether there is a lack of willingness to participate.

These examples show a lack of understanding of the impact of the power imbalance and related dynamics in U.S. society and how that influences participation in diverse settings. The perceived reservation is not necessarily a lack of willingness to participate, but is connected to an inappropriate context or approach. In many settings, European-American values, ways of operation, and cultural standards are the given ones. Many European-American Christians are not aware how their "whiteness," with its inherent privileges,[23] impacts their worldview and faith practice. There have been several books written that reflect on how cultures impact the faith practice of different immigrant groups. However, in the same context there has been little reflection on how European-American culture itself impacts the daily faith practice of its church members.[24] The assumption or mental model is that the European-American culture is "normal" for all Christendom, and everyone else is different. A general inability to identify

---

without Racists.

23. Frankenberg, *Displacing Whiteness.*

24. Parrett, "Becoming," 128. Parrett mentions Wilkerson, *Multicultural Religious Education,* as well as Breckenridge and Breckenridge, *What Color Is your God?* as such examples.

our own European-American cultural traits and their impact on other cultures is prevalent.

Along these lines is the use of the word *ethnic*. In many church settings, *ethnic* is used to describe people with a non-European descent and a more recent migration history. There are "Ethnic Ministries" to reach out to the "ethnic people" in our neighborhood. This usage denies the fact that we all have a distinct ethnic background, hence we all are ethnic. Moreover, it draws a line between "us" and "them." In addition to that, the use of language has generally the potential to create lines of separation.[25]

Fear

Because of the history of slavery in the U.S. and its implications, there is a general feeling of discomfort and fear to talk about race issues. George Yancey points out that "fear prevents European Americans from being willing to enter into genuine dialogue with people of color, because they do not want to say something that will get them categorized as racist. As a result, whites avoid addressing racial issues by favoring a colorblind or Anglo-conformity perspective."[26] For people of color, the fears that their concerns are not taken seriously and that they will be accused of playing the "race card" also prevent them from entering into a dialogue. In short, our society, including the Church, lacks a safe environment to talk about race and wrestle with this and many other issues.[27]

Lack of Dialogue and Polarization

The lack of genuine dialogue, the fear of wrestling with uncomfortable issues, leads to polarization and hinders intercultural unity. The presidential elections in 2012 clearly showed the division and polarization between old and young, women and men, people of color and whites in the United States.[28]

This division is even deeper among different ethnic groups in the Christian community. In their study about attitudes of contemporary

25. It is beyond the scope of this chapter to elaborate on this important aspect, but I recommend Hill, *Everyday Language*.

26. Yancey, *Beyond Racial Gridlock*, 127.

27. Ibid., 132.

28. Statistic Brain, "Presidential Voter."

American evangelicals toward issues of ethnicity and race, Michael O. Emerson and Christian Smith demonstrate the huge division between white evangelicals and black evangelicals in their perception and interpretation of racism:[29] "Based on survey data, white conservative Protestants differ in their explanation from other whites, from theologically liberal white Protestants, from African Americans, and most dramatically from black conservative Protestants."[30]

For many white evangelicals, racism is perceived as an individual sin and not a systemic or structural issue, where action is needed to be taken. Moreover, racism is not perceived as a moral issue like abortion or gay marriage. For most people of color, racism, however, is clearly a moral issue that requires corporate action, rather than being categorized simply as an individual sin.[31]

Another related divergent issue is that of immigration. This discussion, especially around undocumented immigrants, is very polarized and often not based on informed realities. The heated debate around this issue leads away from what the Church is called to do and how it is to act. Theologian Orlando O. Espin said, "Welcoming the stranger (the 'immigrant,' we could say today) is the most often repeated commandment in the Hebrew Scriptures, with the exception of the imperative to worship only the one God. And the love of neighbor (especially the more vulnerable neighbor) is doubtlessly the New Testament's constant command. . .Whatever the cause of immigration today, there can be no doubt as to where the Church must stand when it comes to defending the immigrant."[32]

These fundamental differences in perspectives and experiences pose a huge barrier to genuine collaboration across cultural lines, especially, as they lack genuine dialogue and willingness to wrestle with the issues without dismissing their true depth in the majority culture or demonizing the other person or position.

29. Also their research is focused on African Americans; similar observation can be made within the Hispanic or Asian community.

30. Emerson and Smith, *Divided by Faith*, 97.

31. Yancey, *Beyond Racial Gridlock*, 11.

32. Espin is cited in Soerens and Hwang, *Welcoming the Stranger*, 82. Another resource on this issue is Carroll R., *Christians at the Border*.

Prejudices

Prejudices are ingrained into our thinking. They work as a special type of prejudgment. As I cannot explore the concept of prejudices in depth, I will use Harold D. Fishbein's definition: "Prejudice is an unfavorable and unreasonable negative attitude directed toward others because of their membership in a particular group."[33] Prejudices are applied on a subconscious level when interacting with a certain group. They are reinforced and generalized by negative personal experience, through conversations or stories, and negative media coverage of mostly minority culture groups. For people who encounter prejudices, there is often an experience of discrimination connected; thus, prejudices impact career opportunities, access to housing, health, and mortality.

It is an illusion to think that anyone is free of prejudices, no matter how favorable our attitude toward people of a different ethnic or social group is. In his reflection about hidden prejudices, Jack W. Hayford shared that he suddenly realized that his desire to wash his hands after shaking hands with people of color is rooted in deeply ingrained prejudices that present them as poor and dirty. He said, "I had never allowed this to register in my conscious mind to the degree that I saw my need to repent," and he further emphasizes that "we are going to have to learn to overcome some of the encrusted points of separation in our system. These are not points of bitter resistance, but unperceived points of separation that encrust themselves in our souls."[34] This story and many others show that there is still a lot of work ahead to uncover the blind spots of our souls.

Ethnic, racial, and cultural differences and the reality of human brokenness should not be a barrier for the unity of the body of Christ, as Christ has already destroyed the dividing wall among all people on the cross once and for all. The differences, however, do become barriers when we ignore and deny them. Only through redemption, reconciliation, and celebrating the uniqueness of each diverse group and our respective contributions to the kingdom of God can we progress on our journey toward intercultural unity. In the last part of this chapter, I will, therefore, explore approaches that help us to overcome barriers and to get ready for the challenges of this journey.

33. Fishbein is cited in Conde-Frazier, "Prejudice and Conversion," 109.
34. Hayford, *Confessing*, 21.

Approaches to Embark on a Journey toward Intercultural Unity

Overcoming barriers, prejudices, and fears so that we can change our mental models determines whether our churches become safe environments, whether cross-cultural relationships will have a firm basis that will lead to successful collaboration, and whether we experience intercultural unity, hence establishing the New Jerusalem around us.

Reflecting on these issues, the following question comes to my mind: How can people who do not see the necessity of change or do not think that their actions and attitudes are questionable and counterproductive be challenged to rethink and unlearn?

It certainly is miraculous, the work of the Holy Spirit, when individuals or groups are embarking on a journey toward intercultural unity. This journey is based on intentionality and a conversion experience, as Elizabeth Conde-Frazier describes, "Conversion is the process whereby the grace of God integrates our knowledge of God's will with our practice of it."[35]

Intercultural unity through reconciliation is not reached through a program that has three or seven steps to be implemented, or a magic bullet, but through a lifestyle, a change of mental models. A successful collaboration across cultural lines does not mean the absence of conflict, but a basis to work through hard and challenging questions, to enter in a genuine dialogue with each other. Being together on a journey forces us out of our comfort zones and challenges us to perceive reality through different lenses, no matter whether we belong to the majority or minority culture. In the context of racial reconciliation, George Yancey promotes the mutual-responsibility model: "If white Christians want to be part of the solution to our society's racial problems, they must realize that their perceptions about racial issues are not the only accurate ones. Majority group members must humbly seek to learn about racial minorities and why we feel the way we do."[36] Furthermore, Yancey challenges members of the majority culture to reflect on how they have gained and continue to gain from the racial status quo. Moreover, he puts an emphasis on the concept of corporate repentance, which is an important milestone in the process of reconciliation.

Whites and nonwhites do not have identical responsibility; nevertheless, racial minorities have a different but just as important role to play.

35. Conde-Frazier, "Prejudice and Conversion," 119.
36. Yancey, *Beyond Racial Gridlock*, 99.

Yancey highlights that "we have our own tasks, which are no less challenging than the duties of the majority. Any solution to racism that does not include the proactive actions of people of color is incomplete. Such a solution only encourages racial arrogance and pride on the part of racial minorities, even as it disempowers them from participating in solutions to racial problems."[37]

Having cited that, I want to emphasize that there are no easy answers to these questions. Reconciliation is a lifelong process, a journey that takes time and requires investment. Moreover, each journey looks different, but there are approaches that help to initiate and facilitate transformation. In this part of the chapter, I will focus on three approaches that support the training and preparation of the ambassadors of the New Jerusalem to embark on their journey toward intercultural unity. These approaches are (1) personal growth in intercultural intelligence and competence, (2) creating a safe learning environment, and (3) storytelling.

Personal Growth in Cultural Intelligence

Although intercultural unity and reconciliation always have a corporate element, each individual is responsible for one's own personal growth, expansion, and development of intercultural competence and cultural intelligence. The first steps involve getting theoretically familiar with the concept of culture, general cultural differences,[38] and the particular features of a specific culture. The best way of learning about and from a different culture, however, is through immersion and building personal relationships.

As David Livermore's concept of cultural intelligence is developed in the context of cross-cultural ministry, I refer to it as an example of the many theoretical concepts of the development of cultural intelligence or intercultural competence.

Livermore emphasizes the desire to love our neighbor as a starting point on the pathway to cultural intelligence. Cultural intelligence does not require knowing everything about every culture, but it does involve the capability to

37. Ibid.

38. There are general differences made between hot and cold cultures or primary and secondary cultures, referring to Western and Southern hemisphere. I cannot go into more details about cultural differences, but books such as *Foreign to Familiar: A Guide to Understanding Hot- and Cold-Climate Cultures* by Sarah A. Lanier, and *Many Colors: Cultural Intelligence for a Changing Church* by Soong-Chang Rah are two helpful resources to explore the impact of cultural differences more deeply.

navigate cultural differences and develop respectful learning attitudes toward each other. The cultural intelligence quotient (CQ) consists of four interrelated factors as the CQ map in Figure 1[39] displays: Understanding (knowledge CQ), plus going deep (interpretative CQ), combined with God-honoring motivation (perseverance CQ), leading to action (behavioral CQ).

1. **Knowledge CQ:** Understanding cross-cultural issues and differences on three levels: (a) Understanding our own culture; (b) understanding generally the concept of culture; and (c) understanding the areas where cultural values shape our feelings, thinking, and action.

2. **Interpretive CQ:** The degree of sensitivity in cross-cultural interactions. Steps to develop interpretative CQ include (a) becoming mindful and aware without jumping to quick conclusions; (b) empathizing with others, but at the same time keeping our identity; (c) simultaneously monitoring internal and external worlds, which means nurturing awareness through self-reflection and journaling; and (d) seeking out information in order to confirm or negate interpretations of experiences, thus reflecting with people belonging to the specific cultural background.

3. **Perseverance CQ:** The level of interest, drive, and motivation to adapt cross-culturally, thus, moving from knowing to expressing.

4. **Behavioral CQ:** The extent to which we appropriately change our verbal and non-verbal action when we interact cross-culturally, moving from the desire to love authentically to expressing love in respectful, meaningful ways as manifested in our behavior. The ability to adjust behavior is based on the situation and expectation of others who are culturally different. However, uncritical acceptance of every behavior does not prove cultural intelligence.[40]

In order to help us to assess and reflect on our own cultural intelligence, a set of interpretive questions is available in the appendix.

Creating a Safe Learning Environment

In order to move beyond superficial, polite relationships and to create a basis for dealing with hard questions, a safe learning environment is essential.

39. Livermore, *Cultural Intelligence*, 13.
40. Ibid., 55.

Such a safe environment does not just happen, but needs to be created intentionally, which is not an easy undertaking. All our practical attempts need to be accompanied by prayer and the invitation of the Holy Spirit into the process.

Some of the practices and characteristics that help to create a safe learning environment are confidentiality; being a good listener; not judging one another, but considering the best in one another; and being committed to one another's growth. Moreover, it is important not to look down on those who confess their sins, temptations, or weaknesses. Focusing on our own issues rather than on others' is as important as avoiding "cross-talk," which is being too quick to give unsolicited advice to others or trying to fix the other person.

On the other hand, being in a safe environment does not necessarily mean that we feel at ease and emotionally light. Therefore, it is good to know that a safe environment is not a pain-free environment, as growth is often painful. Moreover, it is not only about "me" feeling safe, but also about helping "others" to feel safe. It is not a place for expressing raw emotions without considering the effect this sharing will have on others. A truly safe environment welcomes different perspectives, so it does not require a uniformity of opinion.

It is easy to describe what a safe environment is and what it is not, but how can we actually create a safe environment? My colleague, Gregg Detwiler, has developed a process diagram that describes "The Process of Creating and Reproducing a Safe Environment."

The starting point for creating a safe environment is (1) willingness. It needs a community or organization that desires to create a safe environment. The next step is (2) skilled leadership to guide and nurture a safe environment. After that, (3) a group-learning process has to take place to agree on and, thus, define qualities of a safe environment. A safe environment is not created once and for all. It is very fragile and requires (4) skilled leadership that will model and maintain a safe environment. Moreover, a regular (5) reality check to assess the status quo is important. A community or organization can only progress if there is the willingness to be honest about where they are in the journey. This leads to the next step, (6) continued practice through "action-reflection" learning, and finally the hope is (7) reproduction, where members of the community or organization reproduce safe environments in their spheres of influence.[41]

41. Detwiler, "Safe Environment."

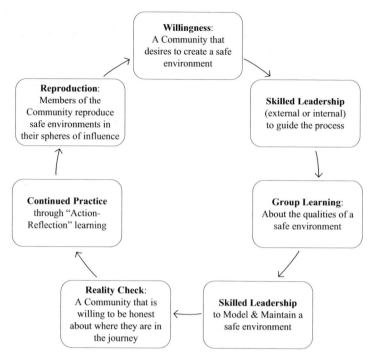

As I mentioned in a previous section, churches and organizations are often not safe environments to discuss sensitive issues such as racism corporately.[42] However, a starting point to enter into a process of reconciliation is to gather people in the immediate surroundings who are interested in digging deeper. The first step to take is the formation of a small group with three or four people who are committed to initiate a safe environment and honestly reflect on racism and reconciliation.[43]

Storytelling

Sharing our stories provides a key to each other's life and a basis for building deeper relationships, hence overcoming prejudices and barriers. Storytelling is an art and method that has long been lost in our "one third" world, driven as it is by facts, statistics, numbers, dates, and mere information.

Henry J. Nouwen rightly advocates that "we need to become storytellers again . . . One of the remarkable qualities of a story is that it creates

42. Yancey, *Beyond Racial Gridlock*, 22.

43. Kang, "Formation Process," 166.

space. We can dwell in a story, walk around, and find our own place. The story confronts but does not oppress; the story inspires but does not manipulate. The story invites us to an encounter, a dialog, a mutual sharing."[44] Stories are entry points into intercultural relationships as they engage emotion and move people. Stories express thoughts, feelings, and values in images we will remember.[45] Stories help us to discover the value each of us bring to the table and lead us away from generalizations and statistics. Stories enable us to share pain and joy.

But, in order to enter into storytelling, a safe learning environment is necessary, especially as "storytelling is the ultimate self-disclosure. It reveals insights into the personality, emotions, content, and identity of the individual. It requires self-disclosure while presenting a way to move the conversation forward."[46]

As everything, storytelling takes practice and dedication. According to Soong-Chan Rah, storytelling consists of four essential aspects: (1) telling the truth, otherwise we lose credibility; (2) revealing yourself beyond sharing facts and figures; (3) sharing pain honestly, including sharing feelings, and (4) sharing your identity, who you are, and how you have been transformed by the power of God.[47]

In summary, storytelling takes time and commitment, and in our busy world it is often hard to create space and time for it. Storytelling also requires listening skills and self-reflection, which are lacking in our society.

Conclusion

The journey toward intercultural unity is a lifelong endeavor; it is a lifestyle. Intercultural unity requires a lifelong commitment to identify and overcome barriers, to transform our mental models again and again. Intercultural unity cannot be treated as a onetime program or event after which we can move on to the next thing; it requires continuous collaboration across cultural lines, the incorporation of the practice of reconciliation into our daily lives.

44. Nouwen, *Living Reminder*, 65–66.

45. Margolis and McLean, "Storytelling," 1.

46. Rah, *Many Colors*, 136.

47. Ibid., 144.

The witness of intercultural unity creates space and invites others to enter the New Jerusalem, to experience the new creation, the reconciliation with God and people.

Questions to Reflect on One's Own Personal Cultural Intelligence

Knowledge CQ: Understand[48]

Am I fluent in a language other than English?

- Do I know the ways other cultures approach conflict?
- Do I know the different role expectations of men and women in other cultures?
- Do I know the basic cultural values of several other cultures?
- Do I understand the primary ways Christians differ in their beliefs and practices in different cultural settings?

Interpretative CQ: Go Deep[49]

Am I conscious of what I need to know about a culture that is unfamiliar to me?

- Am I conscious of how my cultural background shapes the way I read the Bible?
- Do I determine what I need to know about a culture before I interact with people from that culture?
- Do I compare my previous ideas about a culture with what I actually experience during cross-cultural interactions?
- Do I check for appropriate ways to talk about my faith in cross-cultural situations?

48. Livermore, *Cultural Intelligence*, 58.
49. Ibid., 144.

Perseverance CQ: Express[50]

Do I like cross-cultural interactions that are new to me?

- Do I prefer to stay with locals when traveling cross-culturally rather than in a hotel by myself?
- Do I prefer eating local foods when I go to a new place?
- Do I enjoy spending time with people who don't embrace Christianity as their worldview?
- Am I confident I would be effective in cross-cultural ministry?

Behavioral CQ: Express[51]

Do I use pause and silence differently to suit different cross-cultural situations?

- Do I alter my verbal behavior (e.g., accent, tone) according to the culture that I am in?
- Do I display different behaviors based on specifics of the local culture?
- Do I change the manner in which I greet others (shake hands, bow, nod, etc.) when in different cultures?
- Do I change the amount of warmth and enthusiasm I express when talking to others to suit the cultural setting?

References for Further Study

DeYoung, Curtiss Paul, et al. *United by Faith: The Multiracial Congregation as an Answer to the Problem of Race.* New York: Oxford University Press, 2003.

Emerson, Michael O., and Christian Smith. *Divided by Faith: Evangelical Religion and the Problem of Race in America.* New York: Oxford University Press, 2000.

Rah, Soong-Chan. *Many Colors: Cultural Intelligence for a Changing Church.* Chicago: Moody, 2010.

Volf, Miroslav. *Exclusion and Embrace: A Theological Exploration of Identity, Otherness, and Reconciliation.* Nashville: Abingdon Press, 1996.

Yancey, George. *Beyond Racial Gridlock: Embracing Mutual Responsibility.* Downers Grove: InterVarsity, 2006.

50. Ibid., 214.
51. Ibid., 234.

Challenges to Discipleship in the Context of Contemporary Consumer Culture

Teri Elliott-Hart

"Consumer culture" is not just another name for materialism or a framework to explain our relationship to money; it is an ethos. In daily life, we are bombarded by the messages of the consumer age: billboards, sweatshirts, buses, storefronts, coffee cups, and the internet deliver advertisements twenty-four hours a day. Even taxis and buses may invite us to purchase more minutes for a cell phone as we drive by. The breadth and depth of consumer culture reaches into our experiences in unprecedented ways. This includes religious vision—even how we hear and communicate the Christian gospel as North Americans is shaped by the values and practices of the consumer culture, creating a critical issue for the church to face.[1]

Driving the three miles from work to home, I pass "Grove Hall's Mecca" a plaza with its clothing stores, pharmacy, and restaurant. In the adjacent neighborhood, I may go by "Alelu Supermercado" and the "Blessed Assurance Mini-mart." At home in my mailbox among the catalogs for this-and-that sits a bright postcard emblazoned with the entreaty to "Give the One Gift That Really Matters": it is not an announcement from a local church, but a bundle deal on cable, phone, and wireless service from a national telecommunication company. What is the impact of the blending of faith language and images with the language of commerce—is it a blessing for the neighborhoods, or does it contribute to a dulling of the power the language of faith?

---

1. Portions of this chapter are drawn from the author's dissertation, Elliott-Hart, "Educating for Discipleship in a Consumer Culture: Promising Practices Rooted in the Pastoral Circle." Copyright 2011 by ProQuest LLC. Online: http://dcollections.bc.edu/dtl_publish/37/230049.html.

When I consider the blueprints of Jesus as a foundation for establishing communities, secular stores with religious overtones are not included. Instead, I envision gospel values pervading relationships, policies, habits, and identity. The cultural blueprint that life in a typical North American city reflects is the ubiquitous nature of "consumer culture." Everyone lives in relationship to the institutions, practices, and assumptions that constitute the consumer society. The consumer culture socializes people regardless of gender, socioeconomic status, or ethnicity. And the formative aspects of the consumer culture shape the church as well. While many Christians will mentally assent to Jesus' core teachings (on generosity, wealth, or anxiety over material possessions, for example), the actual habits of Christian communities may not look much different than anyone else's when it comes to status seeking, spending and debt, or worry over finances.[2]

These weaknesses are not new, but magnified in the current age. The ancient text called the *Didache* (what scholars call the first teaching documents produced by the early church) is a collection of lessons used in the lengthy rite of initiation for those converting to the Christian Way. Strikingly, it begins with Jesus' teaching on money and possessions. If the disciples' relationship to money and possessions was centrally important for the church two thousand years ago, how much more must we pay attention to Jesus' teachings on such matters in the North American context of capitalism and individualism? This chapter seeks to shed light on some of the mechanisms of a "consumer culture" and paint a picture of challenges to Christian identity and habits in light of it. I also present alternatives to the status quo as exemplified in two examples of formational experiences of holistic discipleship.

Why the Term Consumer Culture?

The study of the consumer society is a relatively new field within sociology with diverse directions in research, such as economic critique, studies of people's relationships to brands, environmentalism and the market, and research on advertising trends, among other topics. Sociologists use the term *culture* in relationship to societies which have not only a free market driven economy, but corresponding attitudes, practices, identity, and morality, which together reflect and uphold the consumer dynamics. In other

2. Explored, for example, in Sider, *The Scandal of the Evangelical Conscience.*

words, such aspects are pervasive and serve as the supporting ethos of the society's institutions and deep beliefs.

One important researcher, Dan Slater, provides the following key elements for identifying consumer culture:

1. Consumer culture is the culture of a market society.

2. Consumer culture is, in principle, universal and impersonal. All social relations, activities, and objects can in principle be exchanged as commodities.

3. Consumer culture identifies freedom with private choice and private life. The relation between freedom and privacy has been crucial to the development of the modern person.

4. Consumer needs are unlimited and insatiable.[3]

Thus, the term *consumer culture* as a descriptor of the foundations of the North American way of life is warranted because of how pervasive and inescapable a life of consumption is. The term does not automatically infer a critique, nor do I presume that the "American" experience can be reduced to consumption habits and values. However, when a people are fixated on living to consume, as opposed to consuming to live, consumption is no longer merely a neutral descriptor but reflective of a cultural ideology.

Of specific concern to me as a practical theologian within the broad topic of consumer culture are two issues: the ethical dangers of overconsumption, and the ways that commercialization shapes human relationships.

Overconsumption and Love of Neighbor

In an urban context where glistening office buildings and cardboard box shelters are juxtaposed on the same block, social inequalities confront us every day. Researchers remind us of the growing concern from Christians and other activists in the public square. First is a growing awareness in popular culture of the breadth of social inequality. The Occupy movement, for example, is trying to speak for the "99 percent": a term referring to economic data that indicate the top 1 percent hold 40 percent of the wealth in the United States, and 20 percent are responsible for 50 percent of the nations' consumer spending.[4] The media delivers scathing stories of the

---

3. Slater, *Consumer Culture and Modernity*, 24–31.
4. Schor and Holt, "Introduction," *The Consumer Society Reader*, vii.

conspicuous consumption of luxury items by people who have stolen and lied in corporate America while others suffer personal bankruptcies and foreclosures. There is also a heightened awareness of global inequality and relative wealth: for example, less than one per cent of what the world spent every year on weapons was needed to put every child into school by the year 2000.[5] When we consider such life and death gaps as knowing that North Americans can spend on candy what it would take to provide malaria control for the entire continent of Africa, how much more should the church stand up in love and take note?[6]

Social scientists also describe growing popular awareness of the devastating environmental impact of the spread of consumerism. "According to a recent estimate by Mathis Wackernagel, co-author of *Our Ecological Footprint*, if everyone consumed at the level of the average North American, it would take four extra planets to provide the necessary resources. Globalization and the marketing of the American consumer lifestyle provoke millions of global consumers to suddenly 'need' sport utility vehicles, big-screen TVs and closets of stuff—something the already overburdened planet can ill-afford."[7] A robust theology of care for our neighbor means practical restraint by consuming a fair share of the earth's resources and using purchasing powers justly.

Underneath the habits that lead to inequalities is the relentless commercialization of all spheres of life. Even values are commodities—not only are objects bought and sold, but brands and products are promoted because of the values they are associated with. The production of news, sports, and entertainment is commodified, i. e., turned into a commercial commodity to be leased and marketed. Actors and athletes can take out insurance on their most desirable body parts. Even relationships are commodified in a culture that privileges taste and choice. People can be treated like disposable objects in a series of intense relationships, trading in and trading up

5. "State of the World." *New Internationalist* 287 (February 1997).

6. According to economist Jeffrey Sachs in the World Malaria Report 2005, "Comprehensive malaria control is the lowest hanging fruit on the planet. For just US $ 3 per person per year in the rich countries, it is possible to fund the comprehensive control of malaria in Africa, ensuring universal access to life-saving nets, effective medicines, and other control measures. Millions of lives in the coming years can be saved, with profound economic benefits as well. This is an historic bargain too great to miss," online: http://www.stopmalarianow.org/what-we-want.html.

7. Tilford, "Why Consumption Matters."

partners when they are no longer satisfying.[8] And, of course, there is growing literature analyzing the commodification of religion such as *Selling God, Consuming Religion*, and an abundance of books on marketing strategies.

Living in a consumer culture poses many ethical dilemmas for the church. And underlying assumptions regarding commodification and disposability can color everything we do, not just what we buy or how we use our finances. Marketers expect people to experience consumption as a part of creating their identities.[9] By attaching brands to certain experiences or attitudes that are already valued in the culture (e.g., a family vacation or being cool), a person attaches that value to the item to be purchased and wants to be identified with it. Miller explains, "Contemporary advertisers do not emphasize the usefulness of a product; instead, they work to associate it with values we desire. Ad values such as control, energy, youth . . . are so well known as to be cliché." Miller continues, "While these values continue to be exploited, more surprising ones have been added to the marketers' repertoires: wisdom, piety, political radicalism, and even simplicity."[10] I agree with Miller that we must be very cautious about how the underlying cultural dynamic of exchange and consumption is applied beyond the world of goods and services to people, relationships, religious identity, and capacity for commitment.

Is it possible to embrace an alternative reality—that the accumulation of goods, seeking status, and giving allegiance to the promises of the marketplace are second best to the abundant life in Christian community described in Scripture? It will be very difficult for the people to develop stronger habits of generosity, self-sacrifice, and simplicity for the sake of the gospel—as difficult as a camel going through a needle. But, such holistic discipleship is what we yearn for as Christian leaders, and we continue to press forward in hope.

Commodification and Being Human

An important theological voice in the discussion of religious life and consumer culture is John Kavanaugh. Kavanaugh began his work *Following Christ in a Consumer Society* in the 1980s, in the midst of the "me-generation" and before the great economic boom of the 1990s, but his analysis

8. Schor and Holt, "Introduction," *The Consumer Society Reader*, viii.

9. Holt, "Why Do Brands Cause Trouble?" *Journal of Consumer Research*, 2002.

10. Miller, "Taking Consumer Culture Seriously," 284.

continues to be informative and a helpful framework for the church. Kavanaugh highlights the differences between a worldview created by consumer culture in America and a worldview birthed by faithfulness to the teachings of Jesus Christ. He asks what "form" human existence takes under the influence of each contrasting formation systems: "Consumer society is a formation system: it forms us and our behavior."[11] Kavanaugh means that the social structures and cultural norms of modern American life form our behavior, inform identity, and tell us our status in the world. In this commodity "form" of life, objects are primary.

Kavanaugh is claiming that in so far as consumerism is both a philosophy and a set of practices, it infuses politics, medicine, and social relations in addition to the economic practices it instigates. Ideologically, he concludes, the process decenters humanity to the margins of the world of objects.[12] This dehumanization is most evident, he says, in examples such as slavery and systematic economic injustices that demonstrate the extreme state of humans being relegated to the status of things. However, this is not the only form such depersonalization takes. For example, to the degree that people know others as commodities, he notes that the objectification of sex in marketing and acceptance of violence as entertainment should not be a surprise.[13]

The more uncritically embedded we are in this commodity formation system, the more people transfer their own deepest longings and vulnerabilities to the material world in longing for products. When we know and are known as "things," our identity is reduced to our external value and attributes. At the most extreme, then, being human is to be "replaceable objects whose goals and values are dependent upon how much we market, produce, and consume."[14] Kavanaugh describes the impact of such commodification on relationships with other people in terms of depersonalization and dispossession. But the Christian understanding of what it means to be human stands in direct contrast to such notions. In a rejection of the glorification of objectivity and efficiency so celebrated in modernity's cultural systems, Kavanaugh is gravely concerned about the ways in which humanity is so easily commodified and ultimately "degraded."[15]

11. Kavanaugh, *Following Christ in a Consumer Society*, 4.

12. Ibid., 19.

13. For a detailed discussion, see ibid., 51–60.

14. Ibid., 64.

15. Ibid., 4.

In Kavanaugh's terms, the theological alternative that refutes the commodification of personhood is called the "personal form." People reflect God's image and are made for covenanting with each other and God. Therefore, relating to people as objects is anathema to the Christian model, which declares that we are all made in God's image and are called to love our neighbors as ourselves. This personal form is demonstrated first in creation, then in the covenant of God with the people in Israel, and the law that provided boundaries for the fulfillment of our truest humanity in community. Finally, it culminates in the continuing revelation of God's self in the form of Jesus.

I would argue that following Jesus as a disciple provides the template for the deepest forms of human flourishing in our communities. By following the model of Christ who lived for others and who brings us into full relationship with the God of freedom and life, people have the power to resist the commodity form. As the church, called to true covenant with others, we need to reject the habits and beliefs that allow others to be objectified and dismissed. The path toward abundant life includes resistance to the commodified culture through the building of the alternative community of disciples. Given how pervasive the reach of commodification is, discipleship must similarly be nurtured in every aspect of life in order for us to live as the alternative community reflecting God's love for our neighbors.

Putting Christ before Consumption

Christian communities at their best provide an alternative space for personal formation. Along with the teaching of Scripture and worship that shape us in Christlikeness, Christian leaders need to work with their congregations to educate them to be aware of the cultural environment. If we begin to make the underlying influence of consumer culture explicit, people in Christian community can begin to compare the cultural narrative of what it means to be human with the Christian story of a life of discipleship. People of faith need to be asking, how do we wrestle back our ultimate concerns from the consumer culture to the heart of God for the world? Christian communities deepen resistance to consumerist practices and ideology at the level of formation, thereby influencing identity development, decision making, problem solving, and practices of generosity and self-sacrifice.

In this next section, I turn to practical examples of allegiance to Christ over consumer culture. There are two contemporary faith movements that provide excellent models for resisting overconsumption, rejecting the commodification of people and values, and demonstrating an alternative culture to the world. First, I describe the Simple Way in Philadelphia, and then present a curriculum called "Lazarus at the Gate" that is impacting Christian communities in the New England area.

The Simple Way is an intentional community in North Philadelphia. It is an example of a small but influential movement called "neomonasticism."[16] Living together in a residential community is the context for their growth in discipleship shaped by shared spiritual practices and a common mission. The Simple Way understands radical discipleship as a choice "to be part of a new community, a new polity, which is formed in Jesus' obedience to the cross. To be a disciple means to share Christ's story, to participate in the reality of God's rule."[17]

Their story begins in 1997 when a group of college students led by then undergraduate Shane Claiborne encountered a group of homeless families living in a church building in North Philadelphia near their campus. The students befriended these people and began to become aware of the complex experiences of the marginalized in their city. As they spent more time listening to and worshiping with the encamped families, the group partnered with them, in advocating for their rights and helping them acquire what they needed from the city. The students also began questioning the theologies they grew up with, which, Claiborne says, had not prepared them for a life of social action or solidarity with suffering people.[18] Eventually, six students moved into a brownstone in the depressed Philadelphia neighborhood where they had met the disenfranchised families. They called themselves "The Simple Way," sharing a home and a common purse and getting involved in the everyday ups and downs of a beleaguered neighborhood.

Today, the Simple Way community is no longer a student movement, but consists of some of those founding young adults as well as others who have joined over the years to become residents and community development

16 A book written from within the movement, *Schools for Conversion,* is a compilation of writings edited by members of the Rutba House, an intentional Christian community. They identified twelve shared values that sustain their various communities. Another helpful book on the subject of intentional discipleship communities is Luther Smith's *Intimacy and Mission.*

17. Hauerwas, *A Community of Character,* 49.

18. Chapter 5 in Claiborne's *The Irresistible Revolution: Living as an Ordinary Radical* tells the story of the genesis of the community/movement.

workers in the neighborhood. Examples of some of their alternative practices include a shared health insurance cooperative that the members participate in along with other people in small Christian communities. They have at times even carried various residents from their neighborhood in their health care co-op when there was an emergency. In avoiding the market economy as much as possible, they attempt to exchange goods and services, instead of money, with neighborhood store owners. This has included sharing second-language lessons, groceries, and child care.

Claiborne speaks of "God's new economy," a phrase he uses to describe the economic that best reflect the theological convictions about wealth, justice, and the common good that they strive for in communal life. Claiborne believes that "charity" and even "generosity" have been co-opted by contemporary culture. Instead, he says, the new economic way of life is "beyond" charity.[19] They value a relational form of redistribution of wealth and resources that comes from a "theology of enough."[20] Adherents of the Simple Way live as they do in part as a spiritual discipline for themselves and as a model for the mainstream church to go beyond a "brokerage model" of sharing resources. Following Christ with full abandon has meant, for the Simple Way members, to refuse the economic rituals that dictate contemporary social institutions and systems.

As I read their story, to me it is clear that they are embodying a theology which resists the presuppositions of consumerism. Their alternative consumer practices have emerged from necessity out of their model of a shared income and their shared residential life, as well as their solidarity with the poor, and their understanding of biblical teaching on stewardship and spirituality. They stand out as people committed to the "blueprints of Christ" for the city.

Their commitment to living out a lifestyle based on the early disciples' way has resulted in creative and effective alternatives to the commodification of self and others. The strengths and appeal to living a life that demonstrates such a degree of counterculture is very attractive to many followers of Jesus; their impact on the development of the neighborhood and spiritual growth is evident. However, it is also important to look at the limits of this lifestyle in order to learn from them. First is the matter that voluntary simplicity has an implicit measure of middle-class

---

19. Claiborne, "Mark 2: Sharing Economic Resources with Fellow Community Members and the Needy among Us," in *Schools for Conversion*, 29.

20. Ibid., 31.

mobility and choice regarding relocation and patterns of work and social action. Some Christians may be called to follow Jesus in this way of moving from comfort to more challenging circumstances because it is the best expression of their devotional and spiritual nourishing. However, for some people, moving out of challenging and demoralizing circumstances can be the most God-breathed expression of their faith. So, rejection of the values and habits of consumer culture will not look the same for all disciples in all communities. Observers also wonder whether intentional residential community is sustainable over time. For example, members often change their perspective after getting married or having children, or young adults discern career and educational callings that take them out of the intentional community they thought they were committed to. And the work itself, often in much-blighted neighborhoods, can lead to burnout in cases where regular self-care and mentorship is not built in.[21]

It is possible for many of the values and practices to be replicated even in non-residential church communities. More mainstream congregations can engage in deep and meaningful relationships with their local community, experience profound fellowship and intimate worship, and also understand themselves as an alternative community of disciples called to a distinct purpose in their neighborhoods. Because of some of the inherent limitations of the relocation/residential community model of discipleship, I present another example of Christians who are attempting to respond to commodification and overconsumption.

Lazarus at the Gate is a small-group curriculum published jointly by Boston Faith and Justice Network, Sojourners Community, and World Vision.[22] They refer to it as more than a small group: it is lifestyle discipleship. It is a twelve-part program rooted in the biblical story of wealth and poverty from the book of Luke 16:19–31. The curriculum encourages participants to develop new practices of economic justice through Bible study and the study of global poverty. As they grow together, each small group sets aside savings out of their new practices of less consuming to give to an international charitable organization at the end of the experience. One key component to the time spent together in small groups is that the participants share specific details of their personal budgets and develop the habit

21. For a helpful book that describes of the challenges facing such communities, see Rausch, *Radical Christian Communities*.

22. A copy of the complete program written by Gary VanderPol et al., can be found at the website of The Micah Challenge. Online: http://www.micahchallenge.us/resources/alphaindex/resources/l.html.

of asking each other how their day-to-day spending reflects their deepest values.

Transformation of values and practices in their everyday living, from conformity to the world to conformity to Christ, is a central outcome hoped for by participants in the Lazarus groups. And, those who commit to the small group experience are also participating in global outreach through their group giving project. The *Lazarus at the Gate* project integrates theology and practice in that the gospel story of Lazarus is woven with the authors' own wrestling with consumer culture and the human propensity toward greed and self-centeredness. The curriculum grew out of questions about the formative influence of consumer culture on the church, and it also invites participants to enter into that analysis for themselves. There is an intersection between studying biblical teachings on wealth, poverty, generosity, discipleship, and reflection on how everyday living lines up with the biblical ideals. While this program has a particular ending point and prescribed social action goal of giving money, the curriculum is designed to be a beginning point for one's conversion away from the trappings of consumer culture. One-time giving of the group donation is not the mark of a transformed life; it is one step in expanding capacity for generosity.

Conclusions

The gospels and the book of Acts characterize the Jesus community as a new people—as leaving their possessions to follow, holding goods in common, giving money to those in need, and carrying on Jesus' ministries of healing and the social restoration that comes with it. One of the strengths of the discipleship practiced by the Simple Way is the commitment to relationships with the marginalized. The Simple Way embraces direct relational connection with the poor, and many members who move to the neighborhood are choosing downward mobility. The *Lazarus at the Gate* groups encourage a lifestyle of radical financial giving/living and examination of spending and saving, in light of the needs of others. I think it is possible that, through their reflection on Scripture and their current practices, those who participate in this program can also develop relationships with the people they serve, beyond just giving money. Contemporary theologian Roberto Goizueta comments in *Caminemos con Jesús*, "As a society, we are happy to help and serve the poor, as long as we don't have to walk with them where they walk, that is, as long as we can minister to them from our safe enclosures."[23] So generosity includes not just stewardship of money but openness to relationships across differences.

I think that both of the examples I share here demonstrate that people cannot seek the status provided by brand identity and accumulation of goods at the same time they are attending deeply to the needs of others in acts of self-giving. Christian leaders can learn from these examples to continue to place a high value on discipleship that runs seamlessly between our inner spiritual life and our actively living out the mission of Christ within our social contexts.

Both of these examples provide resources for resistance and for re-imagining a Christian lifestyle that extricates itself from some of the mechanisms of commodification. As noted earlier, practical theologians Miller and Kavanaugh describe our contemporary culture as one where spiritual longings are being met by substitutes for God and do not require anything of us in return. Just as Jesus invited a new order of allegiance with his disciples in their sociopolitical climate, so can today's discipleship challenge allegiances and attachments.

The Simple Way and *Lazarus at the Gate* are addressing concerns of faith and dominant materialistic culture. Both share a commitment to discipleship as their starting point. By virtue of their intentional discipleship, they demonstrate rich practices that reflect alternatives to the economic values and consumer practices of dominant culture. Both groups long to see justice and social change for the socioeconomically vulnerable. Both groups believe that how they use resources impacts others who have less control over their resources. Members of both movements have cultivated a deep dissatisfaction with the status quo of commodification and overconsumption and are challenging contradictions between beliefs and practices, and asking questions about the intersections of the social context and their theology. Looking at these two distinct discipleship experiments helps demonstrate that there is no one approach all must follow to be faithfully Christian within consumer culture. There will be great diversity in the paths that generate the transformation of religious life out of the "commodity form" to the "personal form."

However, it is interesting to note that these approaches were birthed in the context of cities. And, while cities may call out for our attention for their "problems," we observe that urban areas also present some interesting opportunities for growing in resistance to consumer culture. In our urban

23. Goizueta, *Caminemos con Jesús*, 199.

churches, there are opportunities for covenant relationships across international lines and social class, creating a new "normal" when it comes to definitions of material wants and needs. Because of the presence of people from many countries and multiple generations in our neighborhoods who may not have grown up formed by the ethos of a consumer culture, there is latent wisdom and practices that can embolden churches to live more biblically when it comes to stewardship and consumption. If we are only influenced by people who share our same ethnic and socio-income concerns and presumptions, we may not experience the shift in social consciousness that is needed to outgrow the restrictive context of consumerism.

This chapter has introduced ways that the underlying forms agreed upon by consumer culture are not the underlying forms of a disciple community, as found in the New Testament or seen in the everyday practices of communities such as the Simple Way and *Lazarus at the Gate* groups. Christian leaders who take into consideration the formative impact of the context of consumer culture in their approach to disciple-making need to present both alternate practices and beliefs. The following summary of recommendations is based on my observation of movements such as these and my own reflection and practices in freeing myself, my family, and my church community from the dictates of consumer culture:

(a) Become aware of trends in retail and advertising messages oriented to stimulate desire and consumption;

(b) Undertake media fasts and shopping-free periods to disengage from habits and messages of the marketplace;

(c) Promote theological reflection on culture as a spiritual discipline in the faith community;

(d) Encourage people to see themselves as creators of culture not simply consumers in it;

(e) Create small, intentional communities within the larger church for the practice of spiritual disciplines such as hospitality, Sabbath, and generosity—and to hold each other accountable in them.

This endeavor will require the whole community of disciples to embrace a holistic gospel. Our churches can be formative centers for cultivating a depth of conversion that will sustain new patterns of living, rejecting self-centered accumulation and instead living in service to others. When the church emphasizes the call to an others-centered life of discipleship, it poses a major challenge to the self-serving ethos of a commodified culture.

Consciously cultivating desire for God as more authentic than our desire for things is a crucial antidote to the idolatry of brands, commercial domination, and material hopes and dreams that too often dominate the hearts and minds of the culture, including God's people.

References for Further Study

Beaudoin, Thomas. *Consuming Faith: Integrating Who We Are with What We Buy.* Lanham, MD: Sheed and Ward, 2003.

Clapp, Rodney. *The Consuming Passion: Christianity and the Consumer Culture.* Downers Grove: InterVarsity, 1998.

Simon, Arthur. *How Much Is Enough?* Grand Rapids: Baker, 2003.

Turpin, Katherine. *Branded: Adolescents Converting from Consumer Faith.* Cleveland: Pilgrim, 2006.

A Conceptual Framework for Counseling City People

Carlot D. Celestin

> ... the waywardness of the simple will kill them,
> And the complacency of fools will destroy them. (Prov 1:32 NIV)

Introduction

Just like every city, the city of God, the church, witnesses how people strive to overcome painful and sometimes horrific journeys to build a home, a culture (i.e., a way of life); how they often live in horrific conditions to make money in order to create a better life for themselves, their children, and extended family members; how they work to procure this better life and often end up feeling abandoned by the very people they are striving to serve. Because of indifference and lack of appreciation on the part of the intended beneficiaries, providers may become angry or feel a sense of betrayal, disappointment, despair, and even rejection. Then, bitterness starts to grow. There is division in the nuclear family or in the family of God.

It may be that in the city of Enoch (i.e., the church), people may find themselves confused about how life should be lived. It is in such a time as this, when people's love for each other begins to grow cold, when belief in God is in a crisis mode, and when society begins to lose its raison d'être, that observers need to know what to do. More than any other living context in the world, the city is known for its "multiethnic and cultural diversity," as the place where life is shaped by the cultural mores that characterize it. The city is a place where one is dominated either by an ethnocentric worldview (i.e., the assumption that one's own worldview is the superior mode of thinking), or by a xenocentric worldview (i.e., the assumption that another worldview, particularly that of another culture or social group, is superior to one's own).[1] In every generation, whether or not one is an urbanite or a suburbanite, a Christian church member or a pagan, every human is searching for the understanding of the "self." We are all confronted with the challenges of finding romance in purity; discovering the meaning of life; having children or not, connecting with people (male and female) in the most meaningful way; balancing work, family, church, and pleasure; and solving conflicts with our loved ones and friends. Lack of social support becomes a particular need that may create stress; the need to adapt to a culture that seems hostile to one's worldview and ethnic association also creates stress. Consequently, the choices that we each make to meet those needs lead to life stressors, which may in turn lead to varying kinds of emotional distress, including depression—hence the need for Christian counseling to help eliminate, alleviate, or reduce that distress.

Operating in such a context, counseling can only be effective when a counselor learns how to transform conventions into connections; in other words, he or she learns how to engage in meaningful and mutual expressions of appreciation with others, while offering one's Christian experience and conviction to those of the same or of different faiths. The counseling model is "ethno-socio-cultural" (ESC).[2] The ethno-socio-cultural model is a guide developed by this author to encourage the therapist to be cross-cultural in his or her thinking when dealing with multi-ethnic and multi-generational contexts. The model offers reassurance and support to people in distress. The author assumes that, wherever there is relationship, there is relational stress. Hence, the counseling model must take seriously into consideration ethnicity, sociological perspective, and cultural norms, incorporating them into the counseling process. The ethno-socio-cultural model views people in their living cultural environment, their academic language, their institutional barriers, their stereotypes, their ethno-racial identity, their gender

1. Ethnocentrism—Everyone grows up in a culture that existed before their birth. The concept implies "this is the way things are," versus "the ways things are in this particular society," Fromm (1947, 1962). This is known as "the social unconscious." Egocentrism—each of us, beyond our culture, has specific details in his or her life—genetics, family structure and dynamics, special experiences, education, and so on—that affect the way we think and feel. Dogma—a natural conservative tendency to stick to what has worked in the past.

2. The concept is developed in the author's doctor of ministry thesis, presented to Gordon-Conwell (Celestin, 2008).

discrimination, and their oppression. This author argues that people are relational. Hence, they live in perpetual and inevitable conflict with one another. Therefore, they will need corrective emotional experiences.

This approach calls for "social-cultural adequacy," or the understanding of "cultural relativism," which maintains that each way of life is to be respected. Moreover, it asserts that the message of the gospel spreads most effectively across already existing relationships. Hence, ministry is virtually impossible unless one learns how to conduct interfaith dialogue. This chapter aims to offer a conceptual framework of Christian counseling that maintains Christian orthodoxy and psychotherapy from a pastoral care viewpoint. It will propose a psychotherapeutic strategy that will facilitate counseling from a Christian perspective through "ministerial presence." Having a level of interpersonal relationship will facilitate the therapist's desire to suggest corrective measures to help free clients from hostile or disparaging appraisals of themselves or of other people in their family, their neighborhood, and their church. As individuals and family units, neighborhoods, cities, and church communities are helped to become positive and whole, the New Jerusalem is being built.

What Is Mental Health?

Wherever relationship is required, stress and well-being must be part of the equation. Stress can lead to mental disorder. Hence, it is important to understand mental health. What is mental health? Mental health is a psychological state of well-being. It is characterized by continuing personal growth, a sense of purpose in life, self-acceptance, and positive relations with others. Mental health must be understood as the absence of mental illness. The field of study encompasses both mental health (preventive measures) and mental illness (clinical state of being). Positive factors that influence mental health are self-acceptance, or self-esteem, characterized by a positive evaluation of oneself and one's past experiences. The negative experiences that influence mental health are an unreasonable boss, turbulent family life, divorce, death of a spouse, loss of a job, illness in the family, economic hardship, unemployment, poverty, chronic stress, and unusual traumatic events (such as rape and natural disasters). These events can overwhelm a person's ability to cope and function effectively and may cause post-traumatic stress disorder (PTSD). The method of prevention is intervention. The preventive measure is to teach people coping skills before they encounter adversity, or early in the stages of a crisis, thus helping them to learn effective coping strategies to improve mental health and develop their sense of mastery and self-esteem.

In mental health terms, a crisis refers not to a traumatic event or experience, but to how an individual responds to the situation. Crisis intervention is focused on minimizing the stress of the event while providing emotional support to help the individual improve his or her coping strategies in the here and now context. Crisis counseling involves assessment, planning, and treatment. This involves listening to the client, asking questions, and determining what the individual needs to cope effectively with the crisis. As the counselor gathers information, he or she will define the problem while serving as a source of empathy and support, providing information about the current condition and the steps that the affected people can take to minimize the damage. While offering support, the counselor needs to seek to provide only the things that will contribute to stabilizing the affected persons at this time. Among other things, the most important ones are active listening, unconditional acceptance and reassurance, and nonjudgmental support during the crisis, which can all help reduce stress and improve coping skills.

How to Determine Therapeutic Needs

If there is conflict in a relationship that affects the normal functioning of the person in question, there is a need for intervention. If a child is experiencing conflict with teachers as academic and behavioral demands increase, there is a need for intervention. If a person is experiencing emotional distress (ups and downs) characterized by feelings of sadness, fear, and anger, there is a need for intervention. If there is grief, caused by loss due to parental divorce, separation, death, or displacement, there is a need for intervention. If a person is having relational issues and is emotionally and socially withdrawn, there is a need for intervention. If a child is a bully or is bullied, there is a need for intervention. Anyone who lives under constant stress and is in a perpetual conflict with others needs an appropriate intervention.

Doing a Diagnostic Assessment

Information gathering is discovering the individual's current living situation and life context. Before the interview or the first meeting, the counselor needs to have a clear idea why the person has come for help or has been mandated to receive assistance. This will help you to know what questions to ask. Be concerned about the physical setting or environment of the interview and establish rapport with the interviewee upon arrival. Good rapport produces cooperation and motivation. As the counselor is listening, he or she needs to note and describe symptoms, things that interfere with the person's ability to function. In the assessment, note demographic information, reason for coming, who made the referral, family of origin, family background, and rank in the family tree, any cross-cultural issues, education or vocational factors, background and medical histories. Has an addiction to substances affected relationships with family and friends? Is there trauma history? Are there legal involvements or other agencies involved with the person? Are there physical health and mental health histories for self and family? Counselors should do their own mental status exams by looking at the person's physical appearance and behavior, the apparent emotional state (the client's mood and affect), and by examining the thought processes of the individual, while observing the nonverbal-behaviors, such as attire, eye contact, body positioning, facial expressions, personal space requirements, tendency to touch, voice intonation, and tone.

Understanding the Three Major Theories of Psychotherapy

1. Sigmund Freud coined the method known as *psychoanalysis.* The word is derived from two Greek words: (1) *psyche,* which refers to the spirit or the soul—a term that stresses what happens at the level of the emotions, and (2) *analysis,* which implies the taking apart of something to examine it from a scientific viewpoint. Freud imagined that, by examining what happens to one at the level of spirit or soul (which is mostly emphasized), one can acquaint oneself with those aspects and understand the role they play in one's life. Psychoanalysis preoccupies itself with the understanding of the notion of the "self, identification, personality, the mind and soul, consciousness" and how they all relate to the body. Freud argues that humans are not the captains of their souls or the masters of their fate, but that they are driven by desires. He argues that a human being is tripartite (that is,

having 3 parts): (1) the "conscious" part of the mind that holds what one is currently aware of; (2) the preconscious part of the mind that holds ordinary memory, the ability to recall earlier events in one's life; and (3) the unconscious part of the mind that is not directly accessible to awareness. He correctly argues that humans live in perpetual conflict from the beginning to the end of their lives. Hence, Freud gives rise to the structural model. The *id* (German: es = "it"), which is the original component of personality, and functions entirely in the unconscious (following the "Pleasure Principle"). Then there is the *ego* (German: Ich = "I"), which displays the conscious, the preconscious, and the unconscious. Lastly, Freud talks about the *super-ego* (German: Über-Ich = "over I"), which is what we call our "conscience" and provides us with our prohibitions. To cope with the demands of life, people develop what he calls *defense mechanisms:* repression, denial, projection, rationalization, intellectualization, reaction formation, displacement, sublimation, and religious use of defenses. In so doing, Freud introduced the "talking cure," known as psychotherapy/counseling.

2. Thereafter, a reactive quest developed to disprove the Freudian model. *Behaviorism* was born, which focuses strictly on what is observable. Uninterested in mental processes, behaviorists focus more on action-oriented, classical conditioning or conditional stimulus. They deny that one's actions or behavior has anything to do with one's thought processes or feelings.

3. Much later, a third force of psychotherapy was introduced: *Person-centered and humanistic psychotherapy.* Carl Rogers, Abraham Maslow, and others sought ways to explain how people function and why. In so doing, they proposed a helping way. They asserted that the aim of therapy is to help people to increase their level of actualization. The focus is on free will, spontaneity, and creativity. Rogers talked about therapeutic qualities, in such terms as *congruence,* i.e., *genuineness,* which is resonance between internal experience and external behavior. He argues that the therapist needs to bring to the relationship with the client a transparency so that there is no hindrance in the outcome of the therapeutic process. He argues that the process includes what he calls *unconditional positive regard*: an attitude of interest and respect offered to the client that is unaffected by what the client reveals about himself or herself or how he or she acts. The concept is that the counselor does not belittle the individual as a result of his or her condition. The person-centered theory advocates for the use of *empathy*: the ability to enter the client's experience as if one were "in" the client, without

losing the "as if" quality. This is a skill that the therapist has to develop. It is not sympathy, but a greater response. Without completely merging, the therapist can still stand back and provide a theory of reflection of what he or she has heard. The idea is simply to provide commentary, clarifying the client's own thoughts and feelings. Being empathic is a validation of the client's self. This strategy helps clients develop a sense of self worth, thereby facilitating the desire for making an effort to heal.

Some Forms of Counseling and How They Are Conducted

1. *Family Therapy.* This intervention focuses on changes within the family system. It seeks to discover the nature of the family relationships and the resulting impact on the feelings, behavior, and psychological adjustment of every family member. The goal is to meet with the entire family in a family session to assess everyone's level of functioning in the family system.

2. *Couple's Therapy.* This intervention is the same as marriage counseling and/or marital therapy. The goal is to assess and to appraise the psychological distress that causes the couple to be dysfunctional. The focus is on behavior, emotions, conflicts, thought processes, and interpersonal relationships. In the therapy, the couple will identify what they perceive to be their main issues and resolve as a unit to satisfy their needs and remove the stressors that cause them pain.

3. *Stress Management.* Stress is produced by positive and negative life events and expectations. In therapy, the therapist assesses the client's level of wariness, racing thoughts, anticipation, fear, obsessive planning, depression, anxiety, cognitive rehearsal of expectations, evaluation of self and others involved in one's life events, assessment of potential outcomes from the events, and assessment of the importance of the events (in either a positive or a negative sense) in the client's life. Then, the therapist will seek to desensitize the client to reduce, alleviate, or eliminate the stress. Desensitization is a method to control anxiety and fear. It helps to overcome phobias. In this case, the therapist will need to discover the *informed processing concepts,* that is, the thinking process that drives the person. With such a strategy, the therapist attempts to understand some of the complex behavior that perhaps causes or at least contributes to the many issues that the client

(an individual, couple, or family) faces. In therapy, the therapist looks for speech and perception from the family discipline that may drive the client's pattern of decision-making. The goal is to get the client to realize the consequence of any particular behavior that he or she may choose to do.

4. *Cognitive-Behavioral Therapy (CBT).* There are several approaches to cognitive-behavioral therapy, including rational-emotive behavior therapy, rational-behavior therapy, rational-living therapy, cognitive therapy, and dialectic-behavior therapy. Cognitive-behavioral therapy is based on the idea that our *thoughts* cause our feelings and behaviors, not external things, like people, situations, and events. The benefit of this fact is that we can change the way we think to feel/act better, even if the situation we are in does not change. The therapist must be prepared to discuss explicit issues and behaviors behind the problems that family members face.

Counseling Defined and Applied

The word *counsel* (*sumboulion*) is ordinarily found linked to the verb "to take" or "to give," to express, with the idea of a practical end to be reached. A counselor (*sumboulos*) is an adviser (Rom 11:34). The term is often rendered as a consultation and/or a deliberate act noticed among people who have something in common or are united in a common cause (Matt 12:14; Mark 3:6). In Hebrew, the word for counselor is *yoes*, which means "one who gives advice or counsel" (Prov 24:6b). The word is used as a designation of the Messiah (Isa 9:6). It is also related to *paraklētos*, meaning "to advocate" (1 John 2:1). The word *paraklētos* is derived from the verb *parakaleō*, meaning "to call beside," as a "comforter" (John 14:16, 26; 15:26; 16:7). In John 16:7–33, the idea of a trial is again present, but here the Spirit is the disciple's counselor in relation to the world, and the context (16:7, 13–33; 15:26; 14:16–17, 26) might suggest the broader sense of "helper." In Acts 9:31, it is used to denote the idea of exhortation and encouragement. This is the role of the Holy Spirit in the life of the believer. The help of the Spirit consists in exhortation and encouragement (Matt 10:19–20; Mark 13:11; Luke 12:11–12).

In the Old Testament, we find the use of the word *naham*, which means "comfort." It is used mostly in bereavement (Gen 24:67). It can also mean "to console." Relatives and friends usually come to give comfort and consolation to the sufferers (Job 2:11) and to those who are alone (2 Sam. 10:2). It was a great honor bestowed upon someone when called upon to give counsel in times of sufferings (Job 29:25). However, one must be wary of how to give counsel and not to be incompetent like the miserable counselors of Job 13:4; 16:2. The goal of counseling is to bring comfort to the brokenhearted, to sympathize with the sufferer (Ps 69:20–21).[3] *The means was through ministerial presence.* One would come to visit, bring bread and wine (Jer 16:5, 7), as wine was used to comfort people in times of trouble (Prov 31:6–7). However, it was understood that there is no true comfort apart from God (Ps 69:20; 77:2); hence the major distinction between Christian counseling versus secular counseling[4] (Lam 1:2, 9, 16; Eccl 4:1). The proper work of the Holy Spirit of God is to comfort (Ps 23:4) the people (Isa 54:11–17), and make of "her wastelands like the garden of the LORD" (Isa 51:3 NIV). As the Great Shepherd (Isa 40:11), as one having the compassion of a mother (Isa 66:13), God comforts the sufferers, and in him they delight.

In the New Testament, we find the ordinary use of the word *paraklēsis* (Acts 8:31; 9:38; 16:39; 28:14, 20, etc.) always in general use for comfort (as in Acts 20:12; 1 Thess 3:7; 2 Cor 2:7), and in asking for help in the Synoptic Gospels as a common practice (Matt 8:5; Luke 7:4; Mark 5:18; 6:56; 1:40; 8:22). The Spirit of God encourages by giving us gifts for the perfecting of the church. Second Corinthians 5:20 talks about evangelistic activity as a

---

3. The book of Psalms is one of the most interesting books to help us understand the need for the "talking cure." People want to be listened to. In times of depressive experience, they sense that they are at the end of their rope. Sometimes, people experience life as meaningless and have no strength to go on. They feel forsaken and abandoned; then as a mourner, they cry out for help: "Why, O LORD, do you reject me and hide your face from me?" (Ps 88:14). The question is why and why? In the experience of life, there is an important mix between that which is spiritual and the emotions of the soul. At times people feel isolated, lonely, and desperate. It is at this point of vulnerability when they turn to their pastor for help.

4. Professional Christian Counseling presents a variety of designations, such as Licensed Pastoral Counselors (LPC), Licensed Clinical Pastoral Counselors (LCPC), and Certified Christian Counselors (CCC), or Ordained Pastors who are trained as counselors. Secular counseling refers to those professionals who become licensed by their state or they may work for a licensed clinic or agency to provide a variety of counseling services. Typical designations include Licensed Professional Counselor (LPC), Licensed Marriage and Family Therapist (LMFT), and Licensed Mental Health Counselor (LMHC). The bottom line when seeking a counselor is to find one that is actually motivated to help you from your theological worldview and assumptions.

means of offering help to people in need of salvation. To proclaim the gospel is also part of *paraklēsis* in 1 Thessalonians 2:3, as well as Acts 9:31; 2:40; and Luke 3:18. In so doing, the hearers will be moved to action. The good news about the Thessalonian church "comforts" Paul (1 Thess 3:7), as does the good news from Corinth (2 Cor 7:6). The Bible tells us to "admonish" one another. To admonish is to counsel (Heb 13:22; 1 Pet 5:12; Jude 3; Phil 2:1; Rom 12:1, etc.). We admonish in the name of Christ (Phil 2:1; 1 Cor 1:10; 2 Cor 10:1; Rom 12:1). The Holy Spirit is at work in us when we proclaim his counsel to people (1 Cor 14:3, 31; Acts 15:28, 31). Barnabas was one who was known as a pastoral counselor (Acts 11:24). In Hebrews 6:18 and 12:5, the advice of Paul is understood as comforting by exhortation and encouragement given to people. Paul comforted the churches in their afflictions (cf. Col 2:2; 4:8). He himself is comforted by Philemon (Phlm 7). Paul talked about an eternal comfort and good hope (2 Thess 2:16).

The *Imago Dei* is the concept that humanity is made in the image of God. God created humans male and female (Gen 1:26–27). In this principle, we believe that humans are living spirits because they are from God and that each human is an organic whole because each is created to be in relation with other humans. Hence, every function, both mental and physical, is an activity of a self.[5] This is the Christian dimension, which includes the Greek term *pneuma,* meaning breath or spirit, standing for the self-conscious center of all experience. The mental processes and functions, such as thinking, feeling, willing, and perceiving, we designate by the Greek term *psyche,* meaning soul. The Greek word *soma* is used for body structure and function. In personality theory, the focus is on how the individual person affects others. In the city context, culture and personality are intertwined. The counselor needs to understand the growth and development of personal or social identity as it relates to the surroundings of the individual in community.[6] Hence the focus is on speech and observable posture and/

5. The "self" is a psychoanalytic perspective that speaks of an image to represent the conscious and the unconscious mental representations of oneself. They distinguish between the self-representation, i.e., a person's inner representation of himself by which he experiences life in relation to significant others. The other concept of the "self" is "self-object," indicating a loss of boundaries, where the distinction between the "true self and an object" are blurred.

6. The field of culture and personality is born out of Freud's psychoanalysis. The theory of culture and personality explains relationships between customs and behaviors in different societies. Culture and personality emphasize distinctive characteristics of people in certain cultures and attribute these unique traits to the different methods of living. Personality is the key factor in defining individual uniqueness and shaping an

or facial expression. The focus is holistic, the whole person in life and the whole person in action as one affects others.

Researchers argue the human personality is composed of five core traits, each one being completely independent of the others.[7] These five traits include the following: (1) openness—the general ability of an individual to be imaginative, original, and artistic; (2) conscientiousness—the measure of one's dependableness, organizational skills, and degree of responsibility; (3) extraversion—the degree to which a person is able to relate to and enjoy the presence of other people; (4) agreeableness—whether a person is friendly, cooperative, and trusting; and (5) neuroticism—the degree to which one is high strung, intense, and emotionally unstable. According to the Big Five theory, these five traits are the simplest way to describe a personality accurately.

It is important to give attention to what researchers in the field of psychology refer to as the four temperament types.[8] Knowing these will help the counselor to have a better understanding of a client's personhood. The four temperament types include the following: (1) the sanguine temperament, which is fundamentally impulsive and pleasure-seeking; sanguine people are sociable, charismatic, creative, sensitive, compassionate, thoughtful, forgetful, sarcastic, and confident; (2) the choleric temperament, which is fundamentally ambitious, aggressive, energetic, passionate, and dominant, either highly disorganized or highly organized, assertive, easily falling into deep and sudden depression and prone to mood swings; (3) the melancholic temperament, which is introverted, very thoughtful, creative, compassionate, and perfectionistic; and (4) the phlegmatic temperament, which is fundamentally relaxed and quiet, can be lazy, accepting, and affectionate, shy, enjoying stability, resisting uncertainty and change, being consistent, relaxed, calm, rational, curious, observant, and passive-aggressive. All around us, such persons make up our neighborhoods, our cities, our churches.

---

individual's course through life. To explore and better understand the five-factor model, read James R. Beck, *Jesus and Personality Theory* (1999); and Oliver et al., *Handbook of Personality* (2008).

7. Ibid.

8. Ibid.

Helping Is about the Person, not the Method—How to Do Counseling

Counseling aims to provide insight into the ways core beliefs and values are reflected in one's behavior. In counseling, the client is challenged to discover and/or to reexamine these values. The role of the counselor is to remain open and as nonjudgmental as possible, recognizing that there are multiple paths toward fulfilling the therapeutic needs; however, as a facilitator, the intervener must address some key elements that would lead the client to reorient his or her life. Christian counseling is by nature integrative. It takes a serious view of the psychotherapeutic model within the light of biblical theology. In pastoral counseling, the issue of how spirituality influences the clients must be front and center. Spiritual and religious matters are therapeutically relevant, ethically appropriate, and potentially significant topics for the practice of counseling in both the religious and the secular settings. Hence, Christian counselors must be prepared to deal with spiritual matters when engaging their clients. During the assessment process, it can be ascertained how certain beliefs and practices of the client can be useful focal points for exploration. Theology informs one's way of life. People live according to their belief system. The answer to the question, "Why do people do what they do?" is often simple: their actions flow from their beliefs. Faith, whether obvious or assumed, is a potential source of meaning and a powerful source of purpose. It can contribute to the understanding of one's own powers of thinking, feeling, deciding, willing, and acting. For the healthy Christian religious person, wholesome, godly faith is a critical source of strength where positive values and behaviors lead to physical and psychological well-being. Exploring faith and integrating it with other therapeutic methods will enhance the therapeutic experiences.

Counseling must be first and foremost structured to emphasize the importance of a healthy organizational process for family functioning and the well-being of all family members. One of the most important things that a therapist needs to take into consideration while working with a client is interpersonal relationships. Counseling is about relationship. Relations theory is an offshoot of psychoanalytic theory that emphasizes interpersonal relations, primarily in the family and/or the community. In order for relationship to be all that God intends it to be, particular interest must be placed on the inner images of the self versus others and how those two manifest themselves in this interpersonal, situational relationship. The task of therapy is to alleviate the early anxieties and modify the harshness of internalized objects and inner conflicts. This is done through analyzing, interpreting, focusing on the ills, the transference and resistance, the fantasies, fears, and feelings of dissatisfaction. The very first step in counseling is to help individuals to make sense of their problems in their own eyes to increase the client's awareness about the reality of their situations. The focus is on highlighting the operation of the unconscious mental process of each individual. The counselor needs to seek for the cause of the apparent (and often perpetual) conflict that exists in the mind and soul of the individual.

To arrive at this juncture, the counselor needs first to focus on the observable behaviors and the mental processes leading the individual to actions. Second, the counselor will need to understand the pattern of the individual's decision making. Is he or she making decisions or simply reacting to his/her environment? This is an emphasis on conscious experience. The counselor needs to understand the individual's worldview on issues like grace, acceptance, mercy, and whether the client is weak or strong in judging, truth telling, etc. Third, the counselor will need to interpret what is going on in the mind of the person, while helping the person to listen to him or herself, God, and the web of influences that are affecting personal beliefs and actions. From this vantage point, the counselor will help the individual to realize his or her problem. There will be a focus on free will, spontaneity, and creativity as a means to encourage the person who perhaps has embraced a deterministic view of life. The Christian counselor needs to know that clients want to be all that they can be—both in the manner that God wants them to be and in the way they themselves would like to be seen and understood. If this becomes each client's reality, then the call is for an act of agency. He or she needs to learn empathy for others and how to dialogue with them. These skills are key for surviving in the communities of the city and of the church.

In the treatment process, the counselor needs to create human resources for the person in need. Human connection is the driving force behind behavior. It is in the context of human relationship that clients can look at what happens to themselves and other people in life and learn from these experiences. This is a principle of modeling in learning style, a cognitive revolution approach that teaches people to act on the basis of how they think and experience life. In so doing, the counselor is encouraging individuals to become more transparent, more in touch with their own feelings and, thus, more authentic as integrated human beings. The counselor will help individuals understand that they have choices. The question is what choice would they make when they are left to choose? What would be the outcome of that choice? How would they find meaning in the midst of the apparent chaos some choices may cause? The solution is about being in the moment, being alive, aware, and able to respond correctly to what is going on. The counselor needs to be with the client to guide and to reorient. The client must not be abandoned or left alone in the search process. The counseling process is a partnership, an alliance formed to traverse a long and difficult journey. The story is about the individual in question, not the counselor. Each individual client does possess some potential for growth and perhaps a will to succeed. But being impaired and overwhelmed by the demands of life stressors, one's strength has become faded in the journey. What is needed is guidance to help each person realize his or her potential and discover unused opportunities. In Christian counseling the care is not just for mental health but also for the care of souls.

Conclusion—Listening Is the Heart of Counseling

The counselor should not interfere with the counseling process by his or her inability to be attentive. In this social dynamic interaction, the counselor has an opportunity to discover blind spots that impair the vision of the client. The way to arrive at this juncture is to learn to listen to the client telling his or her story. The story of the person's life is the vehicle to discover not only what troubles the soul but also how to bring about the talking cure. Listening is so important. The Bible says, in Mark 4:23, "If anyone has ears to hear, let him hear" (NKJV). The apostle James tells us, "You must understand this, my beloved: let everyone be quick to listen, slow to speak . . . " (Jas 1:19 NSRV). In Proverbs 18:13, we read, "He who answers before listening—that is his folly and his shame" (NIV). The word *listen* occurs more than two hundred times in the Bible. The counselor needs to learn listening skills and also the roadblocks to listening. Here are some hindrances to listening: preconceived notions, over-quickness to respond, mental distraction, inability to discriminate between the client's issues and one's own issues, emotional responses, and attacking the client. The counselor needs to know that the issues that the client brings to the session are not personal to the counselor but to the client alone. The client must not be interrogated or be put under attack for what he or she has said in a session, no matter how offensive it may be.

Other pitfalls to keep clear of include the following:

1. Avoid sexual misconduct and the abuse of power.

2. Therapists should not engage in sexual intimacies with current or former patients or anyone not their spouses.

3. Do not accept as patient someone with whom you had a prior relationship or for whom you had intimate feelings.

Remember that something may be legal, but unethical and/or immoral. Christian ethics and/or biblical value are the code word for the pastoral counselor. Behave biblically! Also remember the counselor's role is not to agree or to disagree with the client. His or her role is to provide support leading to change. So during the session, he or she must learn to paraphrase what is being said and be empathic (the ability to see things from the perspective of the person who is talking without interference). A key for urban (and all) counselors is to remember Colossians 4:6: "Let your conversation be always full of grace, seasoned with salt, so that you may know how to answer everyone" (NIV).

Counseling people in or connected to or referred to the city church is a key activity in helping bring in God's New Jerusalem of healthy, godly communal living. As all individuals heal, they bring wholeness, empowered by God's Spirit, to the family, the neighborhood, the city, and the church. Not every counselor is competent for every cause. Competence is defined by training. When there is conflict of interest, make a referral.

References for Further Study

Borgman Dean. *Hear My Story: Understanding the Cries of Troubled Youth.* Peabody, MA: Hendrickson, 2003.

Clinebell, Howard. *Basic Types of Pastoral Care and Counseling: Resources for the Ministry of Healing and Growth.* Nashville: Abingdon Press, 1984.

Jones, Stanton L., and Richard E. Butman. *Modern Psychotherapies.* Downers Grove: InterVarsity, 1991.

Miller, William R., and Kathleen A. Jackson. 2nd ed. *Practical Psychology for Pastors.* Eugene, OR: Wipf & Stock, 2010.

Olson, G. Keith. *Counseling Teenagers: The Complete Christian Guide to Understanding and Helping Adolescents.* Loveland, CO: Group Books, 1984.

Sanders, Randolph K. *Christian Counseling Ethics: A Handbook for Therapists, Pastors, and Counselors.* Downers Grove: InterVarsity, 1997.

Spencer, Aída, et al. *Marriage at the Crossroads: Couples in Conversation about Discipleship, Gender Roles, Decision Making, and Intimacy.* Downers Grove: InterVarsity, 2009.

Worthington, Everett L. *Marriage Counseling: A Christian Approach to Counseling Couples.* Downers Grove: InterVarsity, 1989.

Wright Norma, H. *The New Guide to Crisis and Trauma Counseling.* Ventura, CA: Regal. 2003.

Yarhouse, Mark, and James N. Sells. *Family Therapies: A Comprehensive Christian Appraisal.* Downers Grove: InterVarsity, 2008.

Under One Steeple

Biblical and Theological Foundations for Sharing Church Space[1]

LORRAINE CLEAVES ANDERSON

Introduction: Biblical Foundations

> But when the Son of Man comes in his glory, and all the angels with him, then he will sit upon his glorious throne. All the nations will be gathered in his presence, and he will separate the people as a shepherd separates the sheep from the goats. He will place the sheep at his right hand and the goats at his left.
>
> Then the King will say to those on his right, "Come, you who are blessed by my Father, inherit the Kingdom prepared for you from the creation of the world. For I was hungry, and you fed me. I was thirsty, and you gave me a drink. I was a stranger, and you invited me into your home. I was naked, and you gave me clothing. I was sick, and you cared for me. I was in prison, and you visited me."
>
> Then these righteous ones will reply, "Lord, when did we ever see you hungry and feed you? Or thirsty and give you something to drink? Or a stranger and show you hospitality? Or naked and give you clothing? When did we ever see you sick or in prison and visit you?"
>
> And the King will say, "I tell you the truth, when you did it to one of the least of these my brothers and sisters, you were doing it to me!"

---

1. This chapter has been adapted from *Under One Steeple: Multiple Congregations Sharing More Than Just Space.*

Then the King will turn to those on the left and say, "Away with you, you cursed ones, into the eternal fire prepared for the devil and his demons. For I was hungry, and you didn't feed me. I was thirsty, and you didn't give me a drink. I was a stranger, and you didn't invite me into your home. I was naked, and you didn't give me clothing. I was sick and in prison, and you didn't visit me."

Then they will reply, "Lord, when did we ever see you hungry or thirsty or a stranger or naked or sick or in prison, and not help you?"

And he will answer, "I tell you the truth, when you refused to help the least of these my brothers and sisters, you were refusing to help me."

And they will go away into eternal punishment, but the righteous will go into eternal life.[2]

Jesus' injunction strikes terror in our hearts, and rightfully so. How can we be faithful to God in caring for the imprisoned, the hungry, the destitute, the orphan, the widow, the alien—with integrity and uncontrived love? After all, Scripture is replete with references like Psalm 146:7–9:

> He gives justice to the oppressed
> and food to the hungry.
> The Lord frees the prisoners.
> The Lord opens the eyes of the blind.
> The Lord lifts up those who are weighed down.
> The Lord loves the godly.
> The Lord protects the foreigners among us.
> He cares for the orphans and widows,
> but he frustrates the plans of the wicked.

What is God specifically asking of us? How can we, in fact, put ourselves in the shoes of "those who are weighed down," learn from them, and reach out in Jesus' name? And what about those among us who are the weighed-down newcomers? How do we relate to the established church?

One powerful, emerging paradigm, particularly visible in urban areas, is space-sharing within church buildings. As the broader Christian community reaches toward the New Jerusalem-style culture, in our own generation, in our own city, sharing church space is one simple means of creating unity. Wholehearted sharing of more than just space can catapult New Jerusalem-style kingdom of God churches across our cities. The

2. Matt 25:31–46. All citations are from the New Living Translation (NLT), unless otherwise noted.

United States, for example, continues its urbanization trend far beyond the global rate,[3] with proliferating immigrant populations stimulating growth.

> Currently, population growth is fastest among minorities as a whole, and according to the Census Bureau's estimation for 2012, 50.4 per cent of American children under the age of one belonged to minority groups.[4]

Many newcomers arrive bewildered and traumatized, or ecstatic yet homesick, and thus eager to gather for prayer—but where can they congregate for much-needed worship, Bible study, and camaraderie? Often they must live with family members and friends in crowded apartments, while some have no recourse but to live in temporary public shelters. And when they do begin assembling for worship, few groups can afford a mortgage, and rents are often prohibitive.[5]

Places for worship are needed, yet many church buildings are being sold to developers or transferred to non-Christian groups at an alarming rate.[6] In fact, a google search of "Church Buildings for Sale" reaps thousands of listings: "find great deals on churches for sale!"[7]

But Jesus' words that the "gates of Hades will not overcome it [my church]"[8] couldn't be more true! People emigrating from volatile situations bring with them a right-now-in-the-moment trust in God that refuses to neglect meeting together, "as is the habit of some."[9] And so they crowd into living rooms, schools, basements—anywhere they can squeeze—to praise

---

3. Wikipedia states, "As of January 1, 2013 the Unites States had a total resident population of 315,281,000, making it the third most populous country in the world. It is a very urbanized population, with 82% residing in cities and suburbs as of 2008 (the worldwide urban rate is 50.5%)," "Demographics of the United States," online: http://en.wikipedia.org/wiki/Demographics_of_the_United_States.

4. Wikipedia, "Demographics of the United States"; Carol Morello and Ted Mellnik, "Census: Minority Babies Are Now Majority in United States," *Washington Post*, May 17, 2012, online: http://articles.washingtonpost.com/2012-05-17/local/35458407_1_minority-babies-census-bureau-demographers-whites.

5. Retail space in Boston ranges from $10 to $50 per square foot, per 1000 minimum square feet, according to Oodle Marketplace, online: http://officespace.oodle.com/boston-ma/retail-property-for-rent.

6. Tim Reid, "Banks Foreclosing on Churches in Record Numbers," Los Angeles (Reuters), March 9, 2012.

7. Online: http://www.loopnet.com/Churches-For-Sale/.

8. Matt 16:17–18 NIV.

9. Heb 10:25 NRSV.

and pray and support one another in their common sojourn within this foreign, often hostile land.

If only United States congregations would open their eyes to see and their ears to hear how God has used immigrants for decades to answer our prayers for revival! Boston's Emmanuel Gospel Center has tracked and documented what Dr. Douglas Hall has called, "The Quiet Revival," in which "over the last thirty-five years, an average of one new church has been planted in Boston or Cambridge every forty-five days."[10] Immigrant start-up churches have sparked an unprecedented spiritual renewal within our cities, bringing prayer and faith and godliness with them from distant lands. Still, finding worship space remains a huge struggle in our decimated economy. It is an opportunity from God to practice what we preach and extend an open hand of Christian friendship to our new friends, who are, in fact, God's gifts to the U.S. church. Instead, many congregations conclude that sharing their building, their furniture, their antiques, their history, and their nostalgia is an unworthy inconvenience and have very tragically missed God's blessing. Some churches have dissolved rather than share their property with an immigrant group, even though Jesus clearly said,

> "You fool! This very night your life is being demanded of you. And the things you have prepared, whose will they be?" So it is with those who store up treasures for themselves but are not rich toward God.[11]

But, thank God, many churches *are* opening their doors, unlocking cabinets, shuffling furniture, and revamping schedules. In Boston and Cambridge alone, one in three churches shares their building with one or more additional congregations.[12] Many of these churches are alert to the enormous, God-sent blessing in "submit(ting) to one another out of reverence for Christ,"[13] by sharing all that we are and all that we have *out of* our reverence for Christ Jesus—the One who submitted his all in love for us.

What if owners of church buildings could envision themselves as homeless shelters for churches? Rather than sharing a church building for ulterior motives of image or financial survival, what if a church

10. T.C. Moore, "No, Sir: New England Is Already Experiencing Revival—You Just Need Eyes to See It," online: http://www.beingtc.com/new-england-conversion-church-planting-quiet-revival.

11. Luke 12:20–21 NRSV.

12. Duemling, "Shared Worship Space."

13. Eph 5:21 NIV.

re-envisioned her ministry as a "Shelter for Homeless Churches," à la Matthew 25:35–46? What if God poured into us the heart of Oskar Schindler whose desperation to shelter Jews led him to wail after the Allied liberation, "But I could have saved one more!"[14]

In order to align our ministries with the heart of God, we must allow God's passion for the orphan, the widow, and the foreigner—indeed, the literal and figurative beneficiaries of the gospel itself—to saturate our hearts and inform our decisions:

> You must not mistreat or oppress foreigners in any way. Remember, you yourselves were once foreigners in the land of Egypt.
>
> You must not exploit a widow or an orphan. If you exploit them in any way and they cry out to me, then I will certainly hear their cry. My anger will blaze against you, and I will kill you with the sword. Then your wives will be widows and your children fatherless.[15]

In this chapter, we will explore two of many theological/biblical foundations for sharing church space, followed by five of numerous principles, and two of countless true stories, all of which point to the New Jerusalem Church (with a capital C) of Jesus Christ spreading across our great cities. May God renew our minds and ignite our hearts.[16]

Theological Foundations: The Incarnation as Sacrificial Hospitality and the Ascension as Radical Reciprocity

The Incarnation as Sacrificial Hospitality

Articulating the incarnation, with all of its intra/extra-mortal subtleties, has proven a baffling challenge for theologians and disciples for two millennia. How true was Paul's prophetic statement that people would consistently stumble over the person of Christ Jesus,[17] half grasping the enormity of God-in-flesh, half believing it. By becoming a human being, God not only stood in solidarity with humanity, but then welcomed humanity into His very life! The Creator unselfishly became one of those he created, in order to invite those very ones into his perfect world. God did not have to be-

14. Dir. Steven Spielberg, "Schindler's List," 1993.
15. Exod 22:21–24.
16. Sentiment of Rom 12:1–2.
17. 1 Pet 2:4–8.

come human and endure slander, abuse, torture, execution, and relegation by his created ones. Yet, at some point in eternity, God decided to come into the very world he created,[18] in order to bring into his own reality his created ones.[19] Sacrificially, God puts out the welcome mat through justification, cleans our inner homes through purification, turns up the music by sanctification,[20] explains his motives in written, scriptural detail,[21] and woos us to himself,[22] never manipulating or forcing. Jesus simply invites: "Come to me, all of you who are weary and carry heavy burdens, and I will give you rest."[23]

God is in every regard the Consummate Host who sacrifices all for the sake of enlarging his family. Then Jesus takes out a mortgage on us, pays it in full, and moves in, no strings attached, proclaiming, "I am in you."[24] And that's not all. He then goes the additional step of adding a lot onto his spacious new development project and inviting us into the property, rent-free: "Anyone who loves me will obey my teaching. My Father will love them, and we will come to them and make our home with them."[25] Their home with us! Incredible.

Is this not divine, sacrificial hospitality, embodied in the person and work of Jesus, the Christ! Can we make the leap, now, and turn the binoculars on ourselves and the homeless churches knocking on our doors? Can we welcome others into our gathering spaces in the same way that God in Christ welcomes us into his heaven—his presence? "Just as I have loved you," says Jesus, "you should love each another."[26]

By allowing the spectra of incarnation to saturate our understanding, surely we can slide over and share what we have and who we are with other churches. In truth, all that we have—including our buildings and their accouterments—belongs to God, and all that we are (becoming) is the direct result of God's work in our lives:

18. John 1:10–18.
19. John 17:23–24.
20. Ps 40:3.
21. Ps 119:105.
22. John 7:37.
23. Matt 11:28.
24. John 14:20 NIV.
25. John 14:23 NIV.
26. John 13:34.

And so, dear brothers and sisters, I plead with you to give your bodies to God because of all he has done for you. Let them be a living and holy sacrifice—the kind he will find acceptable. This is truly the way to worship him. Don't copy the behavior and customs of this world, but let God transform you into a new person by changing the way you think. Then you will learn to know God's will for you, which is good and pleasing and perfect.[27]

We can never out-sacrifice or out-host God-in-Jesus. We can, however, prayerfully and actively emulate his sacrificial hospitality and seek his grace in extending the hand which has already been extended to us by our Lord:

There is more than enough room in my Father's home. If this were not so, would I have told you that I am going to prepare a place for you? When everything is ready, I will come and get you, so that you will always be with me where I am.[28]

The Ascension as Radical Reciprocity

Secondly, Jesus in his ascension provides an unparalleled model of radical reciprocity by showing us both how to *leave well* and how to *pass the torch*. Consider the succession of farewell scenes between Jesus and his disciples recorded in Luke 24:31–53. He decreases and his disciples increase. Jesus carefully readies them for the end of his earthly ministry and the beginning of theirs in seven steps and seven key Scripture passages: preparation, peace, pain, partaking, perspective, promise, and empowerment.

1. Preparation: Jesus opens the eyes of their understanding. What they could not figure out or discern suddenly became clear when Jesus drew close: "Suddenly, their eyes were opened, and they recognized him. And at that moment he disappeared!"[29]

2. Peace: Jesus bathes them in soul-deep peace. Earlier[30] he spoke about a peace unlike any the world had ever proffered, and now he liberally gives it away:

27. Rom 12:1–2.
28. John 14:2–3.
29. Luke 24:31.
30. John 14:27.

And just as they were telling about it, Jesus himself was suddenly standing there among them. "Peace be with you," he said. But the whole group was startled and frightened, thinking they were seeing a ghost! "Why are you frightened?" he asked. "Why are your hearts filled with doubt?"[31]

3. Pain: Jesus rehearses the indignities and torture inflicted on him, and vicariously on his disciples. He does not dismiss or minimize the trauma, but emphasizes it for balanced review: "'Look at my hands. Look at my feet. You can see that it's really me. Touch me and make sure that I am not a ghost, because ghosts don't have bodies, as you see that I do.' As he spoke, he showed them his hands and his feet."[32]

4. Partaking: Next Jesus eats with them, infusing ordinary with divine; bread and wine into eternal, even daily symbols. Fellowship assumes new depth and tenderness. Over the centuries since that last meal, many Christian groups have come to understand the elements as transcending symbolism to become a means of sacramental grace. Food always strengthens the body, the soul, the mind, and the bond of community—and now, regardless of our theological stance, everyday victuals are permeated with superlative meaning: "Still they stood there in disbelief, filled with joy and wonder. Then he asked them, 'Do you have anything here to eat?' They gave him a piece of broiled fish, and he ate it as they watched."[33]

5. Perspective: Fifthly, Jesus conceptually revolutionizes their outlook on all that occurred during his incarnation. He literally renews their minds[34] and enables them to launch a global movement of forgiveness and peace with God:

> Then he said, "When I was with you before, I told you that everything written about me in the law of Moses and the prophets and in the Psalms must be fulfilled." Then he opened their minds to understand the Scriptures. And he said, "Yes, it was written long ago that the Messiah would suffer and die and rise from the dead on the third day. It was also written that this message would be proclaimed in the authority of his name to all the nations,

31. Luke 24:36–38.
32. Luke 24:39–40.
33. Luke 24:41–43.
34. Rom 12:2.

beginning in Jerusalem: 'There is forgiveness of sins for all who repent.' You are witnesses of all these things."[35]

6. Promise: Next, Jesus reminds them of his binding promise to clothe them with the Holy Spirit, but they must not rush ahead of grace. Instead, he instructs, they are to wait, similar to their resting in the Lord each Sabbath. Then when the Father sends the Holy Spirit, they will be ready to give to others while receiving from God; to minister in Jesus' name while being refilled by the Holy Spirit. There is to be a lifestyle of serving God that is radically reciprocal: "And now I will send the Holy Spirit, just as my Father promised. But stay here in the city until the Holy Spirit comes and fills you with power from heaven."[36]

7. Empowerment: Lastly, Jesus turns everything over to his bewildered disciples and leaves. He ascends to his Father and to theirs, to his God and to theirs. They ecstatically hustle off to wait for their imminent empowering, gradually realizing that their Lord has just entrusted them with a high, holy task. He has passed the baton to them, and they will pass it on to others, but each will pass it back to God regularly for ongoing empowerment. They will fulfill their commission only through a reciprocal relationship with God and with each other, where God works *in* them, then *through* them. This is not to be the work of control freaks, but of brothers and sisters in Christ. Such work is only accomplished in a relationship of give and take with the Creator of the Universe, the Savior of the world. In ascending to heaven, Jesus reciprocated their trust in him by trusting them. What an honor! What a mystery!

> Then Jesus led them to Bethany, and lifting his hands to heaven, he blessed them. While he was blessing them, he left them and was taken up to heaven. So they worshiped him and then returned to Jerusalem filled with great joy. And they spent all of their time in the Temple, praising God.[37]

Ponder the breadth of Jesus' prophecy: "I tell you the truth, anyone who believes in me will do the same works I have done, and even greater works, because I am going to be with the Father."[38] Likewise, he prays pas-

35. Luke 24:44–48.
36. Luke 24:49.
37. Luke 24:50–53.
38. John 14:12.

sionately for his followers of all times to be so united, in such collaboration, that women and men in every culture will be irresistibly drawn into his family:

> Just as you sent me into the world, I am sending them into the world. And I give myself as a holy sacrifice for them so they can be made holy by your truth. I am praying not only for these disciples but also for all who will ever believe in me through their message . . . . I have given them the glory you gave me, so they may be one as we are one. I am in them and you are in me. May they experience such perfect unity that the world will know that you sent me and that you love them as much as you love me . . . . I have revealed you to them, and I will continue to do so. Then your love for me will be in them, and I will be in them.[39]

To share our resources gladly and equitably, we will, by default, find ourselves practicing radical reciprocity with new friends and colleagues. We will discover a freedom indeed that nourishes not the kingdom of "First Urban Church," but the kingdom of God, citywide—the New Jerusalem. We will more easily be able to relinquish our responsibilities to others, and, at the proper time, leave ourselves, entrusting what was never ours to begin with (i.e., property and ministry) to the next generation of called leaders. And they, in turn, will more easily draw on our experience and prayer to help fuel their vision and confidence.

Reciprocity in ministry isn't radical at all, when we realize how Jesus hands off his ministry to us, much like the four-hundred meter relay, and is himself the *relay anchor*. May we live the joy and experience the load-lightening satisfaction of doing likewise.

Practical Principles for Sharing Church Space

Sharing should be kindergarten-easy. But for many adults, inviting a cross-cultural group to move into their building sends shock waves of unexpected challenges.

1. Patterned after the Attributes of God

   Ministry collaboration bears witness, in very practical ways, to the personality of God displayed in his communicable attributes. How we share resources must be patterned after God's character, including

39. John 17:18–20, 22–23, 26.

God's knowledge, wisdom, veracity, goodness, love, grace, mercy, longsuffering, holiness, righteousness, and justice.[40]

If God has entrusted us with resources for spreading the gospel, then we are beholden to pattern our use of them after the very intrinsic nature of the One who shares them with us. We must strive to be knowledgeable and wise, truthful and genuinely good, motivated by love, showing grace and mercy, long-sufferingly slow to anger and avoiding all despicable sin, as righteous as we can be, filled with a heart for justice—all to the best of our ability, by God's grace. People see the excellence of God not through our beautiful rooms or up-to-date technology, not through our worship style or persuasive preaching, not through our compelling programs or riveting outreach, but through something far deeper that requires our submission to the Holy Spirit. *People see the excellence of God through our love*[41]—the over-arching attribute of God embodied in Jesus and his followers, the body of Christ in this world. Love is the most powerful attribute of God, the one at which we his people are the least adept.

2. Guided by Jesus' Commandments

The Torah contains over six hundred laws which Jesus, in his inimitable wisdom, summarized into two commandments:

> Jesus replied, "'You must love the Lord your God with all your heart, all your soul, and all your mind.' This is the first and greatest commandment. A second is equally important: 'Love your neighbor as yourself.' The entire law and all the demands of the prophets are based on these two commandments."[42]

The sharing of our resources, including our buildings, furniture, technology, time, and books, always hails back to Jesus' two commandments. If we could master these two guidelines, the church of Jesus Christ could then literally change the world. Sharing would be second-nature; buildings would be places to gather; turf and stuff wars would end; and the world would know us by our love. People would be attracted to the Messiah in droves: "Lord, forgive us for holding tight to that which perishes—the temporal stuff around us. 'For the things we see now will soon be gone, but the things we cannot see will

---

40. Berkhof, *Systematic Theology*, 64–76.

41. John 13:35.

42. Matt 22:37–40.

last forever."[43] Help us instead to love others sacrificially as you love. O God, help us to love."

3. Joined by Collaborators (Co-labor-ators)

Heaven continues to be populated by people from every nation and tongue and tribe, as attested to in Revelation:

> After this I saw a vast crowd, too great to count, from every nation and tribe and people and language, standing in front of the throne and before the Lamb. They were clothed in white robes and held palm branches in their hands. And they were shouting with a great roar, "Salvation comes from our God who sits on the throne and from the Lamb!"[44]

Our co-labor-ators in Christ are most definitely from every corner of the globe, from all two-hundred-and-twenty-plus countries of the world. An astonishing wealth of insight, Christian experience, human stories, God-sightings—and, yes, humility—awaits those who cross linguistic and cultural bridges. The body of Christ is not to be divided. As a gift to our Lord, let us actually be the answer to his prayer in John 17: "I am in them and you are in me. May they experience such perfect unity that the world will know that you sent me and that you love them as much as you love me."[45]

Paul often referred to his "co-laborers in the gospel," mentioning many of them by name at the end of his letter to Rome. Like them, we too are part of something much bigger than ourselves and our parochial ministries. We benefit greatly by sharing our space and resources with immigrants from around the globe, for, together, we paint a more poignant portrait of Revelation 7 and the body of Christ worldwide. Others in "our space" (which, remember, is God's, not ours) sharpen us and remind us daily that God's kingdom spans time and place and personage and belongs to the One who sits on the throne forever.

4. Challenged by the Expected

Expect challenges. They will come. We cannot be naïve, even when ministering alongside brothers and sisters in Christ. So anticipate the ugly brokenness of human nature to rear its head, but do not allow it

43. 2 Cor 4:18.
44. Rev 7:9–10.
45. John 17:23.

to separate you from your co-laborers, for they are works-in-progress like you. Psalm 55 describes the festering wound that results when one co-laborer hurts another:

It is not an enemy who taunts me—
I could bear that.
It is not my foes who so arrogantly insult me—
I could have hidden from them.

Instead, it is you—my equal,
my companion and close friend.

What good fellowship we once enjoyed
as we walked together to the house of God.[46]

Instead, may we practice the power of the apology and the fruit of forgiveness for the sake of God's kingdom and the salvation of souls. Some have described the late Dr. J. Edwin Orr as the renowned authority on prayer. Dr. Orr "explains how [our] focused prayers can affect [our] community, city, state, nation, and world. [He] illustrates how the spiritual revivals of the past are the direct result of concerted, extraordinary, and united prayer."[47]

There is more to be gained than cooperation and friendship when co-laborers in Christ collaborate well; there are societal implications and revival at stake. We cannot afford to permit inter-personal and inter-church challenges and squabbles to derail the progress of the Holy Spirit. Lives, souls, and shalom itself depend on our unified collaboration and sharing. Challenges are normal; reconciliation is Christ-like.

5. Strengthened by Pure Joy

Lastly, sharing our resources, our buildings, our belongings, our time, and ourselves readies inside us a feast of gourmet quality. When we surmount the challenges that lead to compromise, esteem others better than ourselves,[48] determine to love as Jesus loves, and steep our beings in the attributes and nature of God, we will be surprised by unspeakable joy! Obedience brings joy—not begrudged obedience,

46. Ps 55:12–14.

47. "The Role of Prayer in Spiritual Awakening," featuring Dr. J. Edwin Orr, back cover of DVD, Campus Crusade for Christ (Irvine, CA: Randolf Productions, 2006).

48. Phil 2:3 NIV.

but prayerful, "iron sharpens iron"[49] joy that, over time, forms a deep-down, peaceful contentment that no disappointment or grief can destroy, "for the joy of the Lord is your strength!"[50] Even Jesus, facing unique agony, encountered his executioners, focusing himself on authentic, visceral joy, pretentious in no way.[51] And Peter and Silas, imprisoned for co-laboring in the gospel, emerged with contagious, even mysterious joy![52] Worry, anxiety, and selfishness deplete our joy and consequently our effectiveness. Authentic joy and wise collaboration, on the other hand, infuse us with strength, confidence, and boldness. Remember how Peter and John's challenges before the Jerusalem Council led to remarkable unity among believers? Acts 4 records,

> And now, O Lord, hear their threats, and give us, your servants, great boldness in preaching your word. Stretch out your hand with healing power; may miraculous signs and wonders be done through the name of your holy servant Jesus.
>
> After this prayer, the meeting place shook, and they were all filled with the Holy Spirit. Then they preached the word of God with boldness. All the believers were united in heart and mind. And they felt that what they owned was not their own, so they shared everything they had. The apostles testified powerfully to the resurrection of the Lord Jesus, and God's great blessing was upon them all. There were no needy people among them, because those who owned land or houses would sell them and bring the money to the apostles to give to those in need.[53]

Let the joy of sharing our church space and belongings strengthen us. Enjoy collaborating!

Two True Vignettes[54]

In its heyday, United Church was the hub of the neighborhood, attracting four-hundred-and-fifty regular attendees every Sunday and offering a myriad of weekly smaller groups, pancake breakfasts, AA meetings—you name

49. Prov 27:17 NIV.
50. Neh 8:10.
51. Heb 12:2.
52. Acts 16:25–40.
53. Acts 4:29–35.
54. Actual names have been changed.

it. That was before the demographic shift several decades ago. Now the pastor feels blessed to have ten in worship and forty still on the church roll. When Rev. Z. approached her about *renting* space, she was all too thrilled to offer the side room, for eight hundred dollars per month, from two to four o'clock. Within six months, the renting church desperately needed a much larger space, nursery, Sunday School rooms, and storage for instruments and sound equipment. Could its members meet a couple nights a week for prayer, and would it be okay if they cooked their specialty foods twice a month? Grumbling, whining, irritation ensued—until the only child in United Church's congregation saw some children of Pastor Z.'s at the playground, who called out: "Come to the kids' party at church Saturday night!" The rest is history. The next Sunday, eight of United Church's folks visited the afternoon worship and were so touched by the Spirit of God that within two years United Church sold the building to Pastor Z.'s church and joined their flourishing membership!

Across town, St. Paul's had invited Rev. T.'s group of eighty-five to rent space, and even share worship together. It sounded hospitable enough, until Rev. T. was told their offerings would go into St. Paul's account, their name would be St. Paul's, and seventy-eight-year-old Pastor Grumwold would preach each Sunday, in English, of course. Rev. T. could hold a semi-monthly class for his folks, and visit them in their homes, but they must learn the host church's culture, language, music, liturgy, and respect St. Paul's property and leadership. Naturally, Pastor Grumwold would be *the* pastor, and Rev. T. his part-time assistant. (Naturally.) Coming from a culture where elders are held in high esteem, Rev. T. agreed, assuming this was the honoring way to begin his church. Sadly, five years later they still continue this distorted, upside-down relationship. A wheelchair lift has been installed for Pastor's access to *his* pulpit.

> Is there any encouragement from belonging to Christ? Any comfort from his love? Any fellowship together in the Spirit? Are your hearts tender and compassionate? Then make me truly happy by agreeing wholeheartedly with each other, loving one another, and working together with one mind and purpose.

> Don't be selfish; don't try to impress others. Be humble, thinking of others as better than yourselves. Don't look out only for your own interests, but take an interest in others, too.[55]

55. Phil 2:1–4.

May God enable us not only to reach *for* the New Jerusalem, but to reach it.

Resources for Further Study

Anderson, Lorraine Cleaves. *Under One Steeple: Multiple Congregations Sharing More Than Just Space*. House of Prisca and Aquila Series. Eugene, OR: Wipf & Stock, 2012.

Duemling, Bianca. "Shared Worship Space: An Urban Challenge and a Kingdom Opportunity." *Emmanuel Research Review* 74 (January 2012). No pages. Online: http://www.egc.org/err74.

Johnson, Susan. "Inspired Partnerships." *Amazing Space* 4:2 (1998) 2.

Villafañe, Eldin. *Seek the Peace of the City: Reflections on Urban Ministry*. Grand Rapids: Eerdmans, 1995.

Villafañe, Eldin. *Beyond Cheap Grace: A Call to Radical Discipleship, Incarnation, and Justice*. Grand Rapids: Eerdmans, 2006.

Building *Shalom* in the City

Education Provides a Bridge between the Church and the Secular Community

DAVID MARTINEZ

Introduction

Early in my pastoral career, I became interested in the challenges faced by recent immigrants to the United States from Latin America. As a new arrival myself, from Puerto Rico, I could identify with their struggles. But I had no idea how profoundly this would affect my ministry.

In this chapter,[1] I will begin by describing the conditions that Hispanic immigrants are dealing with, based on experience with my flock. Then I will show how we are helping them cope with their situation at the church where I serve as pastor. Finally, I will discuss the theological basis of our efforts in the context of the New Jerusalem.[2]

---

1. Most of the following material is derived from my thesis for the doctorate in ministry (Complex Urban Settings Track), entitled "The Role of Education as a Tool for Addressing the Social and Spiritual Needs of First-Generation Immigrants: El Tabernáculo Evangelico, A Case Study." I am indebted to my professors at Gordon-Conwell Theological Seminary, Center for Urban Ministerial Education (CUME), Boston, MA, and in particular to my advisors, Eldin Villafañe, Alvin Padilla, Douglas Hall, and William David Spencer for helping me to develop the tools to guide my congregation toward the model of the New Jerusalem.

2. Biblical citations are from the King James Version (KJV), except where otherwise noted as NRSV (New Revised Standard Version), NIV (New International Version), and NKJV (New King James Version). Spanish citations are from the Reina Valera Version (1960).

An Unexpected Transition

One day, more than twenty years ago, I received an unexpected call from my district supervisor, who asked me to consider becoming the pastor of an urban evangelical church in East Boston, Massachusetts. At the time, I was the pastor of a growing congregation in Brockton, about 35 miles from Boston. There I had a full-time professional position with a regular salary and was given living quarters for my family. The inner-city church, however, had only 24 members, nearly all of them undocumented immigrants from Latin America. With scant economic resources, they had little to offer a pastor with a growing family. My wife and I nevertheless decided to accept this challenge, seeing it as a manifestation of God's will. You might say that ours was a mission of faith.

A Story of Struggle

As we could immediately see, my new congregation was a flock with special needs. On the economic level, it is common knowledge that new Hispanic immigrants often live at the edge of subsistence. In extreme cases, people showed up at my church with no money at all or a place to stay. Sometimes church members, or their friends, would take them in temporarily, until they could find an apartment. At other times, church members would contribute clothing and even provide dishes and kitchen utensils where needed.

For recent immigrants, especially those who are undocumented, the battle for survival takes place in the shadows. Often working for cash in the underground economy, they receive few if any company benefits, and enjoy little job security. To economize, Hispanic people often share apartments and look after each other's children, so both husband and wife can work.

On the social level, Hispanics face an array of barriers. Their lack of proficiency in English, as well as their accent, creates the impression that they are mentally slow. Added to this are physical characteristics of skin tone and hair that set them apart from the main population. Prejudices about Hispanics include the beliefs that they are inclined to be dirty, likely to be involved in crime, and live on welfare. While it is not my purpose here to disprove prejudices about Hispanics, I can say with confidence that, especially in the case of undocumented immigrants, the incentive to seek official welfare help or become in any way involved with legal authorities is very weak. With the possibility of deportation looming over their heads, compounded by the difficulty of communication, recent Hispanic immigrants prefer to avoid the scrutiny of police or government agencies.

Lending a Hand

Soon after my arrival in East Boston, I found myself assisting church members who were applying for visas, helping them to complete forms in connection with work and residency permits, and coordinating with paralegals and attorneys handling the cases of people with proceedings before the Immigration and Naturalization Service. All of these activities have one thing in common: they require proficiency in English, including the ability to read and write. Although it is higher now, the educational level of our congregation was equivalent to the fourth or fifth-grade level, by my estimate, when I first arrived. A few members could not read the Bible, even in Spanish.

To address this situation, we began offering literacy classes in Spanish, as well as English as a Second Language (E.S.L.) training. Another effort involved the tutoring of high school students, usually of high school age, by adult volunteers from the congregation. We also launched a G.E.D. high school equivalency program, using materials supplied by the state of Massachusetts.

Such educational activities as these raise questions about our mission as a church. Should the church be expected to do more than supply spiritual guidance? As it is, we may be giving the impression of a church serving as a social service agency disguised in clerical garb. Against this I could counter with the argument that churches flourish when they are relevant to the needs of the people they serve. I could even cite the example of Jesus, to show that the church has an obligation to minister to its parishioners in more than spiritual matters alone. Biblically, this conclusion is expressed by the words, "For I was an hungred, and ye gave me meat: I was thirsty, and ye gave me drink: I was a stranger and ye took me in" (Matt 25:35). But this kind of pragmatic response does not tell us what the Bible has to say about the educational role of the church. Few of us would dispute the notion that education is a good thing. Nevertheless, what are the moral and theological underpinnings, if any, for the church as educator? After all, isn't that what the schools are for? In the rest of this article, I intend to address this question.

The Church as Educator

If I were to ask Hispanic clergy—especially the leader of an immigrant, evangelical congregation, like myself—whether the church is in a position to help its members improve their conditions in this country, I have no doubt the answer would be yes. But if I were to ask whether the church has an obligation to try and raise the educational level of the membership, I would get a more qualified response. Why is the church more reticent in the area of education? Perhaps a little historical investigation can offer some insight.

Are We a Church or a School?

In my experience, I have often encountered Hispanic evangelical pastors who do not have professional career qualifications, beyond Bible Training Institutes. For example, as a teacher in such a Bible school, I had a student who was functionally illiterate, and, therefore, could only take examinations orally. He was subsequently ordained and became the pastor of a Pentecostal Hispanic church in Connecticut.

Among evangelical congregations, especially those with a more fundamentalist outlook, emphasis is placed on literal interpretation of the Bible. In many cases, the pastors of such churches do not encourage their members to develop themselves educationally. They seem to espouse the negative viewpoint of the Old Testament Preacher who warned: "Of making many books there is no end; and much study is a weariness of the flesh" (Eccl 12:12). They also base their attitude toward formal education on such biblical verses as "[God] also hath made us able ministers of the new testament; not of the letter, but of the spirit: for the letter killeth, but the spirit giveth life" (2 Cor 3:6),[3] or Paul's words at his trial before King Agrippa: "And as he [Paul] thus spoke for himself, Festus said with a loud voice, Paul, thou art beside thyself; much learning doth make thee mad" (Acts 26:24).

Cultural Isolationism

The problem for the immigrant church lies deeper than the attitude of pastors. For many of my parishioners, especially those who are foreign

3. In contrast, if Paul had no appetite for scholarship, he wouldn't have requested of his assistant Timothy, "So when you come, . . . bring me my books" (see 2 Tim 4:13).

born, the church represents a cultural and religious refuge in the midst of a strange and sometimes hostile country. It is a place where they can be themselves and affirm their common values. As a Hispanic myself, I understand this deep-seated spiritual and social need. Naturally, people want to feel comfortable in the place where they worship. Such an orientation, however, looks inward. It favors a conservative perspective on religious doctrine and discourages outreach toward the wider community.

As an immigrant church, we do not want to be so preoccupied with matters of doctrine and custom that we descend into cultural narcissism. We could easily forget that Jesus was not Hispanic; nor for that matter is it possible that he ever heard a word of Spanish or English. I fail to see how a bias toward ethnocentrism provides a path toward spiritual growth for a congregation. Theologically, it contravenes our Christian mission, as I understand it, which is to bear witness to the gospel. It also affects the outlook of my flock toward the tool of education.

A Question of Identity

The problem of ethnocentrism raises the question of who we are. Is our identity as an immigrant church consistent with biblical teaching? Certainly, in the Old Testament there are abundant examples of immigration. Many of these immigrants were essentially nomads with no specific destination in mind. Adam, for example, was an involuntary emigrant from the Garden of Eden, but also an immigrant to the unspecified land in which he settled, presumably to the east of Eden (Gen 3:24). Noah, likewise, was a wanderer, although by water instead of land. Abraham is perhaps the archetype among the immigrants of the Bible. Acting on a command from God, he and his family struck out for Canaan, although famine forced them to continue as far as Egypt. All of these biblical personages—including Moses and the children of the Exodus—were responding to a command from God. In my own church, however, I have yet to encounter anyone who gave a call from God as his or her reason for immigrating to this country. Does this mean that the Bible has no message for immigrant churches?

Not surprisingly, I find my answer to this question in the New Testament. Jesus himself has a particular connection with immigrants. As John P. Rossing pointed out, "Jesus was an immigrant."[4] He understood the

4. Rossing, "*Mestizaje* and Marginality," *Theology Today* 45:3 (October 1988) 293–304.

experience of isolation and rejection. Jesus gave an eloquent expression to this situation: "Foxes have holes and birds of the air have nests, but the Son of man has nowhere to lay His head" (Luke 9:58 NKJV).

The birth of the first church at Jerusalem on Pentecost, as described in the book of Acts, reveals one overriding theme: unity across cultures. We find that the birth was attended by a diverse array of followers that included Parthians, Medes, Elamites, Egyptians, Libyans, "strangers of Rome," Cretans, and Arabians (Acts 2:5–11). This was multiculturalism. Yet amidst this diversity of languages and cultures, we learn that these early Jewish Christians were nevertheless "of one heart and one soul . . . they had all things common" (Acts 4:32 NKJV). The manifestations of the Holy Spirit on the day of Pentecost (Acts 2:2–12) represent the culmination of this unifying tendency.

Against this, does the Bible say anything in favor of an educational role for the immigrant church? I believe the answer is yes, and I find that the Bible promotes the values of education in many ways.

The Bible, History, and Educational Theory Promote Education

Old Testament Roots

From the earliest part of the Scriptures, where Cain asks, "Am I my brother's keeper?" (Gen 4:9 NKJV), the church has been confronted with the challenge of how to minister to humanity. Throughout the Old Testament, the clergy are depicted as a literate class. Moses, for example, receives the ten commandments which, according to Jehovah, "I have written; that thou mayest teach them" (Exod 24:12). Moreover, the order applies not to the clergy only, but to the entire people of Israel: "And thou shalt write them [the commandments] upon the posts of thy house, and on thy gates" (Deut 6:9). For the Jewish people, at least, universal literacy is an indispensable part of their religion. The Bible, however, takes the matter a step further: "These are the commandments . . . which the LORD your God commanded to teach you, that ye might do them in the land whither ye go to possess it" (Deut 6:1). Here, admission to the promised land is linked to a knowledge of the law, acquired through instruction.

The book of Proverbs contains numerous exhortations regarding the value of learning: for example, "Take fast hold of instruction; let her not go: keep her; for she is thy life" (4:13). In Proverbs, we find what may be the first advertisement for adult education: "Give instruction to the wise, and they will become wiser still; teach the righteous and they will gain in learning" (9:9 NRSV). Regarding the instruction of children, the advice is equally straightforward: "Train children in the right way, and when old, they will not stray" (22:6 NRSV). Proverbs 31, which describes the capable woman, contains the verse, "She speaks with wisdom, and faithful instruction is on her tongue" (31:26 NIV). Likewise, the book of Psalms is replete with references to wisdom and instruction. The psalmist repeatedly begs to be taught by God and says of those who are blessed, ". . . their delight is in the law of the LORD, and on his law they meditate day and night" (Ps 1:2 NRSV).

In the Old Testament, then, moral law and educational values are inextricably tied together. Beyond this, however, the New Testament adds a further dimension.

New Testament Roots

"Love thy neighbor as thyself" (Matt 22:39) were the words of Jesus to the Pharisees. This commandment asserts the responsibility of the churches for the well-being of their members. Moreover, as if to eliminate any question about the meaning of "neighbor," Jesus provided the parable of the Good Samaritan (Luke 10:29–37), in which a neighbor is defined as anyone who is in need of help. From this viewpoint, the role of the church becomes a broad-based obligation to serve the needs, not only of parishioners, but of humanity in general. In the four books of the gospel, Jesus is frequently cast in the role of teacher. For example, the Sermon on the Mount is preceded by the words, "And he opened his mouth and taught them, saying . . ." (Matt 5:2). On several occasions, Jesus is referred to as rabbi, or teacher of the law. In one particular incident, "Straightway on the sabbath day he entered into the synagogue, and taught. And they were astonished at his doctrine, for he taught them as one who had authority" (Mark 1:21–22).

The Apostle Paul emphasized the importance of teaching in his advice to the early Christian community: "We have gifts that differ according to the grace given to us; prophecy in proportion to faith; . . . the teacher, in teaching" (Rom 12:7 NRSV). Paul clearly saw teachers as an indispensable part of the church: "And God hath set some in the church, first apostles, secondarily prophets, thirdly teachers . . ." (1 Cor 12:28). In his second epistle to Timothy, Paul says, "All scripture is inspired by God and is useful for teaching, for reproof, for correction, and for training in righteousness" (2 Tim 3:16 NRSV).

Historical Roots

The role of the church as a guardian of literacy reaches back to the scribes of the ancient synagogue, who recorded and preserved Jewish law. In the early and medieval Christian era, churches in many areas were the only repositories of books and culture. Through the Middle Ages, the Franciscan, Benedictine, and Jesuit orders were bastions of learning. Several prominent figures of church history also compiled translations of the Bible: for example, St. Jerome, Martin Luther, and John Wycliffe.[5] Many universities in Europe were founded under the auspices of the Roman Catholic church, whose educational role remains conspicuous to this day. The connection between churches and public education continues today with involvement in controversies involving school prayer, creationism, birth control, and abortion.

Educational Theory: Education for Transformation

From my discussions with pastors and church members, I've found that the term *education* means a variety of things to different people. For some, education represents a technique for the development of an organization. But for others—especially those with a more conservative outlook—education is simply training for reading, writing, and basic computation. Education for higher purposes is considered an illusion. Traditional Hispanic believers ask, "Porqué tanto estudio? Jesús viene mañana. Todo se quedará con el anticristo" ("Why study so much? Jesus comes tomorrow. The Antichrist will get everything else.")

This attitude concerning education prevails in many churches of my denomination, among pastors and parishioners alike. Before considering how the traditional outlook might be changed, it seems appropriate to ask: Why should it be changed? The answer, I find, has to do with the very

---

5. Standard works of church history that are widely available include Kenneth Scott Latourette, *A History of Christianity*; Justo L. González, *The Story of Christianity*; and Diarmaid MacCulloch, *A History of Christianity*.

purposes of the church itself, and in particular with the mission of immigrant churches like the one I serve, as well as others in my district.

At the time we initiated educational programs at the Tabernáculo, I envisioned these efforts as helping our members to advance themselves politically and socially, and to adjust to the characteristics of American culture. Later, I saw education as a way of fostering the spiritual development of my flock. But contemporary thinking in this area has taken the process a step further.

Writer Lawrence O. Richards, among others, has described the purpose of Christian education in terms of *transformation*. "Christian education," he explains, "is concerned about a process of personality and character transformation."[6] Thus, while educational activities serve to promote social justice, as well as economic progress, they also incorporate a much larger dimension. James W. Fowler, in discussing the work of analysts in the field of practical theology, pursues the point:

> Practical theologians see this discipline as concerned not just with
> ... the mere formulation of persons for "adjusted" living in society.
> Rather, they see practical theology . . . as intrinsically concerned
> toward personal and social *transformation*.[7]

Jesus described this change as being "born again" (John 3:3 NIV), while the apostle Paul put it this way: "If anyone is in Christ, there is a new creation" (2 Cor 5:17 NRSV). Lawrence O. Richards stresses the need for "a whole-person focus" in any approach to Christian education. That is, we must connect our educational programs to practical, real-life situations. Jesus similarly used illustrations from everyday life to explain his concept of the kingdom to ordinary people. The gospels report that he distinguished himself in formal learning situations by demonstrating skill at teaching in the temple. But he also addressed the physical needs of the people, as in his feeding of the 5,000 (John 6:1–13).

Likewise at the Tabernáculo, we began by focusing on the specific needs of our members, but often ended up serving the church organization as a whole and even the wider community outside. Therefore, initially, our educational programs focused in a secular direction. But, under the auspices of my denomination, the Assemblies of God (A/G), we also established a Bible Institute in 2001. Our purpose was to enable well-motivated

---

6. Richards, *A Theology of Christian Education*, 25.
7. Fowler, "Practical Theology," 42:1 (April 1985).

church members to become certified for the practice of ministry as A/G clergy. Graduates of this four-year curriculum have gone on to serve as faculty, while others have assumed leadership roles in churches throughout the New England region.

In 2001, I traveled to Guatemala together with several other church leaders and attended a seminar on church growth that featured home study groups and leadership development. After I got back, I worked with a few key people in the church to develop a one-year program that we refer to as our Leadership Academy. Our objective was two-fold: First, to show our members how to work together as a team to achieve the goals of the church; second, to provide leaders for our home study groups.

The Leadership Academy offers students an overview of the church in all its various aspects. We explain the biblical motivation for our efforts as a church and provide training in the processes that enable us to function. Over the years, we have developed a team that is fully capable of coordinating a church service or home study group meeting without any intervention from me. Thus, through the Bible Institute and the Leadership Academy in particular, we have been able to develop the talents of some church members to preach the gospel. The benefit accrues not only to our church, but also to other congregations where our members are occasionally invited as guest preachers.

As I read more deeply in educational theory, I realized that our approach to learning at the Tabernáculo has parallels with principles of educational theory. The approach to learning I was following was similar to that advocated by John Dewey, who maintained that students learn best when they become engaged in a process of problem solving. As described by Lois E. LeBar, "Dewey held that education was essentially problem solving, the reconstruction of experience. . . . School should provide . . . a learning situation because it causes him to think."[8] That is, students acquire knowledge most effectively when they are confronted with the challenge of analyzing a set of conditions and devising ways to improve them—an especially apt description of various circumstances faced by members of my immigrant congregation.

Jesus likewise encouraged independent thinking in a subtle way, when he advised, "Render therefore unto Caesar the things which be Caesar's, and unto God the things which be God's" (Luke 20:25). Thus, he left to

8. LeBar, *Education That Is Christian*, 46.

the believer the problem of how to discriminate between the two. Again, he proved himself a champion of the individual vis-à-vis the organization, when he declared, "The sabbath was made for humankind, and not humankind for the sabbath" (Mark 2:27 NRSV). Finally, Jesus affirmed to a crowd of believers, "Ye shall know the truth, and the truth shall make you free" (John 8:32). Clearly, Jesus was not referring to the accepted conventions of his time, the so-called "truth" of his day. Rather he was talking about something yet to be revealed and subsequently understood, using the powers of mind given to us by the Creator for our own emancipation. Thus, Jesus espoused the unfettered use of our mental abilities to meet the challenges of life.

Except insofar as literacy is necessary to read the Bible, is education essentially non-religious in nature, as so many suppose? On the contrary, religious educator Gabriel Moran sees an inseparable link between religion and education. For Moran, education and religion exist in a state of tension. As Moran puts it,

> Abstractly defined, religion and education collide. But placed in relation to the idea of development, the education and the religious achieve a working relationship. Education needs a religious impulse or else its concern to put things in order closes off further development and thereby undoes the meaning of education. Religion needs educational restraint and challenge so that its impulse to transcend the world does not lose touch with the world to be transcended.[9]

Robert W. Pazmiño put it simply: "Education at its best must be God-centered."[10] This connection perhaps explains why, until fairly recently, school prayer was common in public schools. An early proponent of the link between religion and education was John Wesley. Harold W. Burgess cites the example of Methodists who dedicated themselves to educating the poor and working classes of nineteenth-century England during the first decades of the Industrial Revolution:

> For Wesley, education was not secondary to evangelism, it was bound together with it. Wesley was convinced that the results of Methodist revivalism could be made permanent only as new members could be properly educated.[11]

9. Moran, *Religious Educational Development*, 184.

10. Pazmiño, *Fundamental Issues in Religious Education*, 31.

11. Burgess, *Models of Religious Education*, 58.

At the same time, Burgess notes, Wesley recognized wider needs: "Accomplishing his broad vision required addressing the need for basic education, including the essentials of hygiene and medicine."[12] Likewise, in the Tabernáculo, we include topics like AIDS, sexually transmitted diseases, drug addiction, and alcoholism in our curriculum for youth, as presented by some of our members who work in the medical field.

Thus, it becomes clear that the term *secular education*, perceived as a worldly activity, is a misnomer. Education cannot be separated from religious ethics and values. Traditionalists among the Pentecostals I serve seem afraid that education can somehow be divorced from the spiritual. Fundamentalist Hispanics in particular make a distinction between secular and religious education. From their viewpoint, they can legitimately ask, Why should the church get involved in education? After all, isn't our primary role to preach the gospel?

The Response of the Church

The answer to the above question encompasses the mission of the church itself. We recall that Jesus said to Peter, "Upon this rock I will build my church" (Matt 16:18). The image of an inanimate rock may tend to obscure the fact that Peter was a living man, and the church was therefore a living entity. The concept of the church as the "body" of Christ (1 Cor 12:12) emphasizes the organic nature of every congregation, with the potential for growth and decay. Living organisms, of course, need nourishment to survive, as well as the capacity to prevail against hostile circumstances. To Paul, the survival of the church depended on the ability to align itself with the example of Jesus Christ, "who will sustain you to the end" (1 Cor 1:8 ESV).

As a preacher of the gospel, I base my ministry on the Great Commission: "Go ye into all the world, and preach the gospel to every creature" (Mark 16:15). For me, this command of Jesus to his disciples encapsulates my ministry first and foremost. Indeed, before he was taken up, Jesus reiterated this behest to his disciples one last time, enjoining them with the prophecy: "You shall be witnesses to Me in Jerusalem, and in all Judea and Samaria, and to the end of the earth" (Acts 1:8b NKJV). Does this mean that Jesus perceived his ministers to be nothing more than peripatetic spokespeople for the faith, preaching the kingdom as they traveled about?

12. Ibid.

No, because his vision was deeply rooted in a concept of community, which he encapsulated in the prophetic phrase: "Thy kingdom come, Thy will be done in earth, as it is in heaven" (Matt 6:10).

Where does this leave immigrant churches like the Tabernáculo? While modern churches have interpreted the Great Commission as a mandate to send missionaries to remote parts of the world, the immigrant church finds itself in the reverse situation. Instead of traveling to foreign parts, the immigrant church receives believers who are themselves aliens. A biblical precedent is found in the command of Moses: "Love ye therefore the stranger: for ye were strangers in the land of Egypt" (Deut 10:19). Jeremiah too was especially concerned that we "oppress not the stranger" and "do no violence to the stranger" (Jer 7:6; 22:3).

How does the immigrant church go about fulfilling this Old Testament behest? I believe that the success of our mission depends on our collective ability to develop and practice a theology of peace (*shalom*).

A Theology of Peace

St. Paul famously referred to the church as a corporate entity (literally, the *body* of Christ): "For we are members of his body, of his flesh, and of his bones" (Eph 5:30). The church, then, must pick up where Christ left off, when he finished his ministry on earth. At the point of farewell, he said to the disciples, "Peace I leave with you, my peace I give unto you" (John 14:27). Thus, we know that peace was fundamental to his original mission.

How is this peace to be achieved? As Christians, we join together to promote the peace of Jesus Christ. To us, peace is the fruit of God's justice and mercy, to which we bear witness in at least three important ways. To illustrate, I will focus on our unique experience as a marginal church, touching on various ways we have addressed the issues confronting us by strategies like our home study group program and other organized activities.

Response to Contemporary Needs of Addressing the Issues Facing the Modern Immigrant Church

In my home area of southern New England, there has been a considerable influx of Hispanic people in recent years, many with little education and limited economic prospects, as we have seen. As a result, Hispanic churches face major challenges to their traditional religious role in Latino society. In addition to serving their spiritual needs, the churches find themselves dealing with a variety of social, economic, and educational factors confronting their parishioners. Pastors are often asked to supply counseling of various kinds to the members, as they seek help with the transition to American society. Some examples include the following:

- *Careers.* Advice on how to look for work and the types of training available.

- *Legal.* Assistance in applying for work permits, residency, and citizenship.

- *Personal.* Help in managing family relationships and advice on options available.

In many cases, the pastor is the only source for such counseling because, in addition to the language barrier, church members are not familiar with other options that may be open to them. Under such circumstances, the church, in effect, takes on the task of facilitating the adjustment of foreign immigrants to American culture.

At the same time, the second generation of Hispanics is coming along rapidly. These are children and young adults who were either born in the States or who know little of their home in Latin America. Some of them are even losing their Spanish language skills. Growing up between two cultures sometimes creates special problems for them, as we shall see later on. My family confronted an example of this cultural gap soon after we arrived in Boston. Some church members objected to the fact that my young daughters used English during services. These congregants were afraid of cultural contamination since the adults, in particular, speak Spanish as their first language. Our Christian education programs and youth ministries are particularly affected.

Taking Change into Account while Maintaining Focus

When I began my ministry with the Tabernáculo Evangelico (then called the Iglesia Monte Carmelo), we shared a building with two other church groups. Nevertheless, with God's help we acquired our own facility, in the nearby suburb of Malden, two years after my arrival in 1991.

By moving, did we lose our urban focus? Providentially, the answer is no, although the decision was controversial for us at the time. Some members resisted the idea, and we lost a few of our flock as a result. But eventually our losses were compensated by the fact that we were slightly ahead of the curve, demographically speaking. Some families moved to Everett close by, which had relatively few Hispanic immigrants living there at the time. Since then, the foreign-born population of the area has continued to grow.[13]

Having recognized their situation, I began first by preaching regularly to my flock about the obstacles they are dealing with. My purpose wasn't merely to empathize with them, but mainly to address their needs. I wanted to convince them of the need for educational advancement, without which they would remain disadvantaged both socially and economically in American society. Unless they became educated in English, they would continue indefinitely to be victims of political injustice. What does education do for them? It provides them with an avenue to political power by enabling them to communicate credibly about issues affecting Hispanics in particular. In this way, they can be taken seriously by those in the power structure. For those who aspire eventually to become United States citizens, with the right to vote, I tell them that education will enable them to think critically about the choices that they will have to make. Thus, education, when used rightly, serves to promote social justice.

The Struggle for Justice

What should be the scope of service programs in the immigrant church? Jesus had a simple answer; he said to Peter, "Feed my sheep" (John 21:17b). Perhaps it's my cultural bias showing, but I prefer the Spanish rendering of this verse: "Apacentar mis ovejas." The word *apacentar* is especially apt because it evokes the word *paz* or *peace,* and, therefore, expresses the Hebrew concept of *shalom.* But the notion of *paz* implies more than the alleviation of hunger or physical suffering; it also refers to the fruits of social justice, or *shalom.*

J. Alfred Smith of Oakland, California, touched on this distinction in the autobiographical account of his long pastoral career, noting, "By the 1990s I realized that the church had more to do than provide social services for the entire community. We had to fight for social justice."[14] In other

13. Michael Levenson and Yuxing Zheng, "Immigrant numbers up 15% in state since 2000," *Boston Globe* (16 August 2006).

14 Smith, *On the Jericho Road,* 224.

words, feeding the sheep involves more than the satisfaction of material needs. Jesus put it another way when he said, "One does not live by bread alone, but by every word that comes from the mouth of God" (Matt 4:4, quoting Deut 8:3 NRSV).

The situation of my congregants fits the description of the poor and oppressed in the denunciation of Israel by the biblical prophet Amos: "They sell the righteous for silver, and the needy for a pair of sandals—they . . . trample the head of the poor into the dust of the earth, and push the afflicted out of the way" (2:6–7). I might have called this an exaggeration, as it applies to Hispanic immigrants, until I became involved in the case of a parishioner who was employed as an undocumented dishwasher in a local restaurant and who injured himself in a fall while at work. He went home in pain, called, and asked me to take him to the hospital. He was diagnosed with hip injuries and internal hemorrhaging. He was operated on and sent home to recover. Seeking reimbursement for his medical expenses, he asked the company for compensation. The company denied that the accident was work-related, even though coworkers had witnessed it. After he recovered, I visited the company with my parishioner and was told by the owner that nothing could be done by way of compensation for his injuries.

His coworkers, who were also undocumented, were reluctant to speak up for my parishioner. However, I persuaded one of them to make a statement about the incident to a lawyer specializing in worker compensation cases, whom I found for my parishioner. Other employees likewise came forward, and ultimately we obtained a court judgment requiring the company to pay for the medical expenses, lost work time, and physical disability suffered by my parishioner. The case led to another legal action, initiated by my parishioner, for violation of minimum wage regulations. Eventually, the company was fined, and a financial settlement was made in favor of all the underpaid employees.

Such incidents as this are symptomatic of a much broader situation. What we have here is an entire class of people living in a kind of economic slavery that makes them vulnerable to exploitation. How will the Hispanic church respond to this challenge, if at all? If the church is to fulfill its mission, it must become an agent of social change. And in the case of Hispanic immigrants, education should be more than a tool for social advancement or adjustment to American culture. It must be part of a wider moral and spiritual vision.

Building a Vision

A powerful observation from Proverbs declares: "Where there is no vision, the people perish" [29:18*a*].[15] The Babylonian captivity of the Jewish people provides a graphic example of the dynamic here. From biblical history, we recall that, in 586 b.c., several thousand Jews were rounded up during a military invasion by Assyrian forces under King Nebuchadnezzar and deported eastward to the city of Babylon. For the moment, these involuntary "immigrants" to what is now Iraq were unquestionably deprived of a vision for the future. What could they do? The prophet Jeremiah, strangely enough, counseled them to "seek the peace of the city, whither I [God] have caused you to be carried away captives, and pray unto the LORD for it, for in the peace thereof shall ye have peace [*shalom*]" (Jer 29:7). Was this simply a cop-out, a kind of expedient pragmatism telling them to make the best of a bad situation, or is there unexpected wisdom here?

Eldin Villafañe, in his book *Seek the Peace of the City*, sees the barrios of the inner city as fertile ground for the planting of churches and the fulfillment of their spiritual mission. Focusing on Boston, he calls for the churches to enter into partnership with the economically and politically disenfranchised ethnic groups of the city to address their needs through gospel ministry. Villafañe refers to this as a "social spirituality."[16] In the challenging environment of the city, he points out, successful ministry requires an attitude of "burning patience,"[17] that is, a passionate enthusiasm tempered by the recognition that God's work, not humanity's, is what is being done.

Over my years of service to my congregation, I have tried to connect my ministry with the needs of my church members. But this wasn't my original mission. When I started my pastoral career in Connecticut, I saw my role as simple and one-dimensional: it was to win souls for Christ. I felt I had to do everything in my power, with the help of God, to make the church grow. When I came to Boston, however, my pastoral role took a turn in another direction. Over time, I came to the conclusion that immigrant

---

15. King James Version. In a triumph of inspiration over the literal translation of Scripture, the seventeenth-century English scholars got it right, in my view. Other biblical versions include "Where there is no prophecy the people cast off restraint (Revised Standard Version); and, "Where there is no authority, the people break loose" (New English Bible).

16. Villafañe, *Seek the Peace of the City*, 12.

17. Ibid., 43.

churches like mine must also help their parishioners cope with the economic, political, and social problems they face.[18]

Education plays a critical role in the overall ministry of our church. Even more than financial resources, I believe the greatest need of my flock is for education. Earlier I described how we began by offering literacy classes in Spanish, as well as E.S.L. training. However, this is by no means the end of the story. It is only the end of the beginning.

Next Steps: Cell Groups

In 2000, one of our church deacons told me about a training program in Guatemala that was centered on the formation of cell groups. The concept involves small groups of 10 to 30 who meet in homes for Bible study. Neighbors, friends, and coworkers are invited to share in the atmosphere of hospitality and worship. A visitor who expresses interest in attending sessions regularly will be assigned a Hermano Mayor (literally, "Big Brother," but without the Orwellian overtones), and will be thought of as a Hermano Menor ("Little Brother") for the time being. The role of the Hermano Mayor is to follow up with the Hermano Menor in the event of absences and to answer questions as necessary.

Initially, I thought of the cell groups as an evangelical instrument designed to bring about conversions to the Christian faith. For this reason, the Hermano Mayor is required to be baptized and also a regular church member. Those who serve as cell group leaders or co-leaders must have completed the one-year course in our Leadership Academy, previously described.

Over the many years that I have been with this congregation, the home group program has been the single most successful effort we have undertaken. Although attendees are not required to join our church, the effect on our membership growth has been extraordinary. Between 2000 and 2005, our regular membership grew from 75 to 633, and it is still growing.

How are we to explain this unexpectedly high rate of growth? Is our church simply occupying a demographic *sweet spot* that enables us to benefit from the wave of new Latino immigrants to this country, as well as the

---

18. Upon arrival, I became aware of the acute need of our church members for gainful employment. Almost immediately, I began contacting prospective employers about positions available for members. Eventually we organized a committee to establish an information network that we now call a "job bank."

movement of immigrant residents who are leaving the inner city for the suburbs? Perhaps so, but I suspect that our growth is more than a happy accident. The increase comes from a confluence of factors — mostly of an educational nature.

Reaching Out to the Wider Community

In March, 2001, I journeyed with three members of my congregation to El Salvador, as part of an effort to develop a missions program for our church. The idea for the project came from a video tape that one of our parishioners received from his former pastor in El Salvador, showing the virtually complete destruction of the church to which he had belonged there. Ravaged by recent earthquakes, El Salvador had been recovering from massive flooding caused by Hurricane Mitch in November 1998.

Moved by the sad spectacle on tape, we decided as a congregation to mount an independent mission to El Salvador. I went together with my copastor and was joined by the supervisor of our member recruitment program and one of our deacons. My three colleagues were Salvadoran. Until that time, I had never been to Central America, having come to this country directly from my native Puerto Rico.

Earlier, back in Boston, when planning our trip, we had deliberately scheduled activities that would enhance our ability to serve more effectively at home. The most significant of these was attending a three-day seminar on methods for improving church membership growth in Guatemala City, which was the area of El Salvador we would be visiting.[19] There we learned about techniques for increasing membership by means of home study groups, or *grupos celulares*, as we call them. Although we had already been conducting a cell-group program for two years, we nevertheless picked up some practical ideas on how to apply cell groups to our local urban ministry in Boston.

What we have learned is that cell group activities reflect the following three aspects of the church's mission:

- *Fellowship in community.* In cell groups, we share refreshments and social contact before and after meetings; we network within the group, for example, to exchange job information; we discuss common

---

19. Presented by the Misión Cristiana Evangélica, Lluvias de Gracia.

concerns in the light of faith; and afterwards we visit ailing group members.

- *Service ministry*. We share funds in emergency situations, such as a death in the family, or acute financial crisis.

- *Spiritual guidance*. The groups include working toward the solution of personal problems and prayerful support in dealing with circumstances that produce emotional stress, such as domestic abuse, loneliness, and family conflict.

The synergy of these three elements, it seems to me, is greater than their usefulness considered separately, because each home study group is an extension of the Tabernáculo. These groups enable my professional ministry to expand far beyond my own physical limitations, to reach many more people than I could ever get to know directly. More importantly, our educational programs give us a link to the wider immigrant community in surrounding towns. Approximately 50 percent of the students in our Spanish literacy classes, for example, are not affiliated with any church.

What Were We Doing Right and Wrong?

The success of our cell group program could be explained simply as a social phenomenon, but I see it in terms of the fruits of the Holy Spirit. In other words, our continued progress in this area has come through God alone—not from the pastor or anyone else in the congregation. That being said, cell groups clearly provide social support to immigrants who may feel deprived of meaningful interaction with others in their new country. In these small groups, visitors and (we hope) future church members share information about jobs, immigration policies, housing, medical care, language training, and educational opportunities for career development.

On the other hand, to the extent that we recognize it, we all have the potential to become instruments of God's will. Peter Senge, in his book *The Fifth Discipline*, offers a possible reason why cell groups seem to flourish within a much larger organization. Small groups, he points out, "harness the spirit, enthusiasm and knowledge of people throughout the organization."[20]

The book of Exodus provides a practical example of the value of small groups within the church. Faced with pastoral overload, Moses goes to his father-in-law Jethro, seeking advice on how to cope with the demands made

20. Senge, *The Fifth Discipline*, 289.

upon him by the members of his numerous flock. Jethro advises Moses to put men in charge of the people as judges over "thousands, hundreds, fifties, and tens" who will judge small matters by themselves. That way, Jethro assures Moses, "It will be easier for you, and they will bear the burden with you" (18:21–22 NRSV). The soundness of this advice, as a way of preventing pastoral burnout, is unquestionable. Writer Julie A. Gorman provides a simple explanation for the attractiveness of small groups: "People long for a sense of connection to God and other people."[21] This suggests that small groups answer two needs, one spiritual and the other social. The combination, if our membership growth at the Tabernáculo Evangelico provides an indication, is a powerful one.

At this point, I want to avoid giving the impression that cell groups are a panacea or a sure-fire gimmick for energizing church growth. It appears that we owe the success of our educational programs, at least in part, to the natural desire of people to grow. This applies not only to their secular education, but to their spiritual development as well. On several occasions, new members have come to my church who told me that in their previous churches, "No me dan la oportunidad para crecer" (I'm not given a chance to grow). This problem frequently goes unacknowledged, but if it is to be addressed at all, I suspect it will be resolved through some form of education.

At the Tabernáculo, I have found that many people are ready to help out in the church, provided that they have been taught what to do. Behind our educational efforts is the belief that people are a work in progress; in other words, we need to develop our skills in order to use them effectively in God's service. If the laborers are few, as Jesus observed (Luke 10:2), it may in part be due to the fact that they don't have the tools—that is, the knowledge and vision—to pursue our goals as a church community.

In spite of our rapid growth in recent years—which I attribute in part to cell groups—it is clear that the program has to be managed. In other words, cell groups carry risks along with rewards. The proliferation of so many small groups may produce factionalism, when individual cells engage in a degree of empire building. In one case, we had a cell group leader who went so far as to tell his group members, "Don't listen to the pastor," and "Don't listen to the board of deacons." This leader evidently saw himself as the "pastor" of a small congregation.

21. Gorman, "Small Groups in the Local Church," 176.

If left unattended, this matter could have snow-balled into a crisis that would have led to a disaster for our church. As it happened, the leader eventually left the Tabernáculo and took some twenty members with him. Coincidentally, the following month we had an influx of members who had been waiting in the wings for this challenge to our leadership to be resolved. In the wake of this episode, we experienced a period of *shalom* followed by an unexpectedly rapid growth in our membership.

As it turned out, I became convinced of the need to visit cell group meetings regularly to emphasize their connection to our church. This effort is essential because many cell group members do not attend regular services at the Tabernáculo. We also hold weekly meetings of the group leaders, to facilitate the flow of communication between the church and cell groups.

Resolving Difficulties among Hispanic Immigrants

Up to this point, we have been focusing on the needs of first-generation immigrants and have said little about their children, who are growing up bilingual. With time, the adults often become bilingual as well, but often not as soon as their children. Generally, the children embrace the American culture more rapidly than do their parents, perhaps because of peer pressure at school. The resulting "generation gap" can become a problem, if we fail to address it in a pragmatic and compassionate spirit.

As an example from my pastoral experience, one day at church the father of a child in the Sunday school came to me and said that he was considering the possibility of withdrawing his family from membership in our church. He said that his son had complained that he couldn't understand what was going on in the class, which was taught in Spanish. He told me that the church was not meeting the spiritual needs of his family. I was concerned about this because the father was a student at a local theological seminary and also a good friend.

The next Sunday after church, I went with the entire board of deacons to the home of my friend. With all of the family present, we discussed the whole range of areas where the church was failing to meet their needs. The father told me that he sensed a barrier between his family, which is Puerto Rican, and the rest of the congregation, who are mainly Central American. As Puerto Ricans, he said, he and his family are used to attending bilingual churches. He went so far as to say that his family was not readily accepted among the congregation and used the term "raicista" (racist) to describe the climate of the church, as they had experienced it. In the Sunday school, his son said that the teacher insisted that English not be used. On the way back to the church afterwards, one deacon said that we should make some language reforms. Because our children are growing up bilingual, I agreed with him. Clearly, some changes had to be made.

Further discussion revealed that the style of music was also an issue. The young people wanted a more modern and popular type of gospel music, with keyboard instruments and electronic sound systems. The adults preferred more traditional hymns, with acoustic guitar accompaniment, to which they were accustomed in Latin America.

Our initial response was to replace the teacher with a bilingual instructor. To facilitate this change, I took advantage of the fact that the original instructor became pregnant and should be excused from teaching. Later, we introduced instructional materials in both English and Spanish. Currently, we offer separate youth services in English and Spanish, with music styled to their taste. These measures enabled us to retain the family that had been planning to leave the church.

In the area of secular education, we are utilizing the talents of one of our members who is a college graduate to help students in elementary through high school to develop their math skills. Presently, we have a cadre of 15 adult volunteer mentors working with some 50 to 60 of our children at levels from kindergarten through 12th grade. Alarmed by the statistically high drop-out rate among Hispanics, we want to do what we can to ensure their success in school. Often we have found that failing students could in fact do the work, once they understood the assignment.

Who Works in Our Educational Strategy

On a pragmatic level, I would summarize the main features of our educational strategy as follows:

- Address a practical need that is widely shared by members of the congregation, or, in other words, any approach should be grounded in the social and cultural realities of the situation facing the church membership.

- Remember that God produces the fruits of our efforts. This involves recognizing that the results we achieve can never be known ahead of time.

- Recognize the role of serendipity. Although we must always act with purpose, at the same time we need to allow for the unexpected turn of events that can open up new possibilities.

- Be flexible. Consider all serious suggestions, regardless of how improbable of success they may appear to be.

- Take risks. Some of our programs have required a substantial investment up front. For example, to develop the program for our Leadership Academy, we had to send seven of our leaders to Buenos Aires, Argentina, for a week of training.

Recommended Guidelines for Pastors

Although the pastor will likely spearhead the educational effort of the immigrant church, there are some practices to embrace and others to avoid:

- *Programs Require Investment.* Educational programs require a degree of risk. Pastors should alert the congregation to the possibility of failure.

- *Avoid Exhortation.* Don't use the pulpit to push your pastoral vision. The appearance of force may generate resistance. Recognize that vision is developed through education.

- *Yield to Resistance.* Be prepared to put programs on hold. If the undertaking founders, wait for a more favorable time. Put time to work for you, or, as we say in Spanish, "El tiempo es el mejor testigo." (Time is the best witness.)

- *Test the Waters.* Talk about your ideas with church members privately before voicing them publicly.

- *Look at the Big Picture.* Take the cultural background of members into account, for example, by traveling to their native countries as a mission or training project.

- *Pursue Outside Training with Others.* As a matter of policy, never pursue extramural instruction alone. Bring along other key people from the congregation.

- *Education Takes Time.* Although we have implemented both secular and religious programs at our own church, it took many years to get where we are today. In the routine of church life, it is easy to forget that education is a temporal process. The word *education* itself comes from the Latin "edu-care," meaning to lead or draw out.[22] Thus, instant or short-term benefits may not be realistically possible.

Summary

The rapid growth of the Hispanic immigrant population in this country presents challenges and opportunities for the churches that undertake evangelical ministry to them in an urban setting. One of the most critical needs of immigrants from Latin America is for education. The role of education, as a tool for addressing the social and spiritual needs of first generation immigrants, is a subject of controversy. Traditionalist or fundamentalist churches tend to base their position against education on the assumption that secular programs are antithetical to the aims of the church. However, insofar as it serves to promote the values of political justice and social equity, (not to mention) Bible study, training in apologetics (defending the gospel), and strategies to effectuate our growth, education shares goals in common with the mission of the church.

Regardless of orientation or philosophy, the immigrant church is always in transition. Demographics compel the church to prepare for the next generation of North Americans. The question before the church is whether to embrace the reality of cultural assimilation, or insulate itself against it. Education, however, can facilitate this transition and provide a bridge to *shalom*.

References for Further Study

Arias Barahona, Rosario, and Samuel Diaz. *Psicología Pastoral: El Conocimiento Interior de la Grey para un Efectivo Trabajo Pastoral* (in Spanish). Bellflower, CA: Publicaciones Excelencia, 2006.
"Discipleship: The Neglected Mandate," *Enrichment Quarterly*, winter 2008. Springfield, MO: General Council, Assemblies of God.
González, Justo L. *The Story of Christianity: The Early Church to the Present Day.* Peabody, MA: Hendrickson/Prince Press, 1999.

---

22. *The American Heritage Dictionary*, 2100.

Reaching for the New Jerusalem

Latourette, Kenneth Scott. *A History of Christianity.* 2 vols. New York: Harper & Row, 1975.

MacCulloch, Diarmaid. *A History of Christianity: The First Three Thousand Years.* New York: Penguin/Viking, 2010.

Moore, Rebecca, Anthony B. Pinn, and Mary R. Sawyer, eds. *Peoples Temple and Black Religion in America.* Bloomington, IN: Indiana University Press, 2004.

Rivera Miranda, Luz M. *Capellanía Institutional: Nociones Básicas de la Capellanía* (in Spanish). Nashville: Abingdon, 2010.

Senge, Peter M. *The Fifth Discipline: The Art and Practice of the Learning Organization.* New York: Doubleday/Currency, 1990.

Smith, J. Alfred, Sr. *Making Sense of Suffering: A Message to Job's Children.* Elgin, IL: Progressive National Baptist Convention, 1988.

Tillich, Paul. *The Irrelevance and Relevance of the Christian Message.* Cleveland: Pilgrim, 1996.

Villafañe, Eldin. *El Espíritu Libertador: Hacia una Ética Social Pentecostal Hispanoamericana* (in Spanish). Grand Rapids: Eerdmans, 1996.

Volf, Miroslav. *Exclusion and Embrace: A Theological Exploration of Identity, Otherness, and Reconciliation.* Nashville: Abingdon, 1996.

Epilogue

Participating in What God Is Doing

J. ANTHONY LLOYD

IN THESE PRECEDING PAGES of reflection, insight, and investigation, much has been written regarding the building of a New Jerusalem, and much is yet to be written on the landscape of urban ministry.

As Seong Hyun Park points out in his preface, when the New Jerusalem is referenced in Revelation 21:14, the twelve foundations for the wall do not bear the name of God, but the "names of the twelve apostles of the Lamb." Thus, as the heirs of the disciples, we are called to participate in what God is doing in building the New Jerusalem. The task before us is ever so great, but so are the resources. We approach this struggle, grounded in the fundamental understanding that God has been at this work long before we came to it, and he will be at it long after we have left the great work of building. Humbled with this perspective, we must first affirm that it is his work we are doing and not ours. We wear the mantle of building loosely, with an understanding that this is sacred work that God himself initiated and continues to do.

It is our high honor and privilege to be called on to participate in this endeavor. We are not nor ever can we be the central actors on the stage in this construction area. The implications are significant if we will answer the call to be practitioners of his grace and mercy. It is God's work. The glory is God's and his alone. Such a humbled perspective frees us up to be used by God in the building of a New Jerusalem. One knows from any experience in doing urban ministry and reading these chapters before us that the victory is assured in Christ Jesus, and we do the work of the master, as God is building a New Jerusalem through us. To comprehend fully the great privilege that is ours in this new age (for God is still using his church to accomplish his mission), we must heed the lyrics of the old song writer: "To run on and see what the end will be." My mother would always say, "Wash your hands before you come to the table!" We must all have our hands washed by the blood of Christ if we are to share in the building of a New Jerusalem. It will get built because that is God's prerogative, but the question remains: Will we participate in it and bear witness to it? This is what brings us all to the table and ultimately keeps us at the table. As is reflected in the thoughts of the contributors here, the work of God is done by people, called by God, to wash their hands of selfish sin, but then to get those cleansed hands dirty again in ministry, combating crime, abuse, sickness, racism, homelessness, dysfunction, inadequate education, hunger, and the list could go on, as we clean sin up in this world.

The authors have sought to lay before anyone who would answer the call to build a New Jerusalem honest reflections of the sacred task, and they have given us bold propositions on how to engage in the work. They have sought to ensure that this is a collaborative effort on so many fronts. And any discussion of building a New Jerusalem must do justice to the questions of leadership.

I can remember my first visit to Jerusalem, over some twenty-five years ago. I was taken in by the beauty of this ancient city of God, and its beauty remains as I found in my most recent visit last summer. The beauty was then as it is now in its history, stature, collective memory, culture, and peoples past, present, and future. In that encounter, I found myself engulfed by those who came and went through its gates, traveled its streets, and lent their voices to develop the sounds of the city. On the first day, having been caught up in the elegance of this old city and its present-day travelers, my attention was drawn to a weary, disheveled beggar, dirty from the travels of life, making his determined way through the crowd, and hugging the wall of the city as he traveled. I did not know him, but in so many ways I did know him, for to me he symbolized the city, the city of God. In the swiftness of his pace around the wall outside the city I realized that he was on a mission, and he would not allow the sheer numbers in the crowd to deter him from his destination. With my eyes, I sought to keep up with him, not to lose him in the madding crowd, as if where he was going I had to be going as well. Our paths had crossed as if our destinations had to be the same, even though only one of us knew where we were going, and that certainly was not me. In an instance, the weary traveler stopped, reached in his pocket and pulled out a piece of fruit, took a bite, and handed the remainder of the fruit to a beggar who sat on the ground up against the Jerusalem wall, as if the very wall depended on him. Our traveler never said a word, but continued on his journey, and the one who held up the wall with his back never said a word in response.

It was then that I came to realize what urban ministry is all about. It is about beggars sharing with other beggars what is in their hands, in their pockets, and ultimately in their very souls. This new real estate called Jerusalem is occupied by beggars on whom the image of God is stamped, who seek out a journey, not knowing where it leads. Ours as a ministry is to provide leadership at the city wall that embraces all who for too long have traveled in the crowd circling the periphery of the city wall. Such leadership is about building a New Jerusalem, but one where our fellow travelers are invited into the building process of the city itself. The days of circling the periphery must come to an end. There can be no completion of the building of a New Jerusalem until we all sit together at the table, with our hands individually and collectively washed by the blood of Christ. We must clear our voices and sing in harmony as I heard the elders sing when I grew up in the city. A chord was struck in my soul as every now and then they would break out in long meters, dragging the melody as the words bled into one another, the song of invitation by beggars to other beggars on a journey to build a new city, a New Jerusalem:

> I'm going to sit at the Welcome Table,
> I'm going to sit at the Welcome Table one of these days.

Leadership in building a New Jerusalem is distributed by those at the Welcome Table, if we can finally get this right. Membership must be opened to all who inhabit the city, embrace the city, live the city, are the city, by inviting those who up until now have only traveled the exterior walls of the city, on the periphery of life, never being noticed, and never being invited into full participation at the table with full membership through the door of Christ with all its privileges. One such privilege is that of developing the schematic design for the new city. Those who will be the beneficiaries of the New Jerusalem become its residents. They inhabit a city whose maker and builder is God, and God invites all of us to participate in what he is doing. At the table will be the new Nehemiahs, the new Cains, and the new beggars—all of whom God has called inside the city walls and to the welcome table for the miracle of building the New Jerusalem.

I often, when teaching my courses on leadership at Gordon-Conwell Theological Seminary, Boston Campus, am assigned to the classroom lecture hall on the top floor. It is in that classroom that my students and I gather as if in the upper room all over again to dream dreams and see visions of a New Jerusalem. It is from that perch in the evening that, if one pauses long enough, one can take in the panoramic view of the city of Boston. The lights, the buildings, the streets, the energy, the people coming and going, the hustle and bustle of passing fruit from one to another is so all-encompassing. We could become so overwhelmed by the sights and sounds of the city that we want to somehow stay in that upper room cloistered and secure from the challenges with which the landscape of urban ministry confronts us, but our calling is not to refrain from the building process but to engage it boldly in the strength of the Lord. The endeavor is as challenging as these chapters have laid out for us, but it is as bright as the one who builds the city on a hill and who calls us to participate in constructing a New Jerusalem. We must get on with the task because the beggars call to us to join them in the journey, and God will empower us to build. Jerusalem has always been the city of God. A New Jerusalem will be God's as well. Participate with us in what God is doing!

References Cited

Adams, Jay E. *Competent to Counsel.* Grand Rapids: Baker, 1972.

Alexander, Michelle. *The New Jim Crow: Mass Incarceration in the Age of Colorblindness.* Rev. ed. New York: New Press, 2012.

Alexander, T. Desmond. *From Eden to the New Jerusalem: An Introduction to Biblical Theology.* Grand Rapids: Kregel, 2008.

Allen, Roland. *Missionary Methods: St. Paul's or Ours?: A Study of the Church in the Four Provinces.* Grand Rapids: ReadaClassic.com, 2012.

The American Heritage Dictionary of the English Language. 3rd ed. Boston: Houghton Mifflin, 1996.

Anderson, Elijah. *Code of the Street: Decency, Violence, and the Moral Life of the Inner City.* New York: W.W. Norton, 1999.

Anderson, Lorraine Cleaves. *Under One Steeple: Multiple Congregations Sharing More Than Just Space.* House of Prisca and Aquila Series. Eugene, OR: Wipf & Stock, 2012.

Anderson, Ray, and Dennis Guernsey. *On Being Family.* Grand Rapids: Eerdmans, 1985.

Augustine. *The City of God.* Translated by Marcus Dods. New York: Modern Library, 1994.

Balmer, Randall. "Crossing the Borders: Evangelicalism and Migration." In *Religion and Immigration: Christian, Jewish, and Muslim Experiences in the United States,* edited by Yvonne Yazbeck Haddad et al., 53–60. Walnut Creek, CA: AltaMira, 2003.

Barth, Karl. *Church Dogmatics.* 3/3: *The Doctrine of Creation.* Translated by G. T. Thomson et al. Edinburgh: T. & T. Clark, 1936–77.

Bauckham, Richard. *The Theology of the Book of Revelation.* New Testament Theology. Cambridge, UK: Cambridge University Press, 1993.

Beck, Aaron T. *Cognitive Therapy and the Emotional Disorders.* New York: Meridian, 1976.

Beck, James R. *Jesus and Personality Theory: Exploring the Five-Factor Model.* Downers Grove: InterVarsity, 1999.

Benner, David. "The Incarnation as a Metaphor for Psychotherapy." *Journal of Psychology and Theology* 11 (1983) 227–94.

———. *Psychotherapy and the Spiritual Quest.* Grand Rapids: Baker, 1988.

Berkhof, Louis. *Systematic Theology.* Grand Rapids: Eerdmans, 1941.

Berne, Eric. *What Do You Say after You Say Hello?* New York: Grove, 1972.

Bonilla-Silva, Eduardo. *Racism without Racists: Color-Blind Racism and the Persistence of Racial Inequality in the United States.* 2nd ed. Lanham, MD: Rowman and Littlefield, 2006.

Borthwick, Paul. *Western Christians in Global Mission: What's the Role of the North American Church?* Downers Grove: InterVarsity, 2012.

References Cited

Brand, Chad, and Tom Pratt. *Awaiting the City: Poverty, Ecology and Morality in Today's Political Economy.* Grand Rapids: Kregel, 2012.

Breckenridge, James, and Lillian Breckenridge. *What Color Is Your God? Multicultural Education in the Church.* Wheaton, IL: Victor, 1995.

Brenner, Charles. *An Elementary Textbook of Psychoanalysis.* New York: International Universities Press, 1973.

Brown, Francis, S. R. Driver, and Charles A. Briggs. *A Hebrew and English Lexicon of the Old Testament.* Oxford: Clarendon, 1907.

Brown, Stewart J. *Thomas Chalmers and the Godly Commonwealth in Scotland.* Oxford: Oxford University Press, 1983.

Bryan, Steven M. "The Eschatological Temple in John 14." *Bulletin of Biblical Research* 15:2 (2005) 187–98.

Bultmann, Rudolf Karl. *The Presence of Eternity: History and Eschatology.* The Gifford Lectures 1955. New York: Harper, 1957.

Burgess, Harold W. *Models of Religious Education.* Wheaton, IL: Victor, 1996.

Calton and Bridgeton (Scotland) Association for Religious Purposes. "Annual Report for 1816." Mitchell Library, Glasgow.

Capps, Donald. *Biblical Approaches to Pastoral Counseling.* Philadelphia: Westminster, 1981.

Carroll R., M. Daniel. *Christians at the Border: Immigration, the Church, and the Bible.* Grand Rapids: Baker, 2008.

Chalmers, Thomas. *The Christian and Civic Economy of Large Towns.* 3 vols. Glasgow: William Collins, 1819–26.

Chen, Carolyn. *Getting Saved in America: Taiwanese Immigration and Religious Experience.* Princeton: Princeton University Press, 2008.

Claiborne, Shane. "Mark 2: Sharing Economic Resources with Fellow Community Members and the Needy Among Us." In *Schools for Conversion: 12 Marks of a New Monasticism,* edited by The Rutba House. Eugene, OR: Wipf & Stock, 2005.

————. *The Irresistible Revolution: Living as an Ordinary Radical.* Grand Rapids: Zondervan, 2006.

Clinebell, Howard J. *Basic Types of Pastoral Care and Counseling.* Nashville: Abingdon, 1984.

Collins, Kenneth J. *A Real Christian: The Life of John Wesley.* Nashville: Abingdon, 1999.

Conde-Frazier, Elizabeth. "Prejudice and Conversion." In *A Many Colored Kingdom: Multicultural Dynamics for Spiritual Formation,* edited by Elizabeth Conde-Frazier et al., 105–120. Grand Rapids: Baker, 2004.

Crabb, Lawrence J. *Effective Biblical Counseling.* Grand Rapids: Zondervan, 1977.

Currie, David A. "The Growth of Evangelicalism in the Church of Scotland, 1793–1843." PhD diss., University of St. Andrews, 1990.

Danker, Frederick William, et al., eds. *A Greek-English Lexicon of the New Testament and Other Early Christian Literature.* 3rd ed. Chicago: University of Chicago Press, 2000.

Davidson, Richard M. "Cosmic Metanarrative for the Coming Millenium." *Journal of the Adventist Theological Society* 11:1–2 (Spring–Autumn 2000) 102–119.

Detwiler, Gregg. "Developing Safe Environments for Learning and Transformation." *Emmanuel Research Review* 80 (July 2012). Online: http://egc.org/err80.

DeYoung, Curtiss Paul, et al. *United by Faith: The Multiracial Congregation as an Answer to the Problem of Race.* New York: Oxford University Press, 2003.

Dorsett, Lyle W. *A Passion for Souls: The Life of D. L. Moody.* Chicago: Moody, 1997.

Duemling, Bianca. "The Diverse Leadership Project." *Emmanuel Research Review* 69 (August 2011). Online: http://egc.org/err69.

———. "Shared Worship Space: An Urban Challenge and a Kingdom Opportunity," *Emmanuel Research Review* 74 (January 2012). Online: http://www.egc.org/err74.

Egan, Gerard. *The Skilled Helper*. Monterey, CA: Brooks/Cole, 1975.

Ellis, Richard S. *Foundation Deposits in Ancient Mesopotamia*. Yale Near Eastern Researches 2. New Haven: Yale University Press, 1968.

Emerson, Michael O., and Christian Smith. *Divided by Faith: Evangelical Religion and the Problem of Race in America*. New York: Oxford University Press, 2000.

Emmanuel Gospel Center. "The Boston Church Directory." No pages. Online: http://egcbcd.com/.

———. *New England's Book of Acts*. No pages. Online: http://neba.egc.org.

"Epistle of Mathetes to Diognetus." Online: http://www.ccel.org/ccel/richardson/fathers.x.i.ii.html.

Evans, C. Stephen. *Soren Kierkegaard's Christian Psychology*. Grand Rapids: Zondervan, 1990.

Feyerabend, Karl. *Langenscheidt Pocket Hebrew Dictionary of the Old Testament*. Boston: McGraw-Hill, 1969.

Forrester, Jay W. *Urban Dynamics*. Cambridge, MA: MIT, 1969.

Fowler, James W. "Practical Theology and Theological Education: Some Models and Questions." *Theology Today* 42:1 (April 1985).

Frankenberg, Ruth. *Displacing Whiteness: Essays in Social and Cultural Criticism*. Durham: Duke University Press, 1997.

Frankl, Viktor. *Man's Search for Meaning*. New York: Touchstone, 1959.

Fromm, Erich. *Man for Himself: An Inquiry into the Psychology of Ethics*. New York: Rinehart, 1947.

Garelick, Jon. "Thinking Small: A New Book Says 'Smaller' Cities Could Be the Way of the Future." *The Boston Phoenix* 18 (November 2011) 14.

Gesenius, Wilhelm. *Gesenius' Hebrew Grammar*, edited by Emil Kautzsch and A. E. Cowley. 2nd ed. Oxford: Clarendon, 1910.

Gilbreath, Edward. *Reconciliation Blues: A Black Evangelical's Inside View of White Christianity*. Downers Grove: InterVarsity, 2006.

Goizueta, Roberto. *Caminemos con Jesús: Toward a Hispanic/Latino Theology of Accompaniment*. Maryknoll, NY: Orbis, 1995.

Gorman, Julie A. "Small Groups in the Local Church." In *Introducing Christian Education: Foundations for the Twenty-first Century*, edited by Michael J. Anthony, 176. Grand Rapids: Baker, 2001.

Gregory, James N. *The Southern Diaspora: How the Great Migrations of Black and White Southerners Transformed America*. Chapel Hill: The University of North Carolina Press, 2005.

Grigg, Viv. *The Spirit of Christ and the Postmodern City*. Lexington, KY: Emeth, 2009.

"Gutenberg's Legacy." Harry Ransom Center at the University of Texas. Online: http://www.hrc.utexas.edu/educator/modules/gutenberg/books/legacy/.

Hall, Douglas A., with Judy Hall and Steve Daman. *The Cat and the Toaster: Living System Ministry in a Technological Age*. Urban Voice Series. Eugene, OR: Wipf & Stock, 2010.

Harnack, Adolf von. *What Is Christianity?* Fortress Texts in Modern Theology. Philadelphia: Fortress, 1986.

Hart, Archibald. *Coping with Depression in the Ministry*. Waco, TX: Word, 1984.

References Cited

Hattersley, Roy. *Blood and Fire: William and Catherine Booth and Their Salvation Army.* New York: Doubleday, 2000.

Hauerwas, Stanley. *A Community of Character: Toward a Constructive Christian Social Ethic.* Notre Dame: University of Notre Dame Press, 1981.

Hauerwas, Stanley, and William H. Willimon. *Resident Aliens: Life in the Christian Colony.* Nashville: Abingdon, 1989.

Hayford, Jack W. "Confessing What Separates Us." In *Ending Racism in the Church*, edited by Susan E. Davies and Paul Teresa Hennessee, 15–23. Cleveland, OH: United Church, 1998.

Hesselgrave, David J. *Counseling Cross-Culturally.* Grand Rapids: Baker, 1984.

Hill, Jane H. *The Everyday Language of White Racism.* Chichester, UK: Wiley-Blackwell, 2008.

Hollenweger, Walter J. *Erfahrungen der Leibhaftigkeit.* Interkulturelle Theologie I. München: Kaiser, 1979.

Holt, Doug. "Why Do Brands Cause Trouble? A Dialectical Theory of Consumer Culture DN Branding." *Journal of Consumer Culture Research* 29 (June 2002) 70–91.

Hulme, William E. *Pastoral Care and Counseling.* Minneapolis: Augsburg, 1981.

Imade-Babs, Peter, and Oladimeji Lawal. "Nigerian Pastor of Europe's Biggest Church." *Nigerian Compass* (26 August 2012). Online: http://www.compassnewspaper.org/index.php/section-table/35-headlines/6940-nigerian-pastor-of-europes-biggest-church-in-n15-billion-scandal.

Jackson, Darrell, and Alessia Passarelli. *Mapping Migration: Mapping Churches' Responses, Europe Study.* Czech Republic: Churches Commission for Migrants in Europe, 2008.

James, Robert Leoline, and Guy Edward Farquhar Chilver. "Domitian." In *The Oxford Classical Dictionary*, edited by N. G. L. Hammond and H. H. Scullard, 360. 2nd ed. Oxford: Clarendon, 1970.

Johnson, Todd M., and Kenneth R. Ross, eds. *Atlas of Global Christianity 1910–2010.* Edinburgh: Edinburgh University Press, 2009.

Jones, LeAlan, et al. *Our America: Life and Death on the South Side of Chicago.* New York: Scribner, 1997.

Jones, Stanton, ed. *Psychology and the Christian Faith.* Grand Rapids: Baker, 1986.

Kang, S. Steve. "The Formation Process in a Learning Community." In *A Many Colored Kingdom: Multicultural Dynamics for Spiritual Formation*, edited by Elizabeth Conde-Frazier et al., 151–66. Grand Rapids: Baker, 2004.

Kangas, Ron. "'I Saw the Holy City, New Jerusalem'—The Vision of the New Jerusalem as a Corporate God-Man." Living Stream Ministries. *Affirmation & Critique: A Journal of Christian Thought* 16:2 (2012) 3–12.

Kavanaugh, John F. *Following Christ in a Consumer Society: The Spirituality of Cultural Resistance.* 25th anniversary ed. Maryknoll, NY: Orbis, 2006.

Kim, Catherine Y., et al. *The School-to-Prison Pipeline: Structuring Legal Reform.* New York: New York University Press, 2010.

Kirwan, William. *Biblical Concepts for Christian Counseling.* Grand Rapids: Baker, 1984.

Koons, Jennifer. "Urbanization Hasn't Pushed Religion Aside, U.N. Says." *The Washington Post,* July 7, 2007. Online: http://www.washingtonpost.com/wp-dyn/content/article/2007/07/06/AR2007070601843.html..

Lansley, Stewart. *The Cost of Inequality: Why Economic Equality Is Essential for Recovery.* London: Gibson Square, 2012.

Lausanne Congress. "Manila Manifesto" (1989). Online: http://www.lausanne.org/en/documents/manila-manifesto.html.

LeBar, Lois E. *Education That Is Christian*. Wheaton, IL: Victor, 1989.

Levenson, Michael, and Yuxing Zheng. "Immigrant Numbers Up 15% in State since 2006." *The Boston Globe* (16 August 2006).

Liddell, Henry George, and Robert Scott. *A Greek-English Lexicon*, edited by Henry Stuart Jones, et al. 9th ed. Oxford: Clarendon, 1968.

Life Magazine. "The Face of God." December 1990, 52.

Livermore, David A. *Cultural Intelligence: Improving Your CQ to Engage Our Multicultural World*. Grand Rapids: Baker, 2009.

Lupton, Robert D. *Renewing the City: Reflections on Community Development and Urban Renewal*. Downers Grove: InterVarsity, 2005.

Maddi, Salvatore R. *Personality Theories: A Comparative Analysis*. 6th ed. Prospect Heights, IL: Waveland, 2001.

Malanima, Paolo. *Pre-Modern European Economy: One Thousand Years*. Leiden: Brill, 2009.

Margolis, Rhonda, and Sally McLean. "Promoting Cultural Understanding through Storytelling." *National Storytelling Magazine* (July/August 2005) 1–3. Online: http://www.rlmlearninginnovations.ca/pdfs/promoting_cultural_understanding_through_storytelling.pdf.

May, Gerald G. *Care of Mind, Care of Spirit*. San Francisco: Harper & Row, 1982.

McKelvey, R. J. *The New Temple: The Church in the New Testament*. London: Oxford University Press, 1969.

McNeese, Tim. *The Middle Ages*. Dayton, OH: Milliken, 1999.

Meeks, Wayne A. *The First Urban Christians: The Social World of the Apostle Paul*. 2nd ed. New Haven: Yale University Press, 2003.

Meier, Paul D., et al. *Introduction to Psychology and Counseling*. Grand Rapids: Baker, 1982.

Miller, Vincent. "Taking Consumer Culture Seriously." *Horizons* 27 (2000) 284.

Mitchell, Rudy. "An Introduction to Boston's Quiet Revival." *Emmanuel Research Review* 3 (May 2010).

Mitchell, Rudy, et. al. *The Boston Church Directory*. Millennium ed. Boston: Emmanuel Gospel Center, 2001.

Mohr, Holbrook. "Mississippi Criticized on School Discipline: Rights Advocates Say Policies Harsh." *The Boston Globe* (18 January 2013) A11.

Moran, Gabriel. *Religious Educational Development: Images for the Future*. Minneapolis: Winston, 1983.

Mouw, Richard J. *When the Kings Come Marching In: Isaiah and the New Jerusalem*. Grand Rapids: Eerdmans, 1983.

Noguera, Pedro. *The Trouble with Black Boys: And Other Reflections on Race, Equity, and the Future of Public Education*. San Francisco: Jossey-Bass, 2008.

Nouwen, Henri J. M. *The Living Reminder*. New York: Seabury, 1977.

Oliver, John P., et al. *Handbook of Personality: Theory and Research*. 3rd ed. New York: Guilford, 2008.

Ozment, Steven. *The Reformation in the Cities: The Appeal of Protestantism to Sixteenth-Century Germany and Switzerland*. New Haven: Yale University Press, 1980.

References Cited

Parrett, Gary A. "Becoming a Culturally Sensitive Minister." In *A Many Colored Kingdom: Multicultural Dynamics for Spiritual Formation*, edited by Elizabeth Conde-Frazier et al., 121–150. Grand Rapids: Baker, 2004.

———. "The Wondrous Cross and the Broken Wall." In *A Many Colored Kingdom: Multicultural Dynamics for Spiritual Formation*, edited by Elizabeth Conde-Frazier et al., 63–78. Grand Rapids: Baker, 2004.

Parsitau, Damaris Seleina, and Philomena Njeri Mwaura. "God in the City: Pentecostalism as an Urban Phenomenon in Kenya." *Studia Historiae Ecclesiasticae* 36:2 (October 2010) 95–112.

Pazmiño, Robert W. *Foundational Issues in Christian Education.* 2nd ed. Grand Rapids: Baker, 1997.

Perrin, Norman. *The New Testament: An Introduction*, edited by Dennis C. Duling. 2nd ed. New York: Harcourt Brace Jovanovich, 1982.

Pilch, John J., and Bruce Malina, eds. *Handbook of Biblical Social Values.* Peabody, MA: Hendrickson, 1998.

Rah, Soong-Chan. *Many Colors: Cultural Intelligence for a Changing Church.* Chicago: Moody, 2010.

Random House Webster's Unabridged Dictionary. 2nd ed. New York: Random House Reference, 2001.

Rausch, Thomas. *Radical Christian Communities.* Collegeville, MN: Liturgical, 1990.

"Revival Born in a Prayer Meeting." *Knowing and Doing* (Fall 2004). Online: http://www.cslewisinstitute.org/webfm_send/577.

Richards, Lawrence O. *A Theology of Christian Education.* Grand Rapids: Zondervan, 1975.

Rogers, Carl R. *Client-Centered Therapy.* Boston: Houghton Mifflin, 1951.

Rossing, John P. "*Mestizaje* and Marginality: A Hispanic American Theology." *Theology Today* 45: 3 (October 1988) 293–304.

Rumberger, Russell W. *Dropping Out: Why Students Drop Out of High School and What Can Be Done about It.* Cambridge, MA: Harvard University Press, 2011.

The Rutba House, eds. *Schools for Conversion: 12 Marks of a New Monasticism.* Eugene, OR: Wipf & Stock, 2005.

Schor, Juliet, and Doug Holt, eds. *The Consumer Society Reader.* New York: New Press, 2000.

Seitz, Christopher R. "The Two Cities in Christian Scripture." In *The Two Cities of God: The Church's Responsibility for the Earthly City*, edited by Carl E. Braaten and Robert W. Jenson, 11–27. Grand Rapids: Eerdmans, 1997.

Senge, Peter M. *The Fifth Discipline: The Art and Practice of the Learning Organization.* New York: Doubleday/Currency, 1990.

Sider, Ron. *The Scandal of the Evangelical Conscience: Why Are Christians Living Just Like the Rest of the World?* Grand Rapids: Baker, 2005.

"Situation and Trends in Key Indicators, Urban Population Growth." *Global Health Observatory (GHO).* World Heath Organization. Online: http://www.who.int/gho/urban_health/situation_trends/urban_population_growth_text/en/index.html.

Skinner, Burrhus F. *Science and Human Behavior.* New York: MacMillan, 1953.

Slater, Don. *Consumer Culture and Modernity.* Cambridge, UK: Polity, 1997.

Smith, J. Alfred. *On the Jericho Road.* Downers Grove: InterVarsity, 2004.

Smith, Luther. *Intimacy and Mission: Intentional Community as Crucible for Radical Discipleship.* Scottsdale, PA: Herald, 1994.

Snyder, Howard A. *The Community of the King*. 2nd ed. Downers Grove: InterVarsity, 2004.

Soerens, Matthew, and Jenny Hwang. *Welcoming the Stranger: Justice, Compassion and Truth in the Immigration Debate*. Downers Grove: InterVarsity, 2009.

Spencer, Aída Besançon. "'El Hogar' as Ministry Team: Stephana(s)'s Household." In *Hispanic Christian Thought at the Dawn of the 21st Century: Apuntes in Honor of Justo L. González*, edited by Alvin Padilla et al., 69–77. Nashville: Abingdon, 2005.

"State of the World." *New Internationalist* 287 (February 1997). Online: http://www.globalissues.org/article/26/poverty-facts-and-stats.

Statistic Brain. "2012 Presidential Voter Support by Demographic." No pages. Online: http://www.statisticbrain.com/2012-presidential-voter-support-by-demographic/.

Stiglitz, Joseph E. *The Price of Inequality: How Today's Divided Society Endangers Our Future*. New York: W.W. Norton, 2012.

Stout, Harry S. *The Divine Dramatist: George Whitefield and the Rise of Modern Evangelicalism*. Grand Rapids: Eerdmans, 1991.

Stuntz, William J. *The Collapse of American Criminal Justice*. Cambridge, MA: Belknap Press of Harvard University Press, 2011.

Synan, Vinson. *The Holiness-Pentecostal Tradition: Charismatic Movements in the Twentieth Century*. 2nd ed. Grand Rapids: Eerdmans, 1997.

Thayer, Joseph Henry. *Thayer's Greek-English Lexicon of the New Testament*. Marshallton, DE: National Foundation for Christian Education, 1889.

Tilford, David. "Why Consumption Matters." Online: http://www.sierraclub.org/sustainable_consumption/tilford.asp.

Tumber, Catherine. *Small, Gritty, and Green: The Promise of America's Smaller Industrial Cities in a Low-Carbon World*. Cambridge, MA: MIT Press, 2011.

"Urbanization: A Majority in Cities." Online: http://www.unfpa.org/pds/urbanization.htm.

Villafañe, Eldin. *Seek the Peace of the City: Reflections on Urban Ministry*. Grand Rapids: Eerdmans, 1995.

Volf, Miroslav. *Exclusion and Embrace: A Theological Exploration of Identity, Otherness, and Reconciliation*. Nashville: Abingdon, 1996.

Warner, R. Stephen. "Coming to America." *Christian Century* 121:3 (Febuary 2004) 20–23.

Weanzana, Nupanga. "Ezra." In *Africa Bible Commentary*, edited by Tokunboh Adeyemo et al., 531–42. Grand Rapids: Zondervan, 2010.

Wilkerson, Barbara. *Multicultural Religious Education*. Birmingham: Religious Education Press, 1997.

Wilkinson, Richard G., and Kate Pickett. *The Spirit Level: Why Greater Equality Makes Societies Stronger*. New York: Bloomsbury, 2010.

Williams, Monica. "Colorblind Ideology Is a Form of Racism." No pages. Online: http://www.psychologytoday.com/blog/colorblind/201112/colorblind-ideology-is-form-racism.

Winer, Michael Barry, and Karen Louise Ray. *Collaboration Handbook: Creating, Sustaining, and Enjoying the Journey*. Saint Paul: Amherst H. Wilder Foundation, 1994.

Winter, Irene J. "Babylonian Archaeologists of The(ir) Mesopotamian Past." In *Proceedings of the First International Congress on the Archaeology of the Ancient Near East, Rome, May 18th–23rd, 1998*, edited by Paolo Matthiae et al., 1785–99. Roma: Università degli Studi di Roma "La Sapienza," Dipartimento di Scienze Storiche, Archeologiche e Antopologiche dell'Antichità, 2000.

Worden, J. William. *Grief Counseling and Grief Therapy*. New York: Springer, 1991.

World Bank, "6th Urban Research and Knowledge Symposium," October 8–10, 2012. Online: http://web.worldbank.org/WBSITE/EXTERNAL/TOPICS/ EXTURBA NDEVELOPMENT/0,,menuPK:337184~pagePK:149018~piPK:149093~theSite PK:337178,00.html.

Worthington, Everett L. *When Someone Asks for Help: A Practical Guide for Counseling*. Downers Grove: InterVarsity, 1982.

Yancey, George A. *Beyond Racial Gridlock: Embracing Mutual Responsibility*. Downers Grove: InterVarsity, 2006.

Scripture Index

Subject Index

Abel, 3–4
Abraham, 11, 171
Adam, 17, 27, 171
Alexander, Michelle, 76–77
Amos, 182
Anderson, Elijah, 70
Antioch, 41
Augustine, of Hippo, 2–3, 8, 44–45
Babel. *See* Babylon.
Babylon, 8, 22–23, 67, 183
Barth, Karl, 68
Bible Institute, 175–76
Booth, William, and Catherine, 51–52
Boston, 13–14, 55, 69, 81, 96, 99, 153–54, 168–69, 180, 183, 185, 196; Quiet Revival, 53, 82, 84, 86–87, 154
Burgess, Harold W, 177–78
Cain, xiv, 3–5, 7–9, 15, 172, 195
Calvin, 39, 47
Cassidy, Michael, 54
Castro, Fidel, 13
cat, vs. toaster, 38, 80, 87, 89
cell group (s), 184–88
choice(s), 14, 42–43, 47, 56, 123–24, 130, 136, 148, 181

Chalmers, Thomas, 49, 51–52
church: as body, 27–28, 44, 80, 86–87, 99–100, 102–7, 112, 161–62, 178–79; mission, xiii, 11, 13, 15–16, 39–42, 50–52, 54, 59, 63–65, 67, 71, 84–86, 95–96, 100–102, 128, 132, 168–75, 177–79, 180–85, 187, 189–91, 194. *See* city, vs. church.
city: and arts, 6; and diversity, 6–7; defined and described, 2–11, 14–15, 17–21, 24, 41–42, 61, 81–82, 86, 128, 135, 144; feminine, 20; percentage of dwellers, 27n3, 53, 153; types of, 38, 45–47, 56; reclamation of, 13–15; vs. church, 38–40, 43–46, 49–56, 58–62, 65, 129
city, commercial. *See* city, types of.
city, heavenly. *See* Jerusalem, New.
Claiborne, Shane, 128–29
collaboration, 100–102, 106, 108–9, 111, 113, 118, 160, 164
colorblindness, 108, 110
commodification, 124–30, 132
compassion, 59, 61, 63–64, 78, 141, 143, 145, 147, 165, 188